Programming Languages:
Principles and Practices

Programming Languages: Principles and Practices

Hector Nicolson

CLANRYE
INTERNATIONAL
www.clanryeinternational.com

Clanrye International,
750 Third Avenue, 9ᵗʰ Floor,
New York, NY 10017, USA

ISBN: 978-1-63240-905-8

Cataloging-in-Publication Data

Programming languages : principles and practices / Hector Nicolson.
    p. cm.
Includes bibliographical references and index.
ISBN 978-1-63240-905-8
1. Programming languages (Electronic computers). 2. Electronic data processing. I. Nicolson, Hector.
QA76.7 .P76 2019
005.13--dc23

For information on all Clanrye International publications
visit our website at www.clanryeinternational.com

Contents

Preface

A programming language is a set of instructions that are used to develop programs that use algorithms. Some common examples are Java, C, C++, COBOL, etc. The description of a programming language can be divided into syntax and semantics. The description of data and processes in a language occurs through certain primitive building blocks, which are defined by syntactic and semantic rules. The development of a programming language occurs through the construction of artifacts, chief among which is language specification and implementation. This book elucidates the concepts and innovative models around prospective developments with respect to programming languages. Most of the topics introduced in this book cover the principles and practices of developing programming languages. The textbook is appropriate for those seeking detailed information in this area.

To facilitate a deeper understanding of the contents of this book a short introduction of every chapter is written below:

Chapter 1- A formal language which consists of a set of instructions for producing output is termed as a programming language. This chapter provides an introduction to programming languages and includes topics such as programming language implementation, programming language specification, programming language theory, etc.

Chapter 2- A complete understanding of programming languages requires study of the three levels of programming languages- low-level programming language, high-level programming language and very high-level programming language. The following chapter elucidates the varied aspects associated with this area of study.

Chapter 3- Science and technology have undergone rapid advancement in the past decade which has resulted in the development of the five different generations in programming language. They are first-generation, second-generation, third generation, fourth generation and fifth-generation programming languages; which have been extensively detailed in this chapter.

Chapter 4- The set of rules which is used to define a combination of symbols which is considered to be a perfectly structured document in a programming language is referred to as syntax. Semantics is concerned with meaning. It describes the processes followed by a computer when executing a program in a specific language. The aim of this chapter is to explore the important aspects of syntax and semantics in programming languages such as lexical analysis, syntax highlighting, action semantics, etc.

Chapter 5- A classification or categorization of data which enables a compiler or interpreter to know how a programmer intends to use the data is a data type. This chapter has been carefully written to provide an easy understanding of the varied data types such as primitive data type, machine data type, Boolean data type, numeric data type, etc.

Chapter 6- The set of rules through which a computer program is assigned its type on the basis of its property is called type system. The chapter closely examines the different type systems to provide an extensive understanding of the subject. It includes topics like nominal type system, structural type system, duck typing, strong and weak typing, etc.

Chapter 7- A general purpose programming language is a programming language that is designed for writing software in a wide array of application domains. This chapter closely analyzes some general purpose programming languages in detail, such as C, C++, Java and Python.

Finally, I would like to thank the entire team involved in the inception of this book for their valuable time and contribution. This book would not have been possible without their efforts. I would also like to thank my friends and family for their constant support.

Hector Nicolson

An Introduction to Programming Language

A formal language which consists of a set of instructions for producing output is termed as a programming language. This chapter provides an introduction to programming languages and includes topics such as programming language implementation, programming language specification, programming language theory, etc.

A programming language is a language designed to describe a set of consecutive actions to be executed by a computer. A programming language is, therefore, a practical way for us humans to give instructions to a computer.

Languages that computers use to communicate with each other have nothing to do with programming languages. They are referred to as communication protocols, and it is quite different from the former. A programming language is very strict, wherein each instruction corresponds to one processor action.

The language used by the processor is called machine code. The code that reaches the processor consists of a series of 0s and 1s known as (binary data). Machine code is, therefore, difficult for humans to understand, which is why intermediary languages, which can be understood by humans, have been developed. The code written in this type of language is transformed into machine code so that the processor can process it.

The assembler was the first programming language ever used. This is very similar to machine code but can be understood by developers. Nonetheless, it is so similar to machine code that it strictly depends on the type of processor used (each processor type may have its own machine code).

Thus, a program developed for one machine may not be portable to another type of machine. The term portability describes the ability to use a software program on different types of machines. A software program written in assembler code may sometimes have to be completely rewritten to work on another type of computer.

A programming language is, therefore, much more understandable than machine code and allows greater portability.

Imperative and Functional Programming Languages

Programming languages are generally divided into two major groups according to how their commands are processed: imperative languages and functional languages.

Imperative Programming Language

An imperative language programs using a series of commands, grouped into blocks and comprised of conditional statements that allow the program to return to a block of commands if the condition is met. These were the first programming languages in use and, even today, many modern languages still use this principle.

Structured imperative languages suffer, however, from lack of flexibility due to the sequentiality of instructions.

Functional Programming Language

A functional programming language (often called procedural language) is a language that creates programs using functions, returning to a new output state and receiving as input the result of other functions. When a function invokes itself, we refer to this as recursion.

Interpretation and Compilation

Programming languages may be roughly divided into two categories: interpreted languages and compiled languages.

Interpreted Language

A programming language is, by definition, different from machine code. This must, therefore, be translated so that the processor can understand the code. A program written in an interpreted language requires an extra program (the interpreter), which translates the program's commands as needed.

Compiled Language

A program written in a compiled language is translated by an additional program called a compiler, which creates a new stand-alone file that does not require any other program to execute itself. Such a file is called an executable.

A program written in a compiled language has the advantage of not requiring an additional program to run it once it has been compiled. Furthermore, as the translation only needs to be done once, at compilation it executes much faster.

However, it is not as flexible as a program written in an interpreted language, as each modification of the source file means that the program must be recompiled for the changes to take effect.

On the other hand, a compiled program has the advantage of guaranteeing the security of the source code. In effect, interpreted language, being a directly legible language, means that anyone can find out the secrets of a program and, thus, copy or even modify the program. There is, therefore, a risk of copyright violation. On the other hand, certain secure applications need code confidentiality to avoid illegal copying (e.g. of bank transactions, on-line payments, secure communications, etc.).

Intermediary Language

Some languages belong to both categories (i.e. LISP, Java, Python, etc.) as programs written in these languages may undergo an intermediary compilation phase into a file written in a language different from the source file and non-executable (requiring an interpreter). Java applets, small programs often loaded in web pages, are compiled files that can only be executed from within a web browser — these are files with the class extension.

Some Examples of Widely Used Languages

Here is a non-exhaustive list of current programming languages:

Language	Main application area	Compiled/interpreted
ADA	Real-time	Compiled language
BASIC	Programming for educational purposes	Interpreted language
C	System programming	Compiled language
C++	System object programming	Compiled language
Cobol	Management	Compiled language
Fortran	Calculation	Compiled language
Java	Internet oriented programming	Intermediary language
MATLAB	Mathematical calculations	Interpreted language
Mathematical	Mathematical calculations	Interpreted language
LISP	Artificial intelligence	Intermediary language
Pascal	Education	Compiled language
PHP	Dynamic website development	Interpreted language
Prolog	Artificial intelligence	Interpreted language
Perl	Processing character strings	Interpreted language

Programming Language Implementation

Programming Language Implementation describes the method for how your code (such as Java) as an example is converted to a language that the machine (processor etc.) understands. We refer to this as machine code. There are 2 main forms of this, compilation and interpretation.

- Programs in a source language are implemented using:

1. Compilation:

  - Translate program from source language to target language.

  - Program in target language is then executed.

  - Compiler finished before program executed.

  - Diagram:

    o Source -> compiler -> target

    o Input -> target -> output

2. Interpretation:

- Directly execute source language program.

- Fetch source program, decode it, execute it.

- Interpreter executes while program executing.

- Diagram:

  o Source + input -> interpreter -> output

3. Or both:

- Compile source program to intermediate language version.

- Interpret intermediate language version.

- Diagram:

  o source -> compiler -> intermediate

  o intermediate + input -> interpreter -> output

Examples

- Compilation:

  o gnatmake foo.adb creates foo.exe

  o foo.exe contains machine language and OS calls

  o foo.exe is directly executed by machine and OS

- Interpretation:

  o Prolog interpreter (ie xsb on rucs)

  o Python interpreter (ie python on rucs)

  o Actually, these use compilation and interpretation

  o Pure interpretation is rare

- Compilation and Interpretation:

  o Prolog/Python interpreter first converts to intermediate code then executes

  o javac Foo.java creates foo.class

  o java Foo interprets foo.class

Pros and Cons of Compilation and Interpretation

- Compilation: compiled code faster than interpreted

- Interpreters:

  o Easier to write than compilers

- o Allow greater flexibility (eg create and execute programs on the fly)
- o Slower: Why? If a statement is in a loop (for example):
  - ▪ Interpreter analyzes the statement each time through loop
  - ▪ Compiler analyzes the statement once
  - ▪ Combination: provides flexibility of interpretation with increased speed
- • Combination: allows platform independence
  - o Intermediate code runs on any machine with an interpreter
- • Combination: relatively easy to port to new machine
  - o Hand translate byte-code interpreter to existing language
  - o Use interpreter to interpret byte-code version of compiler

Compiled Language

A compiled language is a computer programming language whose source code is typically compiled, or translated into machine code, to produce an executable program.

A compiler is a program, which converts a high-level language program/code into binary instructions (machine language) that our computer can interpret, understand and take the appropriate steps to execute the same.

Let us take an example to understand what does the above definition means.

If you ask any person who is associated with programming, that what the first program he/she wrote was, then the obvious answer would be "Hello World". So let us also start with the same.

```
#include<stdio.h>
Void main()
{
printf("Hello, world!");
}
```

This most basic program prints or displays the words "Hello,World!" on the computer screen. But there is a problem. It is not that simple. Behind the curtains there is lot of complex things going. Let us peep inside these things. The hard truth is that our computer cannot understand the commands/instructions contained in a source file (helloworld.c), because C is a high-level language which means, it contains various characters, symbols, and words that represent complex, numbers-based instructions for eg. printf, main, header files etc. The only instructions a computer can execute are those written in machine language, consisting entirely of numbers that is the binary language in terms of 0 and 1. Before our computer can run our C program, our compiler should convert our helloworld.c into an object file; then a program called a linker should convert the object file into an executable file.

The drawing below illustrates the process.

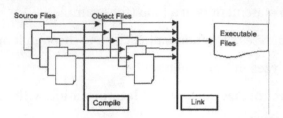

Fig: A Diagram Illustrating the Process Flow of Compiler.

Development

Early compilers were complex in their code and also had large compiling time. But with time, several developments took place which led to advanced compiler. The main reason behind this was the splitting of a compiler into parts. In broad terms compiler can be distributed in 3 parts:

- The front end - It understands the syntax of the source language.

- The mid-end - Its role is to perform the high level optimizations.

- The back end - It produces the assembly language.

Front End

The front-end job is to analyze the source code file and then to make an internal picture of the program (code), called the intermediate representation or IR. It also manages the symbol table which is a data structure which maps or links each symbol in the program or the code with the corresponding information (location and type are few of the information). This is done over several phases:

- Line reconstruction - This phase is required so as to convert the input character sequence into a form, which is ready for the parsing phase.

- Lexical analysis - This phase is required to divide the code into small pieces known as tokens (for example a keyword, identifier or symbol name). This phase is also called lexing or scanning, and the corresponding software for the same is called a lexical analyzer or scanner.

- Preprocessing - Some languages for example C, requires a preprocessing phase which allows the macro substitution and sometimes conditional compilation.

- Syntax analysis - This phase allows parsing the tokens so as to identify the syntactic structure of the code. This phase is used to build a parse tree according to the rules of the grammar of the language.

  - Grammar: The grammar of a language is needed so as to get a meaningful outcome of the language. It doesn't defines it meaning, rather defines rules to get a meaning. Grammars are specified using "productions." Few of the examples of production are as follows:

    Statement -> if (expression) statement else statement

    Statement -> while (expression) statement

o Tree: Basically tree is the data structure used by the compiler internally to represent the meaning of the code. This phase is after the parsing phase in which the grammar of the language is set with the code.

- Semantic analysis - This phase is used to add the semantic information to the parse tree and hence to build the symbol table for the same. This phase performs semantic checks and rejects the incorrect programs or issue warning.

  o Symbol Table: Every subroutine, variable has some information associated with them.

- Variable names – information regarding type, storage location and scope.

- Subroutine names – information regarding locations, argument and types. The information is associated with the help of a "hash map", which is a table that associates a string with the corresponding information.

Back End

In layman language one can say that back end is associated with the generation of the code that is machine independent.

The main phases of the back end include the following:

- Analysis: This phase is the base for the optimization of the code. The typical analyses methods are data flow analysis, dependence analysis, pointer analysis etc.. The call and control flow graph are also built during this phase.

- Optimization: This is the intermediate phase, which converts the language representation into equivalent faster forms. The various optimization methods are inline expansion, dead code elimination, loop transformation, registers allocation etc.

- Code generation: This is generally the last phase in the process as it is associated with output language that is the machine language. This involves resource and storage decisions. Debug data if generated is also generated during this phase.

If we break these three levels then there are total seven levels as follows:

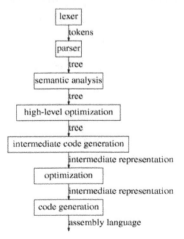

Fig: Flow Chart Representing Different Levels of Development in Compiler.

Out of these few major fields are explained below:

- The Lexer (or lexical analyzer).

- The lexer is the first process in the phase of compiling. Its purpose is to decompose the stream of input characters into discrete sets known as "tokens".

Let us take an example to understand it:

char str[] = "Compiler.";

Decomposes into:

token 1: Keyword, "char"

token 2: Identifier, "str"

token 3: Left square bracket

token 4: Right square bracket

token 5: Equals sign

token 6: String, "Compiler." (Whole strings are token)

token 7: Semicolon

From the above example we can easily say that token is a string of characters, categorized according to the rules that are it may be a Identifier, Number, Comma. The role of lexer is to categorize the token according to a symbol type. The tokens are made so as to make the processing of strings easy.

Parser & Error Detection

The Parser

In today's world when dependency on machines is constantly increasing and lots of complicated tasks are performed by the machines, the phase of parsing is very important. This phase increases the capability of the computer to understand the code and take the corresponding action according to the code.

Parsing is the process of understanding the syntax of a language by representing the code by data structures understood by the compiler.

Generally there are two main methods of parsing that is Top-down parsing and Bottom-up parsing.

- Top-down parsing partitions a program top-down, programs into modules, modules into subroutines, subroutines into blocks.

- Bottom-up parsing group tokens together into terms, then expressions, statements, then blocks and subroutines.

Error Detection

The error detection is a basically not a phase but a process which keeps on going at the background during the various phases. It is an ongoing process occurring throughout.

- Lexer - detects malformed tokens.

- Parser - detects syntax errors.

- Tree - detects annotation type mismatches.

Types and Benefits

Types of Compilers

The compilers are classified according to the machine, input and output. Some of the types of compilers are:

- One-pass compiler

- Threaded code compiler

- Incremental compiler

- Stage compiler

- Just-in-time compiler

- A retargetable compiler

- A parallelizing compiler

Compiler Benefits

- The main benefit of compiler is that it allows you to write the code that is not machine dependent.

- The compiler converts a high-level language into machine code, and it also looks at the source code to make it efficient (by collecting, reorganizing and generating a new set of instructions to make the program run faster on the computer.)

- Compilers help in debugging the code as the font coloring and indentation helps to catch the error by the programmer and they also display warning and error messages.

Advantages of the Compiled Languages

Speed

Compiled languages are always supposed to be fast because of their direct execution by the computer. Speed and performance can change programmer's preference. Especially for large projects, speed and performance is indispensable. Poor speed can crush user experience and can annoy them. C is claimed to be the fastest programming language next to assembly code. It is believed that C is faster than C++ is some instances. One website even says that some algorithms implemented in python may run ten times slower than its equivalent written in C++. It is also obvious that speed always does not matter. There can be places where speed is secondary.

Native Applications are Secured

Even though native applications can be disassembled, the assembly code is not so clear and the source code cannot be that easily obtained. For example it is possible to generate C# code from a .NET assembly using some tools but it is impossible to generate C++ code from an executable.

Large Softwares are Written in Compiled Languages

Large softwares and million dollar projects are often written in compiled languages because of the speed and performance they offer. Many large softwares with huge code bases ranging from Office suites, IDEs, Compilers, Games, time and mission critical applications were written in compiled languages. You can even observe in your computer many softwares are natively compiled. Even the web browser you are viewing this page may be written in compiled languages. Browsers are compiled natively because they need speed. But the parts of a large software may be written in interpreted languages. It is to be noticed that your browser uses many interpreted languages like JScript, VBScript, PHP etc., to view web pages.

Reflection in Compiled Languages

Reflection is not impossible in compiled languages. It is possible with third party libraries like GNU lightning, Boost Serialization etc., Thus it is not true that reflection is impossible in compiled languages. It saves us from creating XML or any other sort of IO routines, which saves our data textually for every persistent data which is time consuming. Some programmers prefer saving their data in binary form rather than simply saving in a textual manner. But writing compilers for native languages that can emit machine code is an advanced step though then there are some libraries like ASMJIT that can be used for real time machine code generation.

Interoperability is possible with .NET, Java and Python

It is possible for a natively compiled application to use .NET(through COM), Java libraries and Python source codes. So if you have a large investment in interpreted languages and planning to move to compiled languages, you can still use your libraries that you have created for .NET, Java and python. There is an option of using .NET controls in your MFC Applications. . NET Assemblies can be accessed by creating a COM wrapper from any program.

Interpreted Language

An interpreted language is any programming language that isn't already in "machine code" prior to runtime. Unlike compiled languages, an interpreted language's translation doesn't happen beforehand. Translation occurs *at the same time as the program is being executed.*

Many of an interpreted language's instructions can be executed directly, without compiling to machine code; however, when certain code is required, an interpreter steps in during runtime and translates it on the spot.

Interpreted languages have a major advantage: they're portable, which means they can run on different operating systems and platforms. Also, because they're translated on the spot, they're going to be optimized for the system on which they're being run. That means there are no middle steps, less memory space is required for interim object code, and there's no need to worry about platform-specific code.

Workings of Interpreting

The interpreter is a program that converts source code—the human-readable code mentioned above—into machine code each time you run the program, one line at a time. It starts interpreting each instruction immediately upon execution, which means that the resulting program runs slower than a compiled program—it's got more going on at runtime. Compiled languages, on the other hand, have already been through this translation before program execution, so they're arguably faster.

Interpreters have some other bonuses, too. They're especially helpful for reviewing, running, and testing an application's functionality during development because they're able to execute high-level programs immediately—and generate helpful error reports. Also, they allow programmers to make small, step-by-step changes during the development process, incrementally, which complements a step-by-step process for adding and then testing smaller sections of an application.

Features that are easier to implement in interpreters than in compilers include (but are not limited to):

- Platform independence (Java's byte code, for example).
- Dynamic evaluation of code (e.g. eval[?] function).
- Ease of debugging (It is easier to get source code information in interpreted language).
- Small program size (Since interpreted languages have flexibility to choose instruction code).
- Object polymorphism.
- Dynamic scoping.

Some languages that are normally interpreted:

- BASIC (although the original version, Dartmouth BASIC, was compiled, as are most modern versions).
- Euphoria
- Forth (traditionally threaded interpreted)
- JavaScript
- Logo (interpretation makes interactivity easier)
- Lisp (traditionally interpreted, modern versions compiled)
- MUMPS (traditionally interpreted, modern versions compiled)
- Perl (compiled to bytecode which is then interpreted)

- Python (compiled to bytecode which is then interpreted)
- Ruby

Pros

When a programmer wants to change a program developed from an interpreted programming language, he will just open the source code and make the change from there. The executables can be easily tweaked with no long compiling services needed. The process of compiling takes several minutes. Therefore, to a serial programmer, those can turn into hours since they have to tweak their programs as they develop them. In the long run, the program developed by an interpreted programming language grows faster.

Another advantage of these languages is that you can run the program as you code just like in python and ruby. When you open the interpreter, you will be provided with a window like a command prompt in which you can perform calculations to cross check with your program. The interpreted programs tend to be more flexible than the compiled ones. The superior features of interpreted languages include:

- They are platform independent, for instance, the byte code in Java.
- They offer dynamic typing as well as dynamic scoping.
- Provides an ease of debugging.
- They use the evaluator reflectively like in a first order evaluation function.
- They provide you with an automatic memory management.

Cons

Interpreted programming languages also have their disadvantages. In these languages, the executable isn't run by the CPU but rather by an interpreter, which is in turn run by the CPU. That creates a huge performance overhead hence much slower than the compiled language. A powerful processor would solve this, but performance intensive programs would make it very slow. Another downside to the interpreted programs is the fact that the executables can only be run by an interpreter. It means that it cannot execute the source code without the interpreter. Besides, the performance of interpreted languages is generally slower than the compiled languages.

Programming Language Theory

Notice how ASTs are *way simpler* than concrete trees. In fact in real compilers, unless the language is extraordinarily simple, you never see a concrete tree! Parsers generally go straight to the abstract syntax tree (though there are exceptions).

Sub-disciplines and Related Fields

There are several fields of study which either lie within programming language theory, or which have a profound influence on it; many of these have considerable overlap. In addition, PLT makes use of many other branches of mathematics, including computability theory, category theory, and set theory.

Formal Semantics

Formal semantics is the formal specification of the behavior of computer programs and programming languages. Three common approaches to describe the semantics or "meaning" of a computer program are denotational semantics, operational semantics and axiomatic semantics.

Type Theory

Type theory is the study of type systems; which are "a tractable syntactic method for proving the absence of certain program behaviors by classifying phrases according to the kinds of values they compute". Many programming languages are distinguished by the characteristics of their type systems.

Program Analysis and Transformation

Program analysis is the general problem of examining a program and determining key characteristics (such as the absence of classes of program errors). Program transformation is the process of transforming a program in one form (language) to another form.

Comparative Programming Language Analysis

Comparative programming language analysis seeks to classify programming languages into different types based on their characteristics; broad categories of programming languages are often known as programming paradigms.

Generic and Metaprogramming

Metaprogramming is the generation of higher-order programs which, when executed, produce programs (possibly in a different language, or in a subset of the original language) as a result.

Domain-specific Languages

Domain-specific languages are languages constructed to efficiently solve problems of a particular part of domain.

Compiler Construction

Compiler theory is the theory of writing *compilers* (or more generally, *translators*); programs which translate a program written in one language into another form. The actions of a compiler are traditionally broken up into *syntax analysis* (scanning and parsing), *semantic analysis* (determining what a program should do), *optimization* (improving the performance of a program as indicated by some metric; typically execution speed) and *code generation* (generation and output of an equivalent program in some target language; often the instruction set of a CPU).

Run-time Systems

Runtime systems refers to the development of programming language runtime environments and their components, including virtual machines, garbage collection, and foreign function interfaces.

Programming Language Specification

Many programming languages are defined in an official document, usually containing a mix of formal notation and informal descriptions. Other languages just have a reference implementation: in that case, the language definition is "whatever that program does."

Some language definitions are sanctioned by an official standards organization (like ISO, IEC, ECMA, ANSI, etc.) while some don't even care about standardization.

Aspects of Language Specifications

Usually a language is defined by considering its

SYNTAX (structure)	SEMANTICS (meaning)	PRAGMATICS (usage)

Syntax

We have a lot of options for defining a syntax:

- CFG (Context Free Grammar)
- BNF (Backus-Naur Form)
- EBNF (Extended Backus-Naur Form)
- ABNF (Augmented Backus-Naur Form)
- Syntax Diagrams (a.k.a. Railroad Diagrams)
- PEG (Parsing Expression Grammar)

The first five forms are all equivalent. They describe exactly the class of context-free languages. PEGs capture a different set of languages, including some context-sensitive languages like $a^n b^n c^n$.

General parsing of CSGs is hard or inefficient. So we normally give a grammar for the context-free parts and leave the context-*sensitive* parts, like "variables must be declared before being used," to the semantics.

Syntax is usually (but not always) divided into:

- A microsyntax, specifying how the characters in the source code stream are grouped into tokens. The microsyntax deals with whitespace, comments, and case sensitivity.

- A macrosyntax, speficying how the tokens are grouped into phrases (such as expressions, statements, declarations, etc.)

- An abstract syntax, which is a much-simplified restructuring of the macrosyntax.

Semantics

A language's semantics is specified by mapping its syntactic forms (often abstract syntax tree fragments) into their meaning. Common approaches include:

- Natural Language (informal)

- "Compile it and run it" (in which the compiler itself defines the language, and thus the compiler correctness problem is trivial—the compiler is by definition always correct)

- Denotational Semantics

- Operational Semantics

- Axiomatic Semantics

- Action Semantics

A hugely important distinction is that between:

- Static Semantics: which deals with legality rules—things you can check without running the code (i.e., "at compile time"), and

- Dynamic Semantics: which deals with the run-time execution behavior.

Pragmatics

Pragmatics does not affect the *formal* specification of programming languages. However, pragmatic concerns must guide your design of a programming language, if you want it to be easy to read, easy to write, and able to be implemented efficiently. Pragmatics encompasses:

- Common programming idioms (the right ways and the wrong ways of doing things).

- Programming environments, e.g., IDEs, REPLs, workspaces, playgrounds, playpens.

- The standard library or libraries.

- The ecosystem for 3rd party libraries (e.g. NPM for JavaScript, Pip for Python, Gems for Ruby, Rocks for Lua, Maven for Java).

An Example Language Specification

Let's consider the language of infix integer arithmetic expressions with optional parentheses, the operators plus, minus, times, divide, and unary negation, and with spaces and tabs allowed between numbers and operators. We'll call the language Ael, for Arithmetic Expression Language.

When designing a language, it's a good idea to sketch forms that you want to appear in your language as well as forms you do *not* want to appear.

Examples	Non-Examples
432	43 2
24* (31/899 +3-0)/(54 /2+ 4+2*3)	24*(31/// /)/(5+---+))
(2)	[fwe]23re 3 1 124efr$#%^@
8*(((3-6)))	--2--

Concrete Syntax

Here is our first try (it will turn out to not be very good, but it works):

```
exp  = space* exp space* op space* exp space*

    | space* numlit space*

    | space* "-" space* exp space*

    | space* "(" space* exp space* ")" space*

op   = "+" | "-" | "*" | "/"

numlit = digit+

digit = "0".."9"

space = " " | "\t"
```

All those "space*" occurrences make the description hard to read. We can make them implicit: if the rule name begins with a capital letter, it will be as if space* appears between all of the expressions on the right hand side. This gives us:

```
Exp  = Exp op Exp

    | numlit

    | "-" Exp

    | "(" Exp ")"

op   = "+" | "-" | "*" | "/"

numlit = digit+

digit = "0".."9"

space = " " | "\t"
```

Some terminology: Lexical categories start with lowercase letters. Phrase categories start with capital letters.

But we still have problems. This grammar can parse the string 9-3*7 in two ways:

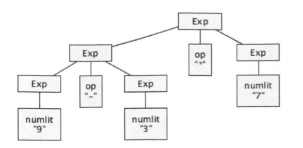 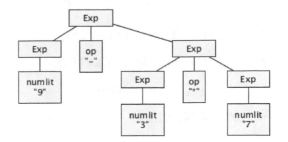

This means our syntax description is ambiguous. We can get rid of the ambiguity and specify an operator precedence at the same time. Like this:

```
Exp    = Term (("+" | "-") Term)*

Term   = Factor (("*" | "/") Factor)*

Factor = "-"? Primary

Primary = "(" Exp ")" | numlit

numlit = digit+

digit  = "0".."9"

space  = " " | "\t"
```

This takes care of precedence concerns, but what if we wanted our grammar to suggest associativity? We can do that too. Here is a way to make our binary operators left-associative:

```
Exp    = Term | Exp ("+" | "-") Term

Term   = Factor | Term ("*" | "/") Factor

Factor = Primary | "-" Primary

Primary = numlit | "(" Exp ")"

digit  = "0".."9"

numlit = digit+

space  = " " | "\t"
```

Abstract Syntax

We had to do a lot of specification work to define expressions as strings of characters. For example, we needed extra tokens (parentheses) and extra categories (Term, Factor, Primary) in order to capture operator precedence. If we just had trees, life would be simpler. So let's define function $\mathscr{A}$ to turn a phrase into an abstract syntax tree. We write trees in the form {*ABC...*} where *A* is the root and *B, C, ...* are the children.

$$\mathscr{A}(E+T)=\{Plus\,\mathscr{A}(E)\,\mathscr{A}(T)\}$$

- $\mathscr{A}(E{-}T)=\{\text{Minus }\mathscr{A}(E).\mathscr{A}(T)\}$

- $\mathscr{A}(T{*}F)=\{\text{Times }\mathscr{A}(T).\mathscr{A}(F)\}$

- $\mathscr{A}(T{/}F)=\{\text{Divide }\mathscr{A}(T).\mathscr{A}(F)\}$

- $\mathscr{A}(-P)=\{\text{Negate }\mathscr{A}(P)\}$

- $\mathscr{A}(n)=\{\text{Numlit }n\}$

- $\mathscr{A}((E))=\mathscr{A}(E)$

Static Semantics

Think of how in a language like Java, an expression like x+5 looks beautifully well formed and well structured. But if x hasn't been declared, or has a type other than a number or string, the expression doesn't *mean* anything. So while it syntactically "correct," it can be determined meaningless without ever running a program containing it.

Ael doesn't have any semantic rules that can be checked statically. Perhaps we could imagine some, if we had, say, limited all integer literals to 64 bits, we would probably put that requirement in the static semantics (even though in theory it is checkable in the syntax).

Dynamic Semantics

A dynamic semantics computes the *meaning* of an abstract syntax tree. In Ael, the meaning of expressions will be integer numeric *values*. Assuming the existence of a function value of for turning number tokens into numeric values, we'll define function $\mathscr{E}$, mapping abstract syntax trees to value, as follows:

- $\mathscr{E}\{\text{Plus }e_1 e_2\}=\mathscr{E}e_1+\mathscr{E}e_2$

- $\mathscr{E}\{\text{Minus }e_1 e_2\}=\mathscr{E}e_1-\mathscr{E}e_2$

- $\mathscr{E}\{\text{Times }e_1 e_2\}=\mathscr{E}e_1\times\mathscr{E}e_2$

- $\mathscr{E}\{\text{Divide }e_1 e_2\}=\mathscr{E}e_1\div\mathscr{E}e_2$

- $\mathscr{E}\{\text{Negate }e\}=-\mathscr{E}e$

- $\mathscr{E}\{\text{Numlit }n\}=value\ of(n)$

Making Sense of the Example

Let's determine the meaning of this string:

-8 * (22-7)

The character string is:

| SPACE | HYPHEN | DIGIT EIGHT | SPACE | TAB | ASTERISK | SPACE | LEFTPAREN |
| DIGIT TWO | DIGIT TWO | HYPHEN | SPACE | SPACE | DIGIT SEVEN | RIGHTPAREN |

Let's apply the lexical rules to tokenize the string. For simplicity, we'll roll up the digits in:

| space | - | numlit(8) | space | space | * | space | (| numlit(22) | - | space | space |
| numlit(7) |) |

The spaces will be skipped eventually, so we can just as well view the token stream like this:

| - | numlit(8) | * | (| numlit(22) | - | numlit(7) |) |

Parsing uncovers the derivation tree, also known as the concrete syntax tree:

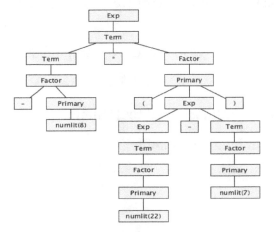

The static semantics is applied to the concrete syntax tree to produce the abstract syntax tree, namely:

```
{Times {Negate {Numlit8}} {Minus {Numlit22} {Numlit7}}}
```

which might be a little easier to read like this:

```
{Times

  {Negate {Numlit8}}

  {Minus {Numlit22} {Numlit7}}}
```

or even easier to read in tree form like this:

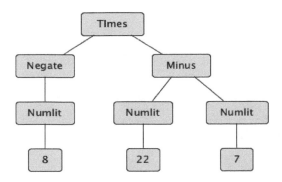

which, *informally* can be shortened to:

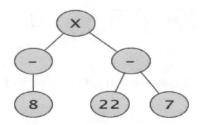

Notice how ASTs are *way simpler* than concrete trees. In fact in real compilers, unless the language is extraordinarily simple, you never see a concrete tree! Parsers generally go straight to the abstract syntax tree (though there are exceptions).

Finally, we apply the dynamic semantics to the AST to compute the meaning:

$\mathcal{E}${Times{Negate{Numlit8}}{Minus{Numlit22}{Numlit7}}}

$=\mathcal{E}${Negate{Numlit8}}$\times$ $\mathcal{E}${Minus{Numlit22}{Numlit7}}}

$=-\mathcal{E}${Numlit8}$\times(\mathcal{E}${Numlit22}$-\mathcal{E}${Numlit7})

$=-8\times(22-7)=-8\times15=-120$

References

- 315-programming-languages: ccm.net, Retrieved 11 June 2018
- What-is-compiler-tutorial: engineersgarage.com, Retrieved 19 April 2018
- Differences-between-compiled-and-Interpreted-Langu-696764: codeproject.com, Retrieved 27 May 2018
- The-basics-of-compiled-languages-interpreted-languages-and-just-in-time-compilers: upwork.com, Retrieved 10 July 2018
- Interpreted-language: encyclopedia.kids.net.au, Retrieved 11 June 2018
- Interpreted-language: itinterviewguide.com, Retrieved 25 April 2018

Three Levels of Programming Languages

A complete understanding of programming languages requires study of the three levels of programming languages- low-level programming language, high-level programming language and very high-level programming language. The following chapter elucidates the varied aspects associated with this area of study.

Low-level Programming Languages

Low level language abbreviated as LLL, are languages close to the machine level instruction set. They provide less or no abstraction from the hardware. A low-level programming language interacts directly with the registers and memory. Since, instructions written in low level languages are machine dependent. Programs developed using low level languages are machine dependent and are not portable.

Low level language does not require any compiler or interpreter to translate the source to machine code. An assembler may translate the source code written in low level language to machine code.

Programs written in low level languages are fast and memory efficient. However, it is nightmare for programmers to write, debug and maintain low-level programs. They are mostly used to develop operating systems, device drivers, databases and applications that require direct hardware access.

Low level languages are further classified in two more categories – Machine language and assembly language.

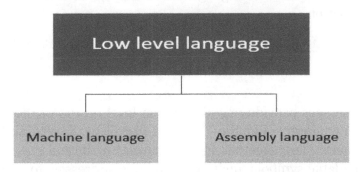

Classification of low level programming language

Machine Language

Machine code, also known as machine language, is the elemental language of computers. It is read by the computer's central processing unit (CPU), is composed of digital binary numbers and looks like a very long sequence of zeros and ones. Ultimately, the source code of every human-readable programming language must be translated to machine language by a compiler or an interpreter, because binary code is the only language that computer hardware can understand.

Each CPU has its own specific machine language. The processor reads and handles instructions, which tell the CPU to perform a simple task. Instructions are comprised of a certain number of bits. If instructions for a particular processor are 8 bits, for example, the first 4 bits part (the opcode) tells the computer what to do and the second 4 bits (the operand) tells the computer what data to use.

```
01001000 01100101 01101100 01101100 01101111 00100001
```

Depending upon the processor, a computer's instruction sets may all be the same length, or they may vary, depending upon the specific instruction. The architecture of the particular processor determines how instructions are patterned. The execution of instructions is controlled by firmware or the CPU's internal wiring.

Human programmers rarely, if ever, deal directly with machine code anymore. If developers are debugging a program at a low level, they might use a printout that shows the program in its machine code form. The printout, which is called a dump, is very difficult and to work with a tool called a dump. Utility programs used to create dumps will often represent four bits by a single hexadecimal to make the machine code easier to read and contain other information about the computer's operation, such as the address of the instruction that was being executed at the time the dump was initiated.

Machine language example:

Below is an example of machine language (binary) for the text "Hello World".

```
01001000 01100101 01101100 01101100 01101111 00100000 01010111 01101111 01110010
01101100 01100100
```

Below is another example of machine language (non-binary), which will print the letter "A" 1000 times to the computer screen.

```
169 1 160 0 153 0 128 153 0 129 153 130 153 0 131 200 208 241 96
```

Assembly

Second-generation languages provide one abstraction level on top of the machine code. In the early days of coding on computers like the TX-0 and PDP-1, the first thing MIT hackers did was write assemblers. Assembly language has little semantics or formal specification, being only a mapping of human-readable symbols, including symbolic addresses, to opcodes, addresses, numeric constants, strings and so on. Typically, one machine instruction is represented as one line of assembly code. Assemblers produce object files that can link with other object files or be loaded on their own.

Most assemblers provide macros to generate common sequences of instructions.

Example: The same Fibonacci number calculator as above, but in x86 assembly language using MASM syntax:

```
fib:
  mov edx, [esp+8]
  cmp edx, 0
  ja @f
  mov eax, 0
  ret


@@:
cmp edx, 2
ja @f
mov eax, 1
ret


@@:
push ebx
mov ebx, 1
mov ecx, 1


@@:
  lea eax, [ebx+ecx]
  cmp edx, 3
  jbe @f
  mov ebx, ecx
  mov ecx, eax
  dec edx
jmp @b


@@:
pop ebx
ret
```

In this code example, hardware features of the x86 processor (its registers) are named and manipulated directly. The function loads its input from a precise location in the stack (8 bytes higher than the location stored in the ESP stack pointer) and performs its calculation by manipulating values in the EAX, EBX, ECX and EDX registers until it has finished and returns. Note that in this assembly language, there is no concept of returning a value. The result having been stored in the EAX register, the RET command simply moves code processing to the code location stored on the stack (usually the instruction immediately after the one that called this function) and it is up to the author of the calling code to know that this function stores its result in EAX and to retrieve it from there. x86 assembly language imposes no standard for returning values from a function (and so, in fact, has no concept of a function); it is up to the calling code to examine state after the procedure returns if it needs to extract a value.

Compare this with the same function in C:

```c
unsigned fib(unsigned n) {
  if (!n)
    return 0;
  else if (n <= 2)
    return 1;
  else {
    unsigned a, c;
    for (a = c = 1; ; --n) {
      c += a;
      if (n <= 3) return c;
      a = c - a;
    }
  }
}
```

This code is very similar in structure to the assembly language example but there are significant differences in terms of abstraction:

- While the input (parameter n) is loaded from the stack, its precise position on the stack is not specified. The C compiler calculates this based on the calling conventions of the target architecture.

- The assembly language version loads the input parameter from the stack into a register and in each iteration of the loop decrements the value in the register, never altering the value in the memory location on the stack. The C compiler could do the same or could update the value in the stack. Which one it chooses is an implementation decision completely hidden from the code author (and one with no side effects, thanks to C language standards).

- The local variables a, b and c are abstractions that do not specify any specific storage location on the hardware. The C compiler decides how to actually store them for the target architecture.

- The return function specifies the value to return, but does not dictate how it is returned. The C compiler for any specific architecture implements a standard mechanism for returning the value. Compilers for the x86 architecture typically (but not always) use the EAX register to return a value, as in the assembly language example (the author of the assembly language example has chosen to copy the C convention but assembly language does not require this).

These abstractions make the C code compilable without modification on any architecture for which a C compiler has been written. The x86 assembly language code is specific to the x86 architecture.

Advantages of low-level Languages

1. Programs developed using low-level languages are fast and memory efficient.

2. Programmers can utilize processor and memory in better way using a low level language.

3. There is no need of any compiler or interpreters to translate the source to machine code. Thus, cuts the compilation and interpretation time.

4. Low-level languages provide direct manipulation of computer registers and storage.

5. It can directly communicate with hardware devices.

Disadvantages of low-level Languages

1. Programs developed using low-level languages are machine dependent and are not portable.

2. It is difficult to develop, debug and maintain.

3. Low level programs are more error prone.

4. Low level programming usually results in poor programming productivity.

5. Programmer must have additional knowledge of the computer architecture of particular machine, for programming in low level language.

High-level Programming Languages

In computer science, a high-level programming language is a programming language with strong abstraction from the details of the computer. In comparison to low-level programming languages, it may use natural language elements, be easier to use, or may automate (or even hide entirely) significant areas of computing systems (e.g. memory management), making the process of developing a program simpler and more understandable relative to a lower-level language. The amount of abstraction provided defines how "high-level" a programming language is.

In the 1960s, low-level programming languages using a compiler were commonly called auto-codes. Examples of autocodes are COBOL and Fortran.

The first high-level programming language designed for computers was Plankalkül, created by Konrad Zuse. However, it was not implemented in his time, and his original contributions were (due to World War II) largely isolated from other developments, although it influenced Heinz Rutishauser's language "Superplan" (and to some degree also Algol). The first really widespread high-level language was Fortran, a machine independent development of IBM's earlier Autocode systems. Algol, defined in 1958 and 1960, by committees of European and American computer scientists, introduced recursion as well as nested functions under lexical scope. It was also the first language with a clear distinction between value and name-parameters and their corresponding semantics. Algol also introduced several structured programming concepts, such as the while-do and if-then-else constructs and its syntax was the first to be described by a formal method, Backus–Naur form (BNF). During roughly the same period Cobol introduced records (also called structs) and Lisp introduced a fully general lambda abstraction in a programming language for the first time.

Features

"High-level language" refers to the higher level of abstraction from machine language. Rather than dealing with registers, memory addresses and call stacks, high-level languages deal with variables, arrays, objects, complex arithmetic or boolean expressions, subroutines and functions, loops, threads, locks, and other abstract computer science concepts, with a focus on usability over optimal program efficiency. Unlike low-level assembly languages, high-level languages have few, if any, language elements that translate directly into a machine's native opcodes. Other features, such as string handling routines, object-oriented language features, and file input/output, may also be present. One thing to note about high-level programming languages is that these languages allow the programmer to be detached and separated from the machine. That is, unlike low-level languages like assembly or machine language, high-level programming can amplify the programmer's instructions and trigger a lot of data movements in the background without their knowledge. The responsibility and power of executing instructions have been handed over to the machine from the programmer.

Abstraction Penalty

High-level languages intend to provide features, which standardize common tasks, permit rich debugging, and maintain architectural agnosticism; while low-level languages often produce more efficient code through optimization for specific system architecture. Abstraction penalty is the border that prevents high-level programming techniques from being applied in situations where computational limitations, standards conformance or physical constraints require access to low-level architectural resources (fi, response time(s), hardware integration). High-level programming exhibits features like more generic data structures/operations, run-time interpretation, and intermediate code files; which often result in execution of far more operations than necessary, higher memory consumption, and larger binary program size. For this reason, code which needs to run particularly quickly and efficiently may require the use of a lower-level language, even if a higher-level language would make the coding easier. In many cases, critical portions of a program mostly in a high-level language can be hand-coded in assembly language, leading to a much faster, more efficient, or simply reliably functioning optimized program.

However, with the growing complexity of modern microprocessor architectures, well-designed compilers for high-level languages frequently produce code comparable in efficiency to what most low-level programmers can produce by hand, and the higher abstraction may allow for more powerful techniques providing better overall results than their low-level counterparts in particular settings. High-level languages are designed independent of a specific computing system architecture. This facilitates executing a program written in such a language on any computing system with compatible support for the Interpreted or JIT program. High-level languages can be improved as their designers develop improvements. In other cases, new high-level languages evolve from one or more others with the goal of aggregating the most popular constructs with new or improved features. An example of this is Scala which maintains backward compatibility with Java which means that programs and libraries written in Java will continue to be usable even if a programming shop switches to Scala; this makes the transition easier and the lifespan of such high-level coding indefinite. In contrast, low-level programs rarely survive beyond the system architecture, which they were written for without major revision. This is the engineering 'trade-off' for the 'Abstraction Penalty'.

Relative Meaning

Examples of high-level programming languages in active use today include Python, Visual Basic, Delphi, Perl, PHP, ECMA Script, Ruby and many others.

The terms high-level and low-level are inherently relative. Some decades ago, the C language, and similar languages, was most often considered "high-level", as it supported concepts such as expression evaluation, parameterized recursive functions, and data types and structures, while assembly language was considered "low-level". Today, many programmers might refer to C as low-level, as it lacks a large runtime-system (no garbage collection, etc.), basically supports only scalar operations, and provides direct memory addressing. It, therefore, readily blends with assembly language and the machine level of CPUs and microcontrollers.

Assembly language may itself be regarded as a higher level (but often still one-to-one if used without macros) representation of machine code, as it supports concepts such as constants and (limited) expressions sometimes even variables, procedures, and data structures. Machine code, in its turn, is inherently at a slightly higher level than the microcode or micro-operations used internally in many processors.

Execution Modes

There are three general modes of execution for modern high-level languages:

Interpreted

When code written in a language is interpreted, its syntax is read and then executed directly, with no compilation stage. A program called an interpreter reads each program statement, following the program flow, then decides what to do, and does it. A hybrid of an interpreter and a compiler will compile the statement into machine code and execute that; the machine code is then discarded, to be interpreted anew if the line is executed again. Interpreters are commonly the simplest implementations of the behavior of a language, compared to the other two variants listed here.

Compiled

When code written in a language is compiled, its syntax is transformed into an executable form before running. There are two types of compilation:

Machine Code Generation

Some compilers compile source code directly into machine code. This is the original mode of compilation, and languages that are directly and completely transformed to machine-native code in this way may be called "truly compiled" languages.

Intermediate Representations

When code written in a language is compiled to an intermediate representation, that representation can be optimized or saved for later execution without the need to re-read the source file. When the intermediate representation is saved, it may be in a form such as byte code. The intermediate representation must then be interpreted or further compiled to execute it. Virtual machines that execute byte code directly or transform it further into machine code have blurred the once clear distinction between intermediate representations and truly compiled languages.

Source-to-Source Translated or Trans-compiled

Code written in a language may be translated into terms of a lower-level programming language for which native code compilers are already widely available. JavaScript and the C programming language are common targets for such translators. See CoffeeScript, Chicken Scheme, and Eiffel as examples. Specifically, the generated C and C++ code can be seen (as generated from the Eiffel programming language when using the EiffelStudio IDE) in the EIFGENs directory of any compiled Eiffel project. In Eiffel, the "Translated" process is referred to as Trans-compiling or Trans-compiled, and the Eiffel compiler as a Transcompiler.

Note that languages are not strictly "interpreted" languages or "compiled" languages. Rather, implementations of language behavior use interpretation or compilation. For example, Algol 60 and Fortran have both been interpreted (even though they were more typically compiled). Similarly, Java shows the difficulty of trying to apply these labels to languages, rather than to implementations; Java is compiled to bytecode and the bytecode is subsequently executed by either interpretation (in a JVM) or compilation (typically with a just-in-time compiler such as HotSpot, again in a JVM). Moreover, compilation, trans-compiling, and interpretation are not strictly limited to just a description of the compiler artifact (binary executable or IL assembly).

High-level Language Computer Architecture

Alternatively, it is possible for a high-level language to be directly implemented by a computer – the computer directly executes the HLL code. This is known as a high-level language computer architecture – the computer architecture itself is designed to be targeted by a specific high-level language.

Advantages of High-level Language

1. Machine Independent – High-level languages are machine independent. This is a very valuable advantage because it means that a company changing computers even one from a different manufacturer, will not be required to rewrite all the programs that it is currently using.

2. Easy to Learn and Use – These languages are very similar to the languages normally used by us in our day-to-day life. Hence they are easy to learn and use.

3. Fewer Errors – In case of high-level languages, since the programmer need not to write the entire small steps carried out by the computer, he is much less likely to make an error.

4. Lower Program Preparation Cost – Writing programs in high-level languages requires less time and effort, which ultimately leads to lower program preparation cost.

5. Better Documentation – A high-level language is designed in such a way that its instructions may be written more like the language of the problem. Thus the statements of a program written in a high-level language can be easily understood by a person familiar with the problem.

6. Easier to Maintain – programs written in high level language are easier to maintain then assembly language or machine language programs.

Disadvantage of High Level Language

Abstraction

What makes high-level languages different from low-level languages is the level of abstraction a language has from system resources. Dealing with system resources on a daily basis can become slow and painful. High-level languages were created to deal with this issue by handling the system for the programmer, freeing her to complete more advanced task while ignoring the minute details of the system, such as memory management. However, this has a drawback in that a programmer might find herself in a situation where system access is required, and a high-level language cannot give that access. A high-level language is typically not suitable for systems programming.

Speed

High-level languages are typically "interpreted" languages rather than the "compiled" low-level languages. "Interpreted" simply means that a language uses an interpreter that executes source code one line at a time, rather than compiling a binary file. However, interpreters are often programs written in compiled languages. Because of this, the interpreted language - Python, as an example - only runs on top of the Python interpreter, which is written in C. This increases the memory and time overhead for interpreted programs, and they often execute more slowly.

System Peculiarities

A seeming strength of high-level code is its portability. High-level code can run on any system that has the appropriate interpreter installed. However, when a program is compiled for a computer, it takes into account the entire environment of that system in its compilation. An interpreted language is already abstracted from the system to such a point that the interpreted program knows nothing about the system except for what the interpreter can supply it.

Programming Limits

Because of the nature of high-level languages, there are certain tasks for which they are not suited for, or at least not yet suited for. Without access to system resources, developing quick, OS-native applications is difficult. Furthermore, even developing an operating system becomes problematic. As more software moves online, this fact becomes less of a concern but, for commercial and industrial usage, interpreted languages may work too slowly, or too far removed from hardware interaction.

Very High-level Programming Languages

Very high-level language (VHLL) is a high level programming language designed to reduce the complexity and amount of source code required to create a program. VHLL incorporates higher data and control abstraction abilities.

A very high level programming language is also known as a goal-oriented programming language.

Sleek and simple, VHLLs supports rapid prototyping of software programs and applications. Generally, VHLLs don't require typical variable declaration and supports autotyping of routine tasks and advanced memory management services. Although designed for limited and specific use, modern very high level languages may be applied to a broad and versatile range of software products and services.

VHLL examples include Python and Ruby.

The reason for using VHLLs is that the solution of a particular problem requires the use of means appropriate to that problem. A typical argument is: "All that remains for the programmer to do is to formulate what the problem is. How the problem is to be solved remains the secret of the VHLL". Unfortunately, it is not quite as easy as that to separate the, *what* from the *how*. Depending on the level of abstraction, they may change places. The *how* of one level turns out to be the, *what* of a lower level. And, even worse, what is possible is determined to some extent by how the problem is tackled. Every mountain-hiker knows that selecting the route (the how) is of crucial importance in order to arrive at the desired destination (what). The *what* and the *how* are, then, linked by economic considerations. That is why the notion of VHLL cannot be defined in contextfree terms of the usual what-how antithesis or in terms of the "very high level" of the languages. We therefore confine ourselves to characterizing VHLLs in terms of features, which many of them have in common. If the purpose of a VHLL is to focus the software developer's attention on describing a problem rather than programming the solution, a VHLL may be characterized as follows:

- Programs written in a VHLL should be compact. By this, we mean, for example, that the formulation of a graph theory problem in a mathematically oriented VHLL such as *Setl* should not be much longer than the mathematical formulation itself.

- VHLLs should have an easily intelligible semantics model; for example:

  o *Setl* is based on the set theory.

  o APL is based on matrix algebra.

  o Snobol4 is based on Markov algorithms.

  o Lisp is based on the A calculus.

  o Prolog is based on Horn logic.

All existing implementations, however, contain constructs, which cannot been xplained in terms of the "easily intelligible" semantic model. VHLLs are designed for use in specific application areas. These application areas correspond well with their semantic model. If VHLLs are used in other areas, they are merely general-purpose languages, offering similar features to any other programming language. This may even result in programs becoming unintelligible.

- VHLLs contain as little explicit flow of control as possible. For example: Lisp uses recursion; Prolog, backtracking as well; Setl is equipped with powerful set constructors.

- VHLLs work with highly powerful data types whose manipulations are very efficiently implemented:

  o *Setl*: sets.

  o *APL*: vectors.

  o *Snobol*: character strings.

  o *Lisp*: lists.

  o *Prolog*: terms.

Today's VHLLs are usually delivered with the following support, which, in our opinion, is practically a must for prototyping purposes:

- A programming environment that facilitates project organization and provides an integrated set of tools. For Lisp, sophisticated programming environments have long been available. Most functional and logical languages are only supplied ready-equipped with a programming environment. Expert system shells are designed as programming environments.

- Means for conversion between data structures and programs (reflexivity). This, for example, enables tools for programming support to be implemented in the VHLL itself. In the case of Lisp and Prolog, reflexivity has proved a decisive factor in speeding up development work, especially in prototype construction.

- Means for their easy combination with other languages and tools.

- An interpreter, an incremental compiler or at least small compilation units in order to ensure sufficient speed of prototype development cycles.

- Incomplete programs written in a VHLL should be executable. This helps speed up the development and debugging cycles.

References

- Levy, Stephen (1994). Hackers: Heroes of the Computer Revolution, Penguin Books. p. 32. ISBN 0-14-100051-1

- Low-level-languages-advantages-disadvantages: codeforwin.org, Retrieved 11 June 2018

- Machine-code-machine-language: whatis.techtarget.com, Retrieved 28 April 2018

- High-level-programming-language, computing: portablecontacts.net, Retrieved 09 July 2018

- What-are-the-merits-and-demerits-of-high-level-language-1342517: technology.blurtit.com, Retrieved 19 March 2018

- The-disadvantages-of-high-level-programming-languages: techwalla.com, Retrieved 11 June 2018

Programming Language Generations

Science and technology have undergone rapid advancement in the past decade which has resulted in the development of the five different generations in programming language. They are first-generation, second-generation, third generation, fourth generation and fifth-generation programming languages; which have been extensively detailed in this chapter.

In the computer industry, these abbreviations are widely used to represent major steps or "generations" in the evolution of programming languages.

1GL or first-generation language was (and still is) machine language or the level of instructions and data that the processor is actually given to work on (which in conventional computers is a string of 0s and 1s).

2GL or second-generation language is assembler(sometimes called "assembly") language. A typical 2GL instruction looks like this:

```
ADD   12,8
```

An assembler converts the assembler language statements into machine language.

3GL or third-generation language is a "high-level" programming language, such as PL/I, C, or Java. Java language statements look like this:

```
public boolean handleEvent (Event evt) {

    switch (evt.id) {

        case Event.ACTION_EVENT: {

            if ("Try me" .equald(evt.arg)) {
```

A compiler converts the statements of a specific high-level programming language into machine language. (In the case of Java, the output is called bytecode, which is converted into appropriate machine language by a Java virtual machine that runs as part of an operating system platform.) A 3GL language requires a considerable amount of programming knowledge.

4GL or fourth-generation language is designed to be closer to natural language than a 3GL language. Languages for accessing databases are often described as 4GLs. A 4GL language statement might look like this:

```
EXTRACT ALL CUSTOMERS WHERE "PREVIOUS PURCHASES" TOTAL MORE THAN $1000
```

5GL or fifth-generation language is programming that uses a visual or graphical development interface to create source language that is usually compiled with a 3GL or 4GL language compiler. Microsoft, Borland, IBM, and other companies make 5GL visual programming products for developing applications in Java, for example. Visual programming allows you to easily envision object-oriented programming class hierarchies and drag icons to assemble program components.

First Generation Programming Language

A first generation (programming) language (1GL) is a grouping of programming languages that are machine level languages used to program first-generation computers. The instructions were given through the front panel switches of these computers, directly to the CPU. There was originally no compiler or assembler to process the instructions in 1GL.

The instructions in 1GL are made of binary numbers, represented by 1s and 0s. This makes the language suitable for the understanding of the machine but very much more difficult to interpret and learn by the human programmer.

Also known as a 1st generation language.

Features of First Geneation

The main features of First Generation are:

- Vacuum tube technology
- Unreliable
- Supported Machine language only
- Very costly
- Generate lot of heat
- Slow Input/output device
- Huge size
- Need of A.C.
- Non portable
- Consumed lot of electricity

Some computer of this generation were:

- ENIAC
- EDVAC
- UNIVAC
- IBM-701
- IBM-650

Advantages of First Generation Language

- They are translation free and can be directly executed by the computers.

- The programs written in these languages are executed very speedily and efficiently by the CPU of the computer system.

- The programs written in these languages utilize the memory in an efficient manner because it is possible to keep track of each bit of data.

Second Generation Programming Language

A second generation (programming) language (2GL) is a grouping of programming languages associated with assembly languages. Unlike the first generation languages, programs can be written symbolically, using English words (also known as mnemonics), in a way that a human can understand and are subsequently converted into machine language by an assembler.

Assembly languages are specific to computer and CPU. The term is used in the distinction between Machine Languages (1GL) and higher-level programming languages (3GL, 4GL, etc.)

Also known as a 2nd generation language.

Assembly Languages originated in the 1940s, and are attributed to the efforts of the American naval officer Grace Hopper, with the introduction of the FLOW-MATIC language for the ENIAC computer.

2GL are mostly used for the implementation of low-level kernels and drivers and for performance-oriented and processing-intensive applications such as computer games, graphic manipulation applications and video editing applications.

The symbolic representation of machine Instructions, registers and memory addresses allows the programmer to produce a human-readable program. For the computer to understand the program it must be converted to a machine-readable format using an Assembler. The Assembler usually converts the Mnemonics via a one-to-one mapping from the mnemonic representation to machine language, for a particular processor family and environment.

Assemblers allow for easier debugging of the program, and also introduce more advanced programming mechanisms such as macro Programming and structured Programming.

Second-Generation Programming Languages Characteristics

Second-generation structures are based on first-generation structures, but the data structures use simple generalizations, such as dynamic arrays and different lower bounds. Like first-generation, they are still linear and closely based on machine-addressing modes. Second-generation languages usually have strong built-in types, hierarchical name structures and better control of name spaces, which allows for efficient dynamic memory allocation. This is because hierarchical structuring increases control flow, which eliminates the need for confusing networks.

These control structures offer recursive procedures, parameter-passing modes and syntactic structures. Second-generation languages use word policies that establish keyword-in-context rules. During their peak of popularity, many second-generation programmers took advantage of the unlimited generalization functionality, which produced both desirable results and undesirable consequences. These languages are specific to a particular type of processor family and processor environment. They are occasionally used in kernels and device drivers to produce processing intensive games and graphics.

Advantages of Second-generation Language

- It is easy to develop understand and modify the program developed in these languages are compared to those developed in the first generation programming language.

- The programs written in these languages are less prone to errors and therefore can be maintained with a great case.

Third Generation Programming Language

A third-generation programming language (3GL), is a programming language that is machine-independent, meaning programs written in that language can be compiled to run on many different devices. Compare this to a first-generation programming language (machine code), or a second-generation programming language (assembly language). In those languages, the program is written specifically for a certain type of CPU and instruction set.

3GLs first appeared in the 1950s with the development of FORTRAN, ALGOL, and COBOL. These languages are considered "high-level," even though they are a much lower level than modern high-level programming languages such as C++, Ruby, and JavaScript.

Moving away from the cryptic commands of Assembly Language and one step below Fourth Generation Languages, programmers in 3GLs are favored by using aggregate data types, variable names and the ability to define sections of code as subroutines. The program in 3GL is called the Source Program or Source Code and it subsequently converted by a specialized program, the Compiler, to Object Code, understandable by the specific computer and CPU.

Since the introduction of the Compiler in 1952, hundreds of 3GLs have been developed, specifically providing benefits for programmers of applications serving various business and scientific domains. In 1957, IBM created FORTRAN (FORmula TRANslator) to facilitate computerized mathematically-intensive scientific research. COBOL (COmmon Business Oriented Language) was instrumental in spurring a surge of programs serving the business arena, with its enhanced ability to provide record keeping and data management services.

Advantages of Third Generation Programming Language

- It is easy to develop, learn and understand the program.

- As the programs written in these languages are less prone to errors they are easy to maintain.

- The program written in these languages can be developed in very less time as compared to the first and second-generation language.

Fourth Generation Programming Language

A fourth generation (programming) language (4GL) is a grouping of programming languages that attempt to get closer than 3GLs to human language, form of thinking and conceptualization.

4GLs are designed to reduce the overall time, effort and cost of software development. The main domains and families of 4GLs are: database queries, report generators, data manipulation, analysis and reporting, screen painters and generators, GUI creators, mathematical optimization, web development and general purpose languages.

Also known as a 4th generation language, a domain specific language, or a high productivity language.

4GLs are more programmer-friendly and enhance programming efficiency with usage of English-like words and phrases, and when appropriate, the use of icons, graphical interfaces and symbolical representations. The key to the realization of efficiency with 4GLs lies in an appropriate match between the tool and the application domain. Additionally, 4GLs have widened the population of professionals able to engage in software development.

Many 4GLs are associated with databases and data processing, allowing the efficient development of business-oriented systems with languages that closely match the way domain experts formulates business rules and processing sequences. Many of such data-oriented 4GLs are based on the Structured Query Language (SQL), invented by IBM and subsequently adopted by ANSI and ISO as the standard language for managing structured data.

Most 4GLs contain the ability to add 3GL-level code to introduce specific system logic into the 4GL program.

The most ambitious 4GLs, also denoted as Fourth Generation Environments, attempt to produce entire systems from a design made in CASE tools and the additional specification of data structures, screens, reports and some specific logic.

Objectives of Fourth Generation Languages

- Increasing the speed of developing programs.
- Minimizing user effort to obtain information from computer.
- Decreasing the skill level required of users so that they can concentrate on the application rather than the intricacies of coding, and thus solve their own problems without the aid of a professional programmer.
- Minimizing maintenance by reducing errors and making programs that are easy to change.

Depending on the language, the sophistication of fourth generation languages varies widely. These languages are usually used in conjunction with a database and its data dictionary.

Five basic types of language tools fall into the fourth generation language category:

1. Query languages

2. Report generators.

3. Applications generators.

4. Decision support systems and financial planning languages.

5. Some microcomputer application software.

Query Languages

Query languages allow the user to ask questions about, or retrieve information from database files by forming requests in normal human language statements (such as English). The difference between the definitions for query language and for database management systems software is so slight that most people consider the definitions to be the same. Query languages do have a specific grammar vocabulary, and syntax that must be mastered, but this is usually a simple task for both users and programmers.

Report Generators

Report generators are similar to query languages in that they allow users to ask questions from a database and retrieve information from it for a report (the output); however, in case of a report generator, the user is unable to alter the contents of the database file. And with a report generator, the user has much greater control over what the output will look like. The user of a report generator can specify that the software automatically determine how the output should look or can create his or her own customized output reports using special report generator command instructions.

Application Generators

Application generators allow the user to reduce the time it takes to design an entire software application that accepts input, ensures data has been input accurately, performs complex calculations and processing logic, and outputs information in the form of reports. The user must key into computer-useable form the specification for what the program is supposed to do. The resulting file is input to the applications generator, which determine how to perform the tasks and which then produces the necessary instructions for the software program.

Decision support systems and financial planning languages combine special interactive computer programs and some special hardware to allow high level managers to bring data and information together from different sources and manipulate it in new ways.

Some microcomputer applications software can also be used to create specialized applications – in other words, to create new software. Microcomputer software packages that fall into this category include many spreadsheet programs (such as Lotus 1-2-3), database managers (Such as dBase IV), and integrated packages (such as Symphony).

Advantages of 4GL

1. Programming productivity is increased. One line of 4GL code is equivalent to several lines of 3GL code.

2. System development is faster.

3. Program maintenance is easier.

4. The finished system is more likely to be what the user envisaged, if a prototype is used and the user is involved throughout the development.

5. End user can often develop their own applications.

6. Programs developed in 4GLs are more portable than those developed in other generation of languages.

7. Documentation is improved because many 4GLs are self-documenting.

Disadvantages of 4GL

1. The programs developed in the 4GLs are executed at a slower speed by the CPU.

2. The programs developed in these programming languages need more space in the memory of the computer system.

Fifth Generation Programming Language

A fifth generation (programming) language (5GL) is a grouping of programming languages build on the premise that a problem can be solved, and an application built to solve it, by providing constraints to the program (constraint-based programming), rather than specifying algorithmically how the problem is to be solved (imperative programming).

In essence, the programming language is used to denote the properties, or logic, of a solution, rather than how it is reached. Most constraint-based and logic programming languages are 5GLs. A common misconception about 5GLs pertains to the practice of some 4GL vendors to denote their products as 5GLs, when in essence the products are evolved and enhanced 4GL tools.

Also known as a 5th generation language.

The leap beyond 4GLs is sought by taking a different approach to the computational challenge of solving problems. When the programmer dictates how the solution should look, by specifying conditions and constraints in a logical manner, the computer is then free to search for a suitable solution. Most of the applicable problems solved by this approach can currently be found in the domain of artificial intelligence.

Considerable research has been invested in the 1980s and 1990s, into the development of 5GLs. As larger programs were built, it became apparent that the approach of finding an algorithm given a problem description, logical instructions and a set of constraint is a very hard problem in itself.

During the 1990s, the wave of hype that preceded the popularization of 5GLs and predictions that they will replace most other programming languages, gave way to a more sober realization.

PROLOG (acronym for PROgramming LOGic) is an example of a Logical Programming Language. It uses a form of mathematical logic (predicate calculus) to solve queries on a programmer-given database of facts and rules.

Advantages of Fifth Generation Languages

- These languages can be used to query the database in a fast and efficient manner.

- In this generation of language, the user can communicate with the computer system in a simple and an easy manner.

References

- Programming-language-generations: whatis.techtarget.com, Retrieved 11 June 2018

- First-generation-programming-language-24304: techopedia.com, Retrieved 28 April 2018

- Generations-of-programming-language, basics: includehelp.com: Retrieved 29 May 2018

- Second-generation-programming-language-24305: techopedia.com, Retrieved 27 March 2018

- Discuss-fourth-generation-languages-advantages-disadvantages: mpstudy.com, Retrieved 15 July 2018

- What-is-a-second-generation-programming-language: computersciencedegreehub.com, Retrieved 07 April 2018

Syntax and Semantics

The set of rules which is used to define a combination of symbols which is considered to be a perfectly structured document in a programming language is referred to as syntax. Semantics is concerned with meaning. It describes the processes followed by a computer when executing a program in a specific language. The aim of this chapter is to explore the important aspects of syntax and semantics in programming languages such as lexical analysis, syntax highlighting, action semantics, etc.

Syntax

In Programming, Syntax is the grammar, structure, or order of the elements in a language statement. (Semantics is the meaning of these elements.) Syntax applies to computer languages as well as to natural languages. Usually, we think of syntax as "word order." However, syntax is also achieved in some languages such as Latin by inflectional case endings. In computer languages, syntax can be extremely rigid as in the case of most assembler languages or less rigid in languages that make use of "keyword" parameters that can be stated in any order.

Modules

To start with, syntax definitions consist of modules that can import other syntax modules. This is useful for dividing a large grammar into parts, but also for reusing a standard language component (e.g. expressions) between language definitions, or for composing the syntax of different languages. We first examine the main syntax module for Calc, which is named after the language and which imports module *CalcLexical* which defines the lexical syntax of the language:

```
module Calc

imports CalcLexical
```

The module defines the sorts Program and Exp as start symbols, which means that parsing starts with these sorts:

```
context-free start-symbols Program Exp
```

Context-free Syntax

Syntactically, a language is a set of well-formed sentences. (In programming languages, sentences are typically known as programs.) Sentences are typically formed by composing different kinds of phrases, such as identifiers, constants, expressions, statements, functions, and modules. In grammar terminology there are two broad categories of phrases, *terminals* and *non-terminals*. In SDF3 we use *sorts* to identify both categories. For Calc we start with defining the Program and Stat sorts:

```
sorts Program Stat
```

A grammar consists of rules (known as productions) for composing phrases from sub-phrases. A Calc program consists of a list of statements that are either bindings that bind the value of an expression to a variable (identifier) or expression statements. This is defined by the following productions:

```
context-free syntax
Program.Program = <<{Stat "\n"}+>>


Stat.Bind = <<ID> = <Exp>;>
Stat.Exp = <<Exp>;>
```

If we take a closer look at the Stat.Bind production we see the following ingredients:

- The production defines one of two altneratives for the Stat sort. The alternatives of a sort are defined by separate productions. This makes it possible to introduce productions in an order that makes sense for presenting a language definition. Instead of defining all productions for a sort in one block, it is rather possible to define the productions for different sorts that together define a language concept together. Furthermore, it enables *modular* definition of syntax.

- The body a production defines the composition of sub-phrases that it corresponds to. Thus, the body <<ID> = <Exp>;> defines a bind statement as the composition of an identifier, followed by an equal sign, followed by an expression, terminated by a semicolon.

- The body is known as a *template* and uses inverse quotation. The template makes everything inside literal elements of the text to be parsed, except for the quasi-quoted sorts (<ID> and <Exp>).

- The sub-phrases are implicitly separated by layout (whitespace and comments). The definition of layout is not built-in. We will see the definition of the layout for Calc when we discuss lexical syntax below.

- The constructor is used to construct abstract syntax tree nodes. Thus, the Bind constructor creates trees with two arguments trees for the identifier (ID) and expression (Exp) subtrees; in abstract syntax we leave out the literals and layout.

Note that a program is defined as a list of one or more statements, which could be expressed with the regular expression operator + as Stat+. The SDF3 notation {Sort sep}+denotes a list of Sort phrases *separated* by sep. For example, {Exp ","}+ is a list of one or more expressions separated by commas. In the definition of statement lists we use a newline as separator. However, this does not imply that statements should be separated by newlines, but rather that newlines are inserted when formatting a program.

Expressions

Sorts and productions give us the basic concepts for defining syntax. Calc programs essentially consist of a sequence of expressions. So, the bulk of the its syntax definition consists of productions for various expression forms denoted by the Exp sort:

```
sorts Exp

context-free syntax

 Exp = <(<Exp>)> {bracket}
```

The *bracket* production defines that we can enclose an expression in parentheses. The bracket annotation states that we can ignore this production when constructing abstract syntax trees. That is, the abstract syntax tree for (x + 1) is the same as the abstract syntax tree for x + 1.

Operator Syntax

Operators are the workhorse of a language such as Calc. They capture the domain-specific operations that the language is built around. We start with the syntax of arithmetic operators:

```
context-free syntax // numbers

 Exp.Num = NUM

 Exp.Min = <-<Exp>>

 Exp.Pow = <<Exp> ^ <Exp>> {right}

 Exp.Mul = <<Exp> * <Exp>> {left}

 Exp.Div = <<Exp> / <Exp>> {left}

 Exp.Sub = <<Exp> - <Exp>> {left, prefer}

 Exp.Add = <<Exp> + <Exp>> {left}
```

Note that the concrete syntax is directly aligned with the abstract syntax. An addition is represented as the composition of two expression and the + symbol. This is best illustrated using term notation for abstract syntax trees. The term C(t1, ..., tn) denotes the abstract syntax tree for a production with constructor C and n sub-trees. For example, the term Add(Num("1"), Var("x")) represents the abstract syntax tree for the expression 1 + x.

The consequence of this direct alignment is that the grammar is ambiguous. According to the Exp. Add production there are two ways to parse the expression 1 + x + y, i.e. as

Add (Add (Num("1"), Var("x")), Var("y")) or as

Add (Num ("1"), Add(Var("x"), Var("y"))).

A common approach to disambiguate the grammar for an expression language is by encoding the associativity and precedence of operators in the productions using additional sorts to represent precedence levels. However, that leads to grammars that are hard to understand and maintain and that do not have a one-to-one correspondence to the desired abstract syntax.

In SDF3, ambiguous expression syntax can be *declaratively* disambiguated using separate associativity and priority declarations. For example, the Exp.Add production above defines that addition is left associative. That is, the expression 1 + x + y should be interpreted as Add(Add(-Num("1"), Var("x")), Var("y")), i.e. (1 + x) + y. The other operators are disambiguated similarly according to standard mathematical conventions. Note that power (exponentiation) is *right* associative, i.e. x ^ y ^ z is equivalent to x ^ (y ^ z).

Comparison operators:

```
context-free syntax // numbers

Exp.Eq = <<Exp> == <Exp>> {non-assoc}

Exp.Neq = <<Exp> != <Exp>> {non-assoc}

Exp.Gt = [[Exp] > [Exp]] {non-assoc}

Exp.Lt = [[Exp] < [Exp]] {non-assoc}
```

Non-assoc means that a phrase such as a < b == true is not syntactically well-formed. One should use parentheses, for example (a < b) == true, to explicitly indicate the disambiguation.

booleans:

```
context-free syntax // booleans


Exp.True = <true>

Exp.False = <false>

Exp.Not  = <!<Exp>>

Exp.And  = <<Exp> & <Exp>> {left}

Exp.Or  = <<Exp> | <Exp>> {left}


Exp.If = <
  if(<Exp>)
    <Exp>
  else
    <Exp>
>
```

variables:

```
context-free syntax // variables and functions


Exp.Var = ID
```

```
Exp.Let = <

  let <ID> = <Exp> in

  <Exp>

>

Exp.Fun = <\\ <ID+> . <Exp>>

Exp.App = <<Exp> <Exp>> {left}
```

Disambiguation

priorities:

context-free priorities

```
Exp.Min

> Exp.App

> Exp.Pow

> {left: Exp.Mul Exp.Div}

> {left: Exp.Add Exp.Sub}

> {non-assoc: Exp.Eq Exp.Neq Exp.Gt Exp.Lt}

> Exp.Not

> Exp.And

> Exp.Or

> Exp.If

> Exp.Let

> Exp.Fun
```

sorts Type

context-free syntax

```
Type.NumT = <Num>

Type.BoolT = <Bool>

Type.FunT = [[Exp] -> [Exp]] {right}

Type    = <(<Type>)> {bracket}
```

template options

```
ID = keyword {reject}
```

Lexical Syntax

lexical syntax:

```
module CalcLexical
```

identifiers:

```
lexical syntax
 ID = [a-zA-Z] [a-zA-Z0-9]*
lexical restrictions
 ID -/- [a-zA-Z0-9\_]
```

numbers:

```
lexical syntax // numbers
 INT   = "-"? [0-9]+
 IntGroup = [0-9][0-9][0-9]
 IntPref = ([0-9] | ([0-9][0-9])) ","
 INT   = IntPref? {IntGroup ","}+
 FLOAT = INT "." [0-9]+
 NUM   = INT | FLOAT
lexical restrictions
 INT  -/- [0-9]
 FLOAT -/- [0-9]
 NUM  -/- [0-9]
```

strings:

```
lexical syntax
 STRING     = "\"" StringChar* "\""
 StringChar   = ~[\"\n]
 StringChar   = "\\\""
 StringChar   = BackSlashChar
 BackSlashChar = "\\"
lexical restrictions
 // Backslash chars in strings may not be followed by "
 BackSlashChar -/- [\"]
```

layout:

```
lexical syntax // layout: whitespace and comments

LAYOUT       = [\ \t\n\r]

CommentChar  = [\*]

LAYOUT       = "/*" InsideComment* "*/"

InsideComment = ~[\*]

InsideComment = CommentChar

LAYOUT       = "//" ~[\n\r]* NewLineEOF

NewLineEOF   = [\n\r]

NewLineEOF   = EOF

EOF       =

lexical restrictions

CommentChar -/- [\/]

// EOF may not be followed by any char

EOF      -/- ~[]

context-free restrictions

// Ensure greedy matching for comments

LAYOUT? -/- [\ \t\n\r]

LAYOUT? -/- [\/].[\/]

LAYOUT? -/- [\/].[\*]
```

Grammar Interpretations

A grammar can be interpreted for (at least) the following operations:

- Parsing

  Recognizing a well-formed sentence and constructing an abstract syntax tree.

- Signature

  Derive schema that defines well-formed abstract syntax trees.

- Formatting

  Map an abstract syntax tree to a well-formed sentence.

- Parse Error Recovery

  When editing programs, the program text is often in a syntactically incorrect state. Since all editor services depend on an AST representation of the program, getting stuck on syntax errors would reduce the utility of an editor. To get a better editing experience, a parser with error recovery does a best effort job to parse as much as possible and still produce an AST.

- Syntactic Completion

  Using a new language

Syntax Error

A syntax error in computer science is an error in the syntax of a coding or programming language, entered by a programmer. Syntax errors are caught by a software program called a compiler, and the programmer must fix them before the program is compiled and then run.

One way to think of a syntax error is that it presents a significant gatekeeping function in the clarity and usability of code. As in other digital technologies such as an email address, the omission or misplacement of just one letter, number or character creates critical problems for a computing system that has to read code in a linear way. It is also helpful to think about the usual causes of syntax errors – either a programmer makes a typographical error, or forgets the format or sequence of some word or command.

Syntax errors are different from errors that affect programs during run time. Many logical errors in computer programming do not get caught by the compiler, because although they may cause grievous errors as the program runs, they do conform to the program's syntax. In other words, the computer cannot tell whether a logical error is going to create problems, but it can tell when code does not conform to the syntax, because the understanding of that syntax is built into the compiler's native intelligence.

Another aspect of understanding syntax errors is that they demonstrate how, unlike humans, computers cannot use input that is not perfectly designed. The lack of a period or comma in a sentence or command, or two swapped letters in a word, confounds the compiler and makes its work impossible. On the other hand, human readers can spot typographical errors and understand them in the context of what they are reading. It is likely that as computers evolve through the coming decades, engineers may be able to create compilers and systems that can handle some types of syntax errors; even now, in some compiling environments, tools can auto-correct syntax errors on site.

Example

Here is an example of a statement containing a syntax error:

```
sum ( where ( a > v , ones ( length ( a ) ) , 0)
```

Let's take a look at what Basis prints out as a result of this error:

```
sum ( where ( a > v , ones ( length ( a ) ) , 0 )
                                  ^ Syntax error.
Attempting to parse after following context:
<lhs> ( <argitem>
which may not be followed by "cr" in this context.
Count of parentheses unbalanced: left = right +  1.
Expected one of the following (?):
 ) ,
Returned to user input level.
```

When the parser echoes the line being parsed, with "Syntax error" underneath the line, the caret points to where the error was detected, not necessarily to where it occurred. In this case, the caret points past the end of the line, a clue that something is missing. The information about the parsing context is useful only to a Basis expert, but the statement that it cannot be followed by "cr" (carriage return) is useful. That seems to say that the line is too short and reinforces our suspicion that something is missing. The next line points out that so far in the line there have been more left parentheses than right, and the next two lines confirm that maybe the parser expected a right parenthesis or a comma. The expression was missing a right parenthesis.

The list of expected symbols (as opposed to the one which actually occurred) is not 100% accurate. It may not contain all possible symbols, which could occur in the given context; or worse yet, it could be such a long list as to be virtually unusable. In the above case it did contain the missing symbol, and it was not needlessly long. Below is a case where the list supplied by the parser is too extensive to be much help:

```
function f(x)
if ( x > 0 ) then return 0
return 1
endf
```

The diagnostic produced by this error is:

```
    endf
   ^ Syntax error.
Attempting to parse after following context:
function <funcdes> <eos> <stlist> if <ifexp> then <stlist>
which may not be followed by "endf" in this context.
Expected one of the following (?):
```

```
( + - : << >> ? Groupname [ ^ ` break call chameleon character
complex complex-constant cr do double double-complex-constant
double-constant else elseif endif for forget function
hex-constant if indirect integer integer-constant list logical
name next octal-constant range read real real-constant return
string while whitespace \{ Returned to user input level.
```

What has happened here is a relatively common error--the programmer has not completed an IF statement. An ENDIF or ELSE clause have been omitted. Deeply buried in the list of "expected" symbols you will find these two reserved words, and also ELSEIF. It is possible to imagine a meaningful continuation of the program starting with any of the other symbols in the list, but the length of the list quite effectively hides the real clues in its depth. Unfortunately, a one-pass, no-backtracking parser with a one token lookahead can not apprehend the entire surrounding context as a human can; it only knows what symbols might, in some circumstances, lead to a correct statement if placed in the current position.

This example also hints at another problem with syntax errors: they may be discovered long after the actual error occurred. In this case, if an ENDIF was intended prior to the return 1 statement, the error was not detected until the ENDF was seen, after that statement had been consumed. There could equally well have been a hundred statements parsed before the ENDF caused the parser to detect the error. Thus our advice is that if you have trouble tracking down a syntax error, don't confine your search to the immediate neighborhood where it was detected. It could have been many lines previous.

Lexical Analysis

The lexer, also called lexical analyzer or tokenizer, is a program that breaks down the input source code into a sequence of lexemes. It reads the input source code character by character, recognizes the lexemes and outputs a sequence of tokens describing the lexemes.

Lexeme

A lexeme is a single identifiable sequence of characters, for example, keywords (such as class, func, var, and while), literals (such as numbers and strings), identifiers, operators, or punctuation characters (such as {, (, and .).

Token

A token is an object describing the *lexeme*. A token has a type (e.g. Keyword, Identifier, Number, or Operator) and a value (the actual characters of the described lexeme). A token can also contain other information such as the line and column numbers where the lexeme was encountered in the source code.

```
/// Enumeration of all types of token.
let TokenType = {
  String:    'string',
  Number:    'number',
  Identifier: 'identifier',
  While:     'while',
  If:        'if',
  // ...
};
class Token {
  /// Initializes a new 'Token' object.
  /// - type.  A 'TokenType' corresponding to the type
  ///      of the newly created 'Token'.
  /// - value. The 'String' value of the token.
  ///      The actual characters of the lexeme described.
  /// - line.  The line number where the token
  ///      was encountered in the source code.
  /// - column. The column number where the token
  ///      was encountered in the source code.
  constructor(type, value, line, column) {
    this.type = type;
    this.value = value;
    this.line = line;
    this.column = column;
  }
}
```

An implementation of a token in JavaScript (ES6). Using this class, the lexeme "Hello, Blink!", for example, could be represented by the token Token(TokenType.String, "Hello, Blink!").

The Lexer in Code

A lexer can be implemented as a class, whose constructor takes an input string in parameter (representing the source code to perform lexical analysis on). It exposes a method to recognize and return the next token in the input.

```
class Lexer {
  constructor(input) {
```

```
    this.input = input;
  }
  // Returns the next recognized 'Token' in the input.
  nextToken() {
    // ...
  }
}
```

Recognition of Tokens

All possible lexemes that can appear in code written in a programming language are described in the specification of that programming language as a set of rules called lexical grammar. Rules in the lexical grammar are often transformed into automata called finite state machines (*FSM*). The lexer then simulates the finite state machines to recognize the tokens.

Lexical Grammar

The lexical grammar of a programming language is a set of formal rules that govern how valid lexemes in that programming language are constructed. For example, the rules can state that a string is any sequence of characters enclosed in double-quotes or that an identifier may not start with a digit. The rules in the lexical grammar are often expressed with a set of regular definitions.

A regular definition is of the form <element_name> <production_rule> where <element_name> is the name given to a symbol or a lexeme that can be encountered in the programming language and <production_rule> is a regular expression describing that symbol or lexeme.

```
letter = [a-zA-Z]
```

For example, the regular definition above defines a *letter* as any lowercase or uppercase alphabet character.

A regular definition can make use, in its regular expression, of any element name defined in the same lexical grammar.

```
letter      = [a-zA-Z]
digit       = [0-9]
identifier  = (letter | _) (letter | digit | _)*
```

As an example, in the regular definitions above, the definition *identifier* reuses the definitions *letter* and *digit*, in its production rule as if *letter* and *digit* were symbols, to define an identifier as *any string starting with a letter or an underscore,* followed by *zero or more occurrences of a letter, a digit or an underscore.*

Finite State Machines

A Finite State Machine or FSM is an abstract machine that is in *one and only one* state at any point in time. The FSM can change from one state to another as a result of an event. Changing from a state to another is called a transition. To better understand this, let's consider the following example.

A light bulb can be thought of as a FSM. A light bulb can be in only one of two states at any point in time, ON or OFF. The light bulb transitions from the state ON to the state OFF by the press of a switch and transitions from the state OFF to ON by the press of the same switch.

FSMs are often represented with state diagrams.

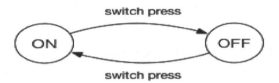

A FSM simulating a light bulb. States are represented with circles and transitions with labeled arrows.

Lexical Grammar and FSMs

To recognize a token described by a regular definition, the regular expression in the definition is often transformed into a FSM. The resulting FSM has a finite number of states comprising an initial state and a set of accepting states.

The FSM moves from one state to another by *consuming one of the characters or elements* in the regular expression. Following the transitions from the initial state to one of the accepting states yields a valid string described by the regular expression.

For example, the regular expression $a \mid b$ can be converted into the following FSM.

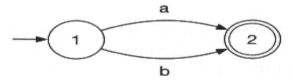

The above FSM has two states labeled 1 and 2. The arrow pointing to 1 and coming out from nowhere indicates that 1 is the initial state and the inner circle on 2 indicates that 2 is an accepting state of this FSM.

From 1 to 2, we can either follow the top transition by consuming the character a yielding the string a or follow the bottom transition by consuming the character b yielding the string b. a and b are effectively the two possible strings described by the regular expression $a \mid b$.

Another example.

Following the transitions from the initial state 1 to the accepting state 6 on the above FSM can yield only one string, *Blink*.

From Regular Expression to FSM

We can transform any regular expression into a FSM by building on top of the following three basic rules.

A | B

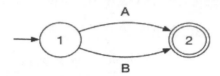

The regular expression $A \mid B$ is represented by a FSM with two states. From the state **1**, we can either consume A and move to the accepting state **2** or consume B and also move to the accepting state **2**.

AB

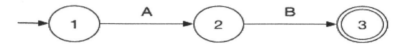

The concatenation AB is represented by a FSM with three states. From **1**, first we move to **2** by consuming A, and then we move to the accepting state **3** by consuming B.

A*

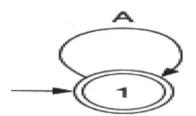

A^* is represented by a FSM with only one state being both the initial and the accepting state with a transition to itself, creating a loop. From **1**, we can either go nowhere because **1** is also the accepting state, thus yielding the *empty string* or we can follow the transition by consuming A which will lead back to **1**; again we can either go nowhere or follow the transition. That will generate the stringsA, AA, AAA, AA...AAA and the *empty string*.

Any other regular expression can be transformed into a *FSM* by reusing one or any combination of the basic rules above.

Let's take a look at some examples.

R = (a|b)c

R is $a \mid b$ followed by c. First, the FSM for $a \mid b$ is

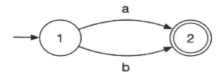

Then, the concatenation to *c* is represented by a transition from the state **2** to a new accepting state.

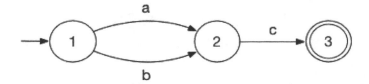

The two possible strings that can be generated by simulating this FSM are acand bc.

R = (a|b)*c

First the FSM for *(a|b)** is a loop with two options *a* and *b* at each iteration.

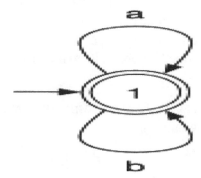

Then we add a new transition to concatenate *c*.

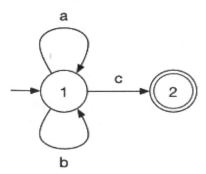

Simulating or running the above FSM can yield such strings as c, ac, abc, bac, bc, bbabaabbc, aaaaac or abbbaabbbaabbc.

R = a(bc)*

*a(bc)** is the character *a* followed by zero or more repetitions of the concatenation *bc*. The FSM for *a* is simple.

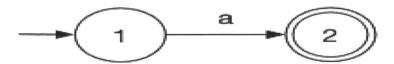

The FSM for *(bc)** would be represented with a loop on *bc*.

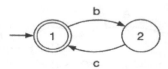

Concatenating the two FSMs will give us the FSM for *a(bc)**.

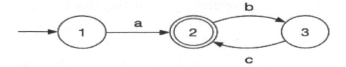

Running this FSM, we have to consume a to move from the state 1 to the accepting state 2. At 2, we can either stop and yield the string a or consume b to move to the state 3. From 3, we have no choice but consume c to go back to the accepting state 2; again at 2, we can either stop or go to 3 by consuming b and the loop goes on. The possible strings that can be generated by this FSM are a, abc, abcbc, abcbc, abc...bc.

As a final example, let's take a look at the FSM corresponding to a regular definition that could describe identifiers in a programming language.

```
letter      = [a-zA-Z]
digit       = [0-9]
identifier  = (letter | _) (letter | digit | _)*
```

First, the FSM for *letter* | _ is a basic *A* | *B* FSM.

Then the FSM for *(letter | digit | _)** will be a loop with 3 different options at each iteration.

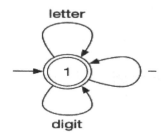

We get the final FSM for *identifier* by concatenating the above 2 *FSMs*.

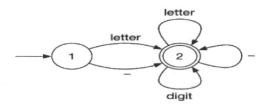

The FSM in Code

A FSM is a combination of:

- The set of all the possible states the FSM can be in.
- The initial state the FSM is in.
- A set of accepting states.
- And the set of all transitions.

We can start by implementing a FSM as a class with properties for the states, the initial state and the accepting states.

```
class FSM {
  constructor(states, initialState, acceptingStates) {
    this.states = states;
    this.initialState = initialState;
    this.acceptingStates = acceptingStates;
  }
}
```

The transitions of a FSM can be modeled with a function that takes a state `currentState` and a character or symbol `input` in parameters and returns the state the FSM will be in after consuming input while in state `currentState`. We can call that function the transition function and name it `nextState()`.

Most often, the transition function will be a switch statement on the parameter `currentState`, with each case returning the next state according to the parameter input.

```
nextState(currentState, input) {
  switch (currentState) {
    case 1:
      // Return the next state after consuming 'input' while in state 1.
    case 2:
      // Return the next state after consuming 'input' while in state 2.
    // ...
  }
}
```

Skeleton for a Transition Function

To assist in the implementation of the transition function, the FSM can first be converted into a transition table. The transition table maps each state S and input I to a state S', where S' is the state the FSM will be in when the input I is consumed from the state S.

As an example, let's consider the FSM below:

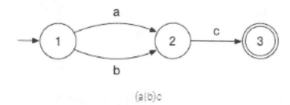

(a|b)c

The corresponding transition table is

	letter	digit	_
1	2	-	2
2	2	2	2

Transition table for (a|b)c

The rows of the transition table are labeled with the states of the FSM and the columns with all the characters or elements that can possibly be consumed. Each cell of the table contains the state the FSM will be in, if the character at the corresponding column is consumed while the FSM is in the state at the corresponding row. A cell containing—means that there is no transition in the FSM for the corresponding state and character.

The transition table provides a quick visual reference when writing a transition function. The transition function for the FSM above will be:

```
nextState(currentState, input) {

  switch (currentState) {

    case 1:

      if (input === 'a' || input === 'b') {

       return 2;

      }

    break;


    case 2:

      if (input === 'c') {

      return 3;

      }
```

```
      break;
    default:
      break;
  }


  return NoNextState; // 'NoNextState' here is a constant to specify that there
  is no next state for the provided parameters.

}
```

Now, to complete the constructor of our FSM class, let's add a parameter nextState of type Function representing the transition function to it.

```
class FSM {
  constructor(states, initialState, acceptingStates, nextState) {
    this.states = states;
    this.initialState = initialState;
    this.acceptingStates = acceptingStates;
    this.nextState = nextState; // The transition function.
  }
}
```

The next step in the implementation of our FSM is to add a function allowing to run, simulate or execute the FSM on an input string. The function will return a boolean specifying whether the input string (or a subset of the input string) matches the regular expression corresponding to the FSM.

The implementation of the run function is straightforward. The function will read the input character by character while keeping track of the current state the FSM is in. For each character read, it updates the current state with the next state the FSM will be in, by calling the transition function nextState( ). At the end of the execution of the loop, if the current state is one of the accepting states of the FSM, then the input string (or a subset of the input string) matches the regular expression corresponding to the FSM.

```
Class FSM {

  constructor(states, initialState, acceptingStates, nextState) {

    this.states = states;

    this.initialState = initialState;

    this.acceptingStates = acceptingStates;
```

```
        this.nextState = nextState; // The transition function.
    }
    /// Runs this FSM on the specified `input` string.
    /// Returns `true` if `input` or a subset of `input` matches
    /// the regular expression corresponding to this FSM.
    run(input) {
        // ...
    }
}
class FSM {
    constructor(states, initialState, acceptingStates, nextState) {
        this.states = states;
        this.initialState = initialState;
        this.acceptingStates = acceptingStates;
        this.nextState = nextState; // The transition function.
    }
    /// Runs this FSM on the specified `input` string.
    /// Returns `true` if `input` or a subset of `input` matches
    /// the regular expression corresponding to this FSM.
    run(input) {
        let currentState = this.initialState;

        for (let i = 0, length = input.length; i < length; ++i) {
            let character = input.charAt(i);
            let nextState = this.nextState(currentState, character);

            // If the next state is one of the accepting states,
            // we return `true` early.
            if (this.acceptingStates.has(nextState)) {
                return true;
            }

            if (nextState === NoNextState) {
                break;
```

```
        }

        currentState = nextState;
    }


    return this.acceptingStates.has(currentState);
    }

}
```

Usage of a FSM

To conclude this part on FSMs, let's see how we can use our newly implemented FSM class to recognize identifiers.

Let's reuse the following regular definitions.

```
letter       = [a-zA-Z]
digit        = [0-9]
identifier   = (letter | _) (letter | digit | _)*
```

Below is the corresponding FSM.

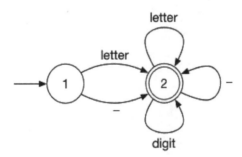

And the corresponding transition table.

	letter	digit	_
1	2	-	2
2	2	2	2

Now we can create a new instance of our FSM class and configure it to recognize identifiers.

```
let

fsm =

FSM();
```

```
fsm.states = new Set([1, 2]);

fsm.initialState = 1;

fsm.acceptingStates = new Set();

fsm.nextState = (currentState, character) => {

  switch (currentState) {

    case 1:

      // Assuming 'CharUtils' is a class with static helper

      // methods allowing us to answer simple questions about

      // characters. For example 'CharUtils.isLetter(c)'

      // determines if the character 'c' is a letter.

      if (CharUtils.isLetter(character) || character === '_') {

        return 2;

      }

      break;


    case 2:

        if (CharUtils.isLetter(character) || CharUtils.isDigit(character) ||
character === '_') {

        return 2;

      }

      break;

  }


  return NoNextState;

}
```

Our FSM instance can then be used to recognize identifiers.

```
fsm.run("camelCaseIdentifier"); // => true

fsm.run("snake_case_identifier"); // => true

fsm.run("_identifierStartingWithUnderscore"); // => true

fsm.run("1dentifier_starting_with_digit"); // => false

fsm.run("ident1f1er_cont4ining_d1g1ts"); // => true
```

Note that the call fsm.run("lisp-case-identifier") will return true even though lisp-case-identifier is not a valid identifier since—is not present in the regular expression. It returns true because the subset lisp in lisp-case-identifier is a valid Blink identifier. In the last part of this article, when working on your own lexer, you will have to update our FSM implementation so that the run method returns in addition of a boolean, the subset of the input that matched the regular expression.

Putting it All Together

Armed with all the necessary tools (lexical grammar, regular expressions, FSMs, transition tables, etc.), we can now have a look at how they all come together in the implementation of a lexer.

Let's consider a simple language for performing mathematical operations. The language supports the four basic arithmetic operators (+, -, * and /), comparison operators (>, ≥, <, ≤ and ==), and grouping using parenthesis. It also has basic support for variables and assignment using the = symbol.

Below are examples of valid instructions in our mini language:

```
1 + 2

(5 - 4) + 7

12.34 * 5e-9

pi = 22 / 7

radius = 5

circle_circumference = 2 * pi * radius
```

The valid lexemes for this language, identifiers, numbers, parenthesis, and operators are described with the following regular definitions.

```
letter       = [a-zA-Z]
digit        = [0-9]
digits       = digit digit*
identifier   = letter | (letter | digit | _)*
fraction     = . digits | ε
exponent     = ((E | e) (+ | - | ε)) digits) | ε
number       = digits fraction exponent
operator     = + | - | * | / | > | >= | < | <= | = | ==
parenthesis  = ( | )
```

Let's build a lexer for this language by completing the skeleton of the Lexerclass we introduced at the beginning of the article.

TokenType

The first step in implementing a lexer is to add a token type for each valid lexeme:

```
let

TokenType

= {

  Identifier: 'identifier',
```

```
    Number: 'number',

    Operator: 'operator',

    Parenthesis: 'parenthesis'

};
```

Because there is a finite number of operators and parenthesis, we will gain in clarity and granularity by adding a specific token for each type of operator and parenthesis. It will also be helpful to add a special token EndOfInput to be returned when all the characters in the input have been read.

```
let

TokenType

= {

  /// Identifiers and literals

  Identifier:      'identifier',

  Number:          'number',


  /// Arithmetic operators

  Plus:          'plus',          // +

  Minus:         'minus',         // -

  Times:         'times',         // *

  Div:           'div',           // /


  /// Comparison operators

  GreaterThan:      'greater than',          // >

  GreaterThanOrEqual: 'greater than or equal', // >=

  LessThan:         'less than',             // <

  LessThanOrEqual: 'less than or equal',    // <=

  Equal:           'equal',                 // ==


  /// Assignment operator

  Assign:          'assign',          // =


  /// Parenthesis

  LeftParenthesis: 'left parenthesis',    // (
```

```
RightParenthesis:   'right parenthesis',   // )


/// Special tokens
EndOfInput:       'end of input'
};
```

The next step is to complete the implementation of the Lexer class.

The Lexer Class

Let's start by adding properties to the Lexer class to keep track of the current position in the input, as long as the current line and column.

```
class
Lexer
{
  constructor(input) {
    this.input = input;
    this.position = 0;
    this.line = 0;
    this.column = 0;
  }


  /// Returns the next recognized 'Token' in the input.
  nextToken() {
    // ...
  }
}
```

Now, let's implement the nextToken() method.

A strategy we could use for nextToken() is to read the character at the current position. If the character matches the starting character in the production rule of one of the lexemes, we delegate the recognition of the lexeme to a helper method corresponding to that production rule.

```
class Lexer {
  constructor(input) {
    this.input = input;
    this.position = 0;
    this.line = 0;
```

```
    this.column = 0;
}


/// Returns the next recognized 'Token' in the input.
nextToken() {
  if (this.position >= this.input.length) {
    return new Token(TokenType.EndOfInput);
  }


  let character = this.input.charAt(this.position);


  if (CharUtils.isLetter(character)) {
    return this.recognizeIdentifier();
  }


  if (CharUtils.isDigit(character)) {
    return this.recognizeNumber();
  }


  if (CharUtils.isOperator(character)) {
    return this.recognizeOperator();
  }


  if (CharUtils.isParenthesis(character)) {
    return this.recognizeParenthesis();
  }


  // ...
}


/// Recognizes and returns an identifier token.
recognizeIdentifier() {
  // ...
}
```

```
/// Recognizes and returns a number token.
recognizeNumber() {
  // ...
}


/// Recognizes and returns an operator token.
recognizeOperator() {
  // ...
}


/// Recognizes and returns a parenthesis token.
recognizeParenthesis() {
  // ...
}
}
```

Let's take a look at the helper methods from the simplest to the most complex.

Recognizing Parenthesis

parenthesis = (|)

```
/// Recognizes and returns a parenthesis token.
recognizeParenthesis() {
  let position = this.position;
  let line = this.line;
  let column = this.column;
  let character = this.input.charAt(position);

  this.position += 1;
  this.column += 1;

  if (character === '(') {
    return new Token(TokenType.LeftParenthesis, '(', line, column);
  }
```

```
    return new Token(TokenType.RightParenthesis, ')', line, column);
}
```

Recognizing parenthesis is straightforward. We just check whether the current character is (or) and return the appropriate token. We also increment the current position in the input, as well as the current column.

Recognizing Operators

$$operator = + \mid - \mid * \mid / \mid > \mid >= \mid < \mid <= \mid = \mid ==$$

In the definition for the operator lexeme, we can notice that we basically have 2 types of operator, *arithmetic* and *comparison* operators (technically we have a third one, the assignment operator = but to simplify the implementation, we'll add it to the comparison operators group here).

For readability, we can delegate the recognition of each type of operator to a specific helper function.

```
/// Recognizes and returns an operator token.
recognizeOperator() {
  let character = this.input.charAt(this.position);

  if (CharUtils.isComparisonOperator(character)) {
    return recognizeComparisonOperator();
  }

  if (CharUtils.isArithmeticOperator(operator)) {
    return recognizeArithmeticOperator();
  }

  // ...
}
recognizeComparisonOperator() {
  let position = this.position;
  let line = this.line;
  let column = this.column;
  let character = this.input.charAt(position);

  // 'lookahead' is the next character in the input
  // or 'null' if 'character' was the last character.
```

```
let lookahead = position + 1 < this.input.length ? this.input.charAt(posi-
tion + 1) : null;


// Whether the `lookahead' character is the equal symbol `='.
let isLookaheadEqualSymbol = lookahead !== null && lookahead === `=';


this.position += 1;
this.column += 1;


if (isLookaheadEqualSymbol) {
  this.position += 1;
  this.column += 1;
}


switch (character) {
  case `>':
    return isLookaheadEqualSymbol
      ? new Token(TokenType.GreaterThanOrEqual, `>=', line, column)
      : new Token(TokenType.GreaterThan, `>', line, column);


  case `<':
    return isLookaheadEqualSymbol
      ? new Token(TokenType.LessThanOrEqual, `<=', line, column)
      : new Token(TokenType.LessThan, `<', line, column);


  case `=':
    return isLookaheadEqualSymbol
      ? new Token(TokenType.Equal, `==', line, column)
      : new Token(TokenType.Assign, `=', line, column);


  default:
    break;
}
```

```
    // ...
    }

  recognizeArithmeticOperator() {
    let position = this.position;
    let line = this.line;
    let column = this.column;
    let character = this.input.charAt(position);

    this.position += 1;
    this.column += 1;
    switch (character) {
      case '+':
        return new Token(TokenType.Plus, '+', line, column);

      case '-':
        return new Token(TokenType.Minus, '-', line, column);

      case '*':
        return new Token(TokenType.Times, '*', line, column);

      case '/':
        return new Token(TokenType.Div, '/', line, column);
    }

    // ...
  }
```

Lookahead: The implementation of recognizeComparisonOperator()makes use of a variable named lookahead. Because an operator can, for example, be > or >=, once we read the character >, we need to know what the next character is before deciding what kind of operator we have. If the next character is =, the recognized operator is >=; if the next character is any other character, the recognized operator is >. That is the purpose of the lookahead variable, to literally look ahead in the input.

Recognizing Identifiers

```
letter     = [a-zA-Z]
digit      = [0-9]
identifier = letter | (letter | digit | _)*
```

We could build an FSM for this and use it to recognize identifiers but these rules are simple enough to be implemented with a loop. We just have to keep reading characters in the input until we encounter a character that is not a letter, a digit or an underscore.

```
/// Recognizes and returns an identifier token.

recognizeIdentifier() {

  let identifier = '';

  let line = this.line;

  let column = this.column;

  let position = this.position;


  while (position < this.input.length) {

    let character = this.input.charAt(position);


    if (!(CharUtils.isLetter(character) || CharUtils.isDigit(character) ||
character === '-')) {

      break;

    }


    identifier += character;

    position += 1;

  }


  this.position += identifier.length;

  this.column += identifier.length;


  return new Token(TokenType.Identifier, identifier, line, column);

}
```

Recognizing Numbers

```
digit        = [0-9]
digits       = digit digit*
fraction     = . digits | ε
exponent     = ((E | e) (+ | - | ε)) digits) | ε
number       = digits fraction exponent
```

Note: With these regular definitions, strings such as 00, 00.42 or 00e-00 are considered numbers.

According to the regular definitions, a number is a succession of one or more digits. The digits can be followed by a fractional part (described by the fraction production rule) or an exponent part (described by the exponentproduction rule) or again by both. Both the fractional and exponent parts are optional as indicated by the | ε in their regular expressions.

Some examples of valid numbers are 42, 3.14 or 6.6262e-34. The regular expressions describing a number are complex enough to dissuade us to try to recognize numbers manually like we did for the identifiers. A FSM will greatly ease up the implementation here.

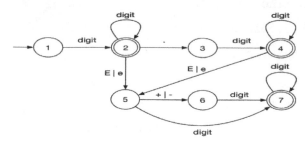

The regular expression for a number can be transformed into the FSM above and below is the corresponding transition table.

	digit	.	E|e	+|-
1	2	-	-	-
2	2	3	5	-
3	4	-	-	-
4	4	-	5	-
5	7	-	-	6
6	7	-	-	-
7	7	-	-	-

With the transition table, we can build a *FSM* and use it in our recognizeNumber() method.

```
/// Recognizes and returns a number token.
recognizeNumber() {
  let line = this.line;
  let column = this.column;
  // We delegate the building of the FSM to a helper method.
  let fsm = this.buildNumberRecognizer();

  // The input to the FSM will be all the characters from
  // the current position to the rest of the lexer's input.
  let fsmInput = this.input.substring(this.position);
```

```
    // Here, in addition of the FSM returning whether a number
    // has been recognized or not, it also returns the number
    // recognized in the 'number' variable. If no number has
    // been recognized, 'number' will be 'null'.
    let { isNumberRecognized, number } = fsm.run(fsmInput);

    if (isNumberRecognized) {
      this.position += number.length;
      this.column += number.length;

      return new Token(TokenType.Number, number, line, column);
    }

    // ...
}
buildNumberRecognizer() {
    // We name our states for readability.
    let State = {
      Initial: 1,
      Integer: 2,
      BeginNumberWithFractionalPart: 3,
      NumberWithFractionalPart: 4,
      BeginNumberWithExponent: 5,
      BeginNumberWithSignedExponent: 6,
      NumberWithExponent: 7,
      NoNextState: -1
    };

    let fsm = new FSM()
    fsm.states = new Set([State.Initial, State.Integer, State.BeginNumberWith-
FractionalPart, State.NumberWithFractionalPart, /* ... */]);
    fsm.initialState = State.Initial;
    fsm.acceptingStates = new Set([State.Integer, State.NumberWithFractional-
Part, State.NumberWithExponent]);
```

```
fsm.nextState = (currentState, character) => {
  switch (currentState) {
    case State.Initial:
      if (CharUtils.isDigit(character)) {
        return State.Integer;
      }

      break;

    case State.Integer:
      if (CharUtils.isDigit(character)) {
        return State.Integer;
      }

      if (character === '.') {
        return State.BeginNumberWithFractionalPart;
      }
if (character.toLowerCase() === 'e') {
        return State.BeginNumberWithExponent;
      }

      break;

    case State.BeginNumberWithFractionalPart:
      if (CharUtils.isDigit(character)) {
        return State.NumberWithFractionalPart;
      }

      break;

    case State.NumberWithFractionalPart:
      if (CharUtils.isDigit(character)) {
        return State.NumberWithFractionalPart;
      }
```

```
            if (character.toLowerCase() === 'e') {

                return State.BeginNumberWithExponent;

            }


            break;


        case State.BeginNumberWithExponent:
            if (character === '+' || character === '-'){

                return State.BeginNumberWithSignedExponent;

            }
    if (CharUtils.isDigit()) {

                return State.NumberWithExponent;

            }


            break;


        case State.BeginNumberWithSignedExponent:
            if (CharUtils.isDigit()) {

                return State.NumberWithExponent;

            }


            break;


        default:
            break;
        }


            Return State.NoNextState;
        };


    return fsm;
    }
```

With the completion of recognizeNumber(), the lexer for our little language for performing mathematical operations is almost complete.

For our lexer to be fully complete, we need to update our nextToken()method to ignore white spaces (so that 1+2, 1 + 2 or 1+ 2, for example, all yield the same sequence of tokens) and to handle errors.

```
class Lexer {
  constructor(input) {
    this.input = input;
    this.position = 0;
    this.line = 0;
    this.column = 0;
  }


  /// Returns the next recognized 'Token' in the input.
  nextToken() {
    if (this.position >= this.input.length) {
      return new Token(TokenType.EndOfInput);
    }


    // We skip all the whitespaces and new lines in the input.
    this.skipWhitespacesAndNewLines();


    let character = this.input.charAt(this.position);


    if (CharUtils.isLetter(character)) {
      return this.recognizeIdentifier();
    }
    if (CharUtils.isDigit(character)) {
      return this.recognizeNumber();
    }


    if (CharUtils.isOperator(character)) {
      return this.recognizeOperator();
    }
```

```
      if (CharUtils.isParenthesis(character)) {
        return this.recognizeParenthesis();
      }


      // Throw an error if the current character does not match
      // any production rule of the lexical grammar.
      throw new Error(`Unrecognized character ${character} at line ${this.line}
and column ${this.column}.`);
    }


  skipWhitespacesAndNewLines() {
      while (this.position < this.input.length && CharUtils.isWhitespaceOrNew-
Line(this.input.charAt(this.position)) {
        this.position += 1;


        if (CharUtils.isNewLine(this.input.charAt(this.position)) {
          this.line += 1;
          this.column = 0
        } else {
          this.column += 1;
        }
      }
    }
}
```

Lexer Class with Complete NextToken() Method

This completes our Lexer implementation. We can easily get all the tokens in an input by repetitively calling nextToken() until an EndOfInput token is returned.

```
class Lexer {
  // ...


  allTokens() {
    let token = this.nextToken();
    let tokens = [];
```

```
while (token.type !== TokenType.EndOfInput) {

    tokens.push(token);

    token = this.nextToken();

}

  return tokens;

}


// ...

}
```

Regular Expressions

A regular expression, simply put, is a rule that describes all the strings that can be built from a set of basic characters/symbols.

The simplest regular expression possible is the exact string being described. For example, let R be the regular expression *lang*, $R = lang$. R describes strings whose first character is l, followed by a, followed by n and followed by g. There is only one such string and that string is lang.

To describe more complex strings, we make use of regular expression operators.

Operators

- Union: The | operator is used to specify union or alternatives. For example, for $R = a \mid b$, a is a valid string described by R, so is b. | can be called the *OR* operator.

- Concatenation: Concatenation is implied in the absence of an operator between characters/symbols. For example $R = ab$ describes the unique string ab.

- Zero or more occurrences: A postfix * is used to specify that the element it's applied to can be repeated *zero or multiple times*. For example, $R = a*$describes strings such as a, aa, aaa, aaaa, aaaaa ... *and the empty string*. *is more formally known as the *Kleene Closure* named after Stephen Cole Kleene who helped formalize the concept of regular expressions.

- Grouping: Just like in mathematical expressions, parenthesis () are used for grouping. For example, $R = (a|b)*c$ concatenates $(a|b)*$ to c and describes strings such as c, ac, aac, bc, bbc, abbc and abbbabababc.

- Character classes: Characters classes can be used to shorten long *OR* regular expressions. For example, the regular expression $a \mid b \mid c \mid d$ can be replaced by the character class *[abcd]*. If all the characters in a character class form a logical sequence, the character class can be abbreviated further using a range notation *[a1–an]* where $a1$ is the first element of the sequence and *an* the last. For example $0 \mid 1 \mid 2 \mid 3 \mid 4 \mid 5 \mid 6 \mid 7 \mid 8 \mid 9$ can be converted to the character class which can be abbreviated further as *[0–9]*.

- Empty string: The empty string is described by ε (epsilon). For example, $R = a \mid ε$ describes the string a or the *empty string*.

Operator Precedence

The Kleene Closure (*) has the highest precedence, followed by the concatenation operator. The union operator (|) has the lowest precedence.

For example, in the regular expression $ab^*|c$, b^* is evaluated first, then ab^* and finally the union with c. Rewritten with parenthesis, that regular expression will be equivalent to $((a(b^*))|c)$.

Syntax Analysis

Syntax analysis or parsing is the second phase of a compiler.

We have seen that a lexical analyzer can identify tokens with the help of regular expressions and pattern rules. But a lexical analyzer cannot check the syntax of a given sentence due to the limitations of the regular expressions. Regular expressions cannot check balancing tokens, such as parenthesis. Therefore, this phase uses context-free grammar (CFG), which is recognized by push-down automata.

CFG, on the other hand, is a superset of Regular Grammar, as depicted below:

It implies that every Regular Grammar is also context-free, but there exists some problems, which are beyond the scope of Regular Grammar. CFG is a helpful tool in describing the syntax of programming languages.

Context-Free Grammar

We will first see the definition of context-free grammar and introduce terminologies used in parsing technology.

A context-free grammar has four components:

- A set of non-terminals (V). Non-terminals are syntactic variables that denote sets of strings. The non-terminals define sets of strings that help define the language generated by the grammar.

- A set of tokens, known as terminal symbols (Σ). Terminals are the basic symbols from which strings are formed.

- A set of productions (P). The productions of a grammar specify the manner in which the terminals and non-terminals can be combined to form strings. Each production consists of a non-terminal called the left side of the production, an arrow, and a sequence of tokens and/or on- terminals, called the right side of the production.

- One of the non-terminals is designated as the start symbol (S); from where the production begins.

The strings are derived from the start symbol by repeatedly replacing a non-terminal (initially the start symbol) by the right side of a production, for that non-terminal.

Example

We take the problem of palindrome language, which cannot be described by means of Regular Expression. That is, $L = \{ w \mid w = w^R \}$ is not a regular language. But it can be described by means of CFG, as illustrated below:

$$G = (V, \Sigma, P, S)$$

Where:

$$V = \{ Q, Z, N \}$$

$$\Sigma = \{ 0, 1 \}$$

$$P = \{ Q \to Z \mid Q \to N \mid Q \to \varepsilon \mid Z \to 0Q0 \mid N \to 1Q1 \}$$

$$S = \{ Q \}$$

This grammar describes palindrome language, such as: 1001, 11100111, 00100, 1010101, 11111, etc.

Syntax Analyzers

A syntax analyzer or parser takes the input from a lexical analyzer in the form of token streams. The parser analyzes the source code (token stream) against the production rules to detect any errors in the code. The output of this phase is a parse tree.

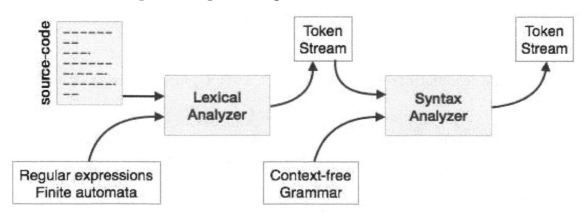

This way, the parser accomplishes two tasks, i.e., parsing the code, looking for errors and generating a parse tree as the output of the phase.

Parsers are expected to parse the whole code even if some errors exist in the program. Parsers use error recovering strategies, which we will learn later in this chapter.

Derivation

A derivation is basically a sequence of production rules, in order to get the input string. During parsing, we take two decisions for some sentential form of input:

- Deciding the non-terminal which is to be replaced.

- Deciding the production rule, by which, the non-terminal will be replaced.

To decide which non-terminal to be replaced with production rule, we can have two options.

Left-most Derivation

If the sentential form of an input is scanned and replaced from left to right, it is called left-most derivation. The sentential form derived by the left-most derivation is called the left-sentential form.

Right-most Derivation

If we scan and replace the input with production rules, from right to left, it is known as right-most derivation. The sentential form derived from the right-most derivation is called the right-sentential form.

Example

Production rules:

$$E \rightarrow E + E$$

$$E \rightarrow E * E$$

$$E \rightarrow id$$

Input string: id + id * id

The left-most derivation is:

$$E \rightarrow E * E$$

$$E \rightarrow E + E * E$$

$$E \rightarrow id + E * E$$

$$E \rightarrow id + id * E$$

$$E \rightarrow id + id * id$$

Notice that the left-most side non-terminal is always processed first.

The right-most derivation is:

E → E + E

E → E + E * E

E → E + E * id

E → E + id * id

E → id + id * id

Parse Tree

A parse tree is a graphical depiction of a derivation. It is convenient to see how strings are derived from the start symbol. The start symbol of the derivation becomes the root of the parse tree. Let us see this by an example from the last topic.

We take the left-most derivation of a + b * c

The left-most derivation is:

E → E * E

E → E + E * E

E → id + E * E

E → id + id * E

E → id + id * id

Step 1:

E → E * E

Step 2:

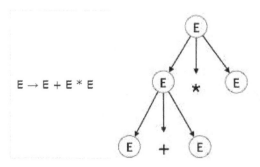

E → E + E * E

Step 3:

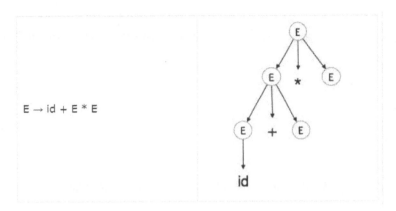

$E \rightarrow id + E * E$

Step 4:

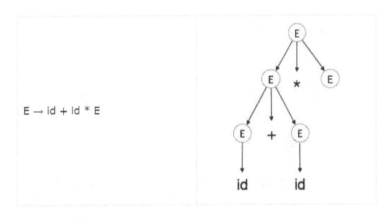

$E \rightarrow id + id * E$

Step 5:

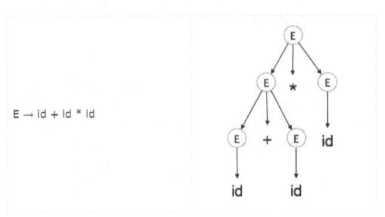

$E \rightarrow id + id * id$

In a parse tree:

- All leaf nodes are terminals.

- All interior nodes are non-terminals.

- In-order traversal gives original input string.

A parse tree depicts associativity and precedence of operators. The deepest sub-tree is traversed first, therefore the operator in that sub-tree gets precedence over the operator which is in the parent nodes.

Ambiguity

A grammar G is said to be ambiguous if it has more than one parse tree (left or right derivation) for at least one string.

Example

$$E \rightarrow E + E$$
$$E \rightarrow E - E$$
$$E \rightarrow id$$

For the string id + id – id, the above grammar generates two parse trees:

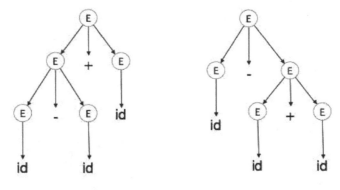

The language generated by an ambiguous grammar is said to be inherently ambiguous. Ambiguity in grammar is not good for a compiler construction. No method can detect and remove ambiguity automatically, but it can be removed by either re-writing the whole grammar without ambiguity, or by setting and following associativity and precedence constraints.

Associativity

If an operand has operators on both sides, the side on which the operator takes this operand is decided by the associativity of those operators. If the operation is left-associative, then the operand will be taken by the left operator or if the operation is right-associative, the right operator will take the operand.

Example

Operations such as Addition, Multiplication, Subtraction, and Division are left associative. If the expression contains:

id op id op id

it will be evaluated as:

(id op id) op id

For example, (id + id) + id

Operations like Exponentiation are right associative, i.e., the order of evaluation in the same expression will be:

id op (id op id)

For example, id ^ (id ^ id)

Precedence

If two different operators share a common operand, the precedence of operators decides which will take the operand. That is, 2+3*4 can have two different parse trees, one corresponding to (2+3)*4 and another corresponding to 2+(3*4). By setting precedence among operators, this problem can be easily removed. As in the previous example, mathematically * (multiplication) has precedence over + (addition), so the expression 2+3*4 will always be interpreted as:

$$2 + (3 * 4)$$

These methods decrease the chances of ambiguity in a language or its grammar.

Left Recursion

A grammar becomes left-recursive if it has any non-terminal 'A' whose derivation contains 'A' itself as the left-most symbol. Left-recursive grammar is considered to be a problematic situation for top-down parsers. Top-down parsers start parsing from the Start symbol, which in itself is non-terminal. So, when the parser encounters the same non-terminal in its derivation, it becomes hard for it to judge when to stop parsing the left non-terminal and it goes into an infinite loop.

Example:

(1)　　A => Aα | β

(2)　　S => Aα | β

　　　　A => Sd

(1) Is an example of immediate left recursion, where A is any non-terminal symbol and α represents a string of non-terminals.

(2) Is an example of indirect-left recursion.

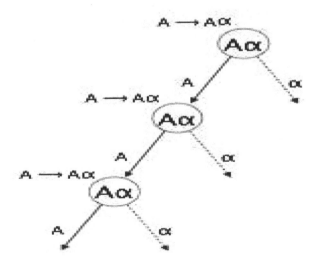

A top-down parser will first parse the A, which in-turn will yield a string consisting of A itself and the parser may go into a loop forever.

Removal of Left Recursion

One way to remove left recursion is to use the following technique:

The production

$$A => A\alpha \mid \beta$$

is converted into following productions

$$A => \beta A'$$

$$A' => \alpha A' \mid \epsilon$$

This does not impact the strings derived from the grammar, but it removes immediate left recursion.

Second method is to use the following algorithm, which should eliminate all direct and indirect left recursions.

```
START


Arrange non-terminals in some order like A1, A2, A3,…, Aₙ


  for each i from 1 to n
   {
   for each j from 1 to i-1
     {
     replace each production of form Aᵢ ⟹Ajγ
     with Aᵢ ⟹ δ1γ | δ2γ | δ3γ |…| γ
     where Aⱼ ⟹ δ₁ | δ₂|…| δₙ are current Aⱼ productions
     }
   }

  eliminate immediate left-recursion


END
```

Example

The production set

$$S => A\alpha \mid \beta$$

```
A => Sd
```

after applying the above algorithm, should become

```
S => Aα | β
A => Aαd | βd
```

and then, remove immediate left recursion using the first technique.

```
A => βdA'
A' => αdA' | ε
```

Now none of the production has either direct or indirect left recursion.

Left Factoring

If more than one grammar production rules has a common prefix string, then the top-down parser cannot make a choice as to which of the production it should take to parse the string in hand.

Example

If a top-down parser encounters a production like

$$A \Longrightarrow \alpha\beta \mid \alpha\gamma \mid ...$$

Then it cannot determine which production to follow to parse the string as both productions are starting from the same terminal (or non-terminal). To remove this confusion, we use a technique called left factoring.

Left factoring transforms the grammar to make it useful for top-down parsers. In this technique, we make one production for each common prefixes and the rest of the derivation is added by new productions.

Example

The above productions can be written as

$$A => \alpha A'$$

$$A' => \beta \mid \gamma \mid ...$$

Now the parser has only one production per prefix which makes it easier to take decisions.

First and Follow Sets

An important part of parser table construction is to create first and follow sets. These sets can provide the actual position of any terminal in the derivation. This is done to create the parsing table where the decision of replacing T[A, t] = α with some production rule.

First Set

This set is created to know what terminal symbol is derived in the first position by a non-terminal.

For example,

$$\alpha \rightarrow t\,\beta$$

That is α derives t (terminal) in the very first position. So, $t \in \text{FIRST}(\alpha)$.

Algorithm for Calculating First Set

Look at the definition of FIRST(α) set:

- if α is a terminal, then FIRST(α) = { α }.

- if α is a non-terminal and $\alpha \rightarrow \varepsilon$ is a production, then FIRST(α) = { ε }.

- if α is a non-terminal and $\alpha \rightarrow \gamma_1\ \gamma_2\ \gamma_3\ ...\ \gamma_n$ and any FIRST(γ) contains t then t is in FIRST(α).

First set can be seen as:

$$\text{FIRST}(\alpha) = \{\,t \mid \alpha \xrightarrow{*} t\beta\,\} \cup \{\,\varepsilon \mid \alpha \xrightarrow{*} \varepsilon\,\}$$

Follow Set

Likewise, we calculate what terminal symbol immediately follows a non-terminal α in production rules. We do not consider what the non-terminal can generate but instead, we see what would be the next terminal symbol that follows the productions of a non-terminal.

Algorithm for Calculating Follow Set:

- If α is a start symbol, then FOLLOW() = $

- If α is a non-terminal and has a production $\alpha \rightarrow AB$, then FIRST(B) is in FOLLOW(A) except ε.

- If α is a non-terminal and has a production $\alpha \rightarrow AB$, where B ε, then FOLLOW(A) is in FOLLOW(α).

Follow set can be seen as: FOLLOW(α) = { t | S *αt*}

Limitations of Syntax Analyzers

Syntax analyzers receive their inputs, in the form of tokens, from lexical analyzers. Lexical analyzers are responsible for the validity of a token supplied by the syntax analyzer. Syntax analyzers have the following drawbacks -

- It cannot determine if a token is valid,

- It cannot determine if a token is declared before it is being used,

- It cannot determine if a token is initialized before it is being used, and

- It cannot determine if an operation performed on a token type is valid or not.

These tasks are accomplished by the semantic analyzer, which we shall study in Semantic Analysis.

Types of Parsing

Syntax analyzers follow production rules defined by means of context-free grammar. The way the production rules are implemented (derivation) divides parsing into two types: top-down parsing and bottom-up parsing.

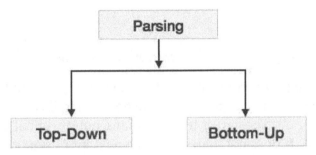

Top-down Parsing

The top-down parsing technique parses the input, and starts constructing a parse tree from the root node gradually moving down to the leaf nodes. The types of top-down parsing are depicted below:

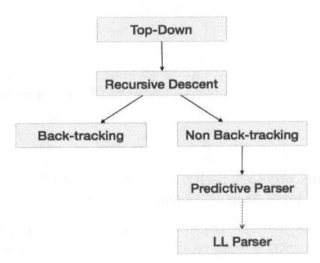

Recursive Descent Parsing

Recursive descent is a top-down parsing technique that constructs the parse tree from the top and the input is read from left to right. It uses procedures for every terminal and non-terminal entity. This parsing technique recursively parses the input to make a parse tree, which may or may not require back-tracking. But the grammar associated with it (if not left factored) cannot avoid back-tracking. A form of recursive-descent parsing that does not require any back-tracking is known as predictive parsing.

This parsing technique is regarded recursive as it uses context-free grammar which is recursive in nature.

Back-tracking

Top- down parsers start from the root node (start symbol) and match the input string against the production rules to replace them (if matched). To understand this, take the following example of CFG:

S → rXd | rZd

X → oa | ea

Z → ai

For an input string: read, a top-down parser, will behave like this:

It will start with S from the production rules and will match its yield to the left-most letter of the input, i.e. 'r'. The very production of S (S → rXd) matches with it. So the top-down parser advances to the next input letter (i.e. 'e'). The parser tries to expand non-terminal 'X' and checks its production from the left (X → oa). It does not match with the next input symbol. So the top-down parser backtracks to obtain the next production rule of X, (X → ea).

Now the parser matches all the input letters in an ordered manner. The string is accepted.

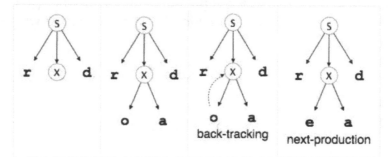

Predictive Parser

Predictive parser is a recursive descent parser, which has the capability to predict which production is to be used to replace the input string. The predictive parser does not suffer from backtracking.

To accomplish its tasks, the predictive parser uses a look-ahead pointer, which points to the next input symbols. To make the parser back-tracking free, the predictive parser puts some constraints on the grammar and accepts only a class of grammar known as LL(k) grammar.

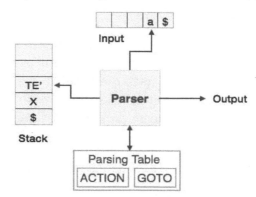

Predictive parsing uses a stack and a parsing table to parse the input and generate a parse tree. Both the stack and the input contains an end symbol $ to denote that the stack is empty and the input is consumed. The parser refers to the parsing table to take any decision on the input and stack element combination.

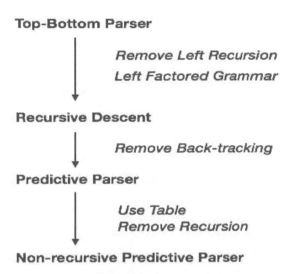

In recursive descent parsing, the parser may have more than one production to choose from for a single instance of input, whereas in predictive parser, each step has at most one production to choose. There might be instances where there is no production matching the input string, making the parsing procedure to fail.

LL Parser

An LL Parser accepts LL grammar. LL grammar is a subset of context-free grammar but with some restrictions to get the simplified version, in order to achieve easy implementation. LL grammar can be implemented by means of both algorithms namely, recursive-descent or table-driven.

LL parser is denoted as LL(k). The first L in LL(k) is parsing the input from left to right, the second L in LL(k) stands for left-most derivation and k itself represents the number of look aheads. Generally k = 1, so LL(k) may also be written as LL(1).

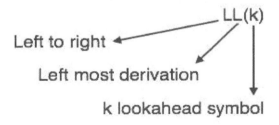

LL Parsing Algorithm

We may stick to deterministic LL(1) for parser explanation, as the size of table grows exponentially with the value of k. Secondly, if a given grammar is not LL(1), then usually, it is not LL(k), for any given k.

Given below is an algorithm for LL(1) Parsing:

Input:

```
string ω

parsing table M for grammar G
```

Output:

```
If ω is in L(G) then left-most derivation of ω,
error otherwise.
```

Initial State : $S on stack (with S being start symbol)

```
ω$ in the input buffer


SET ip to point the first symbol of ω$.


repeat
  let X be the top stack symbol and a the symbol pointed by ip.

    if X∈ Vt or $
     if X = a
        POP X and advance ip.
     else
        error()
     endif


    else    /* X is non-terminal */
     if M[X,a] = X → Y1, Y2,... Yk
        POP X
        PUSH Yk, Yk-1,... Y1 /* Y1 on top */
        Output the production X → Y1, Y2,... Yk
     else
        error()
     endif
    endif
  until X = $       /* empty stack */
```

A grammar G is LL(1) if A → α | β are two distinct productions of G:

- For no terminal, both α and β derive strings beginning with a.

- At most one of α and β can derive empty string.

- If β → t, then α does not derive any string beginning with a terminal in FOLLOW(A).

Bottom-up parsing starts from the leaf nodes of a tree and works in upward direction till it reaches the root node. Here, we start from a sentence and then apply production rules in reverse manner in order to reach the start symbol. The image given below depicts the bottom-up parsers available.

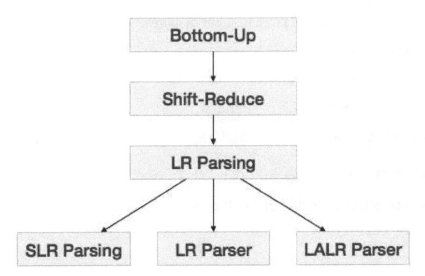

Shift-Reduce Parsing

Shift-reduce parsing uses two unique steps for bottom-up parsing. These steps are known as shift-step and reduce-step.

- Shift step: The shift step refers to the advancement of the input pointer to the next input symbol, which is called the shifted symbol. This symbol is pushed onto the stack. The shifted symbol is treated as a single node of the parse tree.

- Reduce step: When the parser finds a complete grammar rule (RHS) and replaces it to (LHS), it is known as reduce-step. This occurs when the top of the stack contains a handle. To reduce, a POP function is performed on the stack which pops off the handle and replaces it with LHS non-terminal symbol.

LR Parser

The LR parser is a non-recursive, shift-reduce, bottom-up parser. It uses a wide class of context-free grammar which makes it the most efficient syntax analysis technique. LR parsers are also known as LR(k) parsers, where L stands for left-to-right scanning of the input stream; R stands for the construction of right-most derivation in reverse, and k denotes the number of lookahead symbols to make decisions.

There are three widely used algorithms available for constructing an LR parser:

- SLR(1) – Simple LR Parser:
    - Works on smallest class of grammar.
    - Few number of states, hence very small table.
    - Simple and fast construction.
- LR(1) – LR Parser:
    - Works on complete set of LR(1) Grammar.
    - Generates large table and large number of states.
    - Slow construction.
- LALR(1) – Look-Ahead LR Parser:
    - Works on intermediate size of grammar.
    - Number of states are same as in SLR(1).

LR Parsing Algorithm

Here we describe a skeleton algorithm of an LR parser:

```
token = next_token()


repeat forever
  s = top of stack


  if action[s, token] = "shift si" then
   PUSH token
   PUSH si
   token = next_token()


  else if action[s, token] = "reduce A::= β" then
   POP 2 * |β| symbols
   s = top of stack
   PUSH A
   PUSH goto[s,A]


  else if action[s, token] = "accept" then
   return
```

```
    else
      error()
```

LL vs. LR

LL	LR
Does a leftmost derivation.	Does a rightmost derivation in reverse.
Starts with the root nonterminal on the stack.	Ends with the root nonterminal on the stack.
Ends when the stack is empty.	Starts with an empty stack.
Uses the stack for designating what is still to be expected.	Uses the stack for designating what is already seen.
Builds the parse tree top-down.	Builds the parse tree bottom-up.
Continuously pops a nonterminal off the stack, and pushes the corresponding right hand side.	Tries to recognize a right hand side on the stack, pops it, and pushes the corresponding nonterminal.
Expands the non-terminals.	Reduces the non-terminals.
Reads the terminals when it pops one off the stack.	Reads the terminals while it pushes them on the stack.
Pre-order traversal of the parse tree.	Post-order traversal of the parse tree.

Syntax Highlighting

Syntax Highlighting is what makes the editor automatically display text in different styles/colors, depending on the function of the string in relation to the purpose of the file. In program source code for example, control statements may be rendered bold, while data types and comments get different colors from the rest of the text. This greatly enhances the readability of the text, and thus helps the author to be more efficient and productive.

```cpp
Theme Repository::defaultTheme(Repository::DefaultTheme t)
{
    if (t == DarkTheme)
        return theme(QLatin1String("Breeze Dark"));
    return theme(QLatin1String("Default"));
}
```

A C++ function, rendered with syntax highlighting.

```cpp
Theme Repository::defaultTheme(Repository::DefaultTheme t)
{
    if (t == DarkTheme)
        return theme(QLatin1String("Breeze Dark"));
    return theme(QLatin1String("Default"));
}
```

The same C++ function, without highlighting.

Premade Syntax Highlighting Styles

The syntax highlighting element comes with four pre-set visual styles to choose from to suit most if not all websites "look and feel". There are two light themes and two dark themes to choose from.

```css
/* Light 1 - Style */


body{
    margin: 0;
    padding: 0;
    border: 0;
}

    h1{
    font-size: 40;
    font-weight: bold;
}
/* Light 2 - Style */


body{
    margin: 0;
    padding: 0;
    border: 0;
}

    h1{
    font-size: 40;
    font-weight: bold;
}
```

```css
1   /* Dark 1 - Style */
2
3   body{
4       margin: 0;
5       padding: 0;
6       border: 0;
7   }
8
9   h1{
10      font-size: 40;
11      font-weight: bold;
12  }
```

```css
1   /* Dark 2 - Style */
2
3   body{
4       margin: 0;
5       padding: 0;
6       border: 0;
7   }
8
9   h1{
10      font-size: 40;
11      font-weight: bold;
12  }
```

Select your Code Language

Do you want a bit more control over your highlighted syntax on your website? The syntax high-lighting element lets you select the code language you are using.

Code Line Control Options

Choose if your code shows line numbers next to it or not, and with our Line Wrapping option you can choose if lines of code continue with a horizontal scroll bar or break into a new line so no scrolling is needed.

With Line Numbers

```html
<html>
  <body>
    <h1>This showcases line numbers</h1>
  </body>
</html>
```

Without Line Numbers

```html
<html>
  <body>
    <h1>This showcases no line numbers</h1>
  </body>
</html>
```

With Horizontal Scroll

```html
<html>
  <body>
```

```
   <h1>This showcases the horizontal scroll functionality for syntax boxes
that has a lot of horizontally spanning content</h1>

  </body>

</html>
```

Without Horizontal Scroll

```
<html>

  <body>

    <h1>This showcases the horizontal scroll functionality for syntax boxes
that has a lot of horizontally spanning content</h1>

  </body>

</html>
```

Copy to Clipboard Option For Easy Code Sharing

Do you want to share your code with your visitor? The Syntax Highlighter "Copy to Clipboard" option makes it so easy! Share an add banner, call to action, widget or other code with your visitors to embed on their own website! This option sits neatly in the top right corner of the box and with just a click it will copy the entire block of code. You can even customize what it says or disable this option entirely.

```
1   <form method="get" action="https://themeforest.net/item/avada-responsive-multipurpose-theme/2833226?ref=ThemeFusion">
2       <button type="submit">Buy Avada Now!</button>
3   </form>
```

Custom Styling

We offer several customization options that allow you to control exactly how your code & block look. You can control the overall font size of the code, the border size, color and style of the entire box, the background color of the box, overall margins and even the line number text and background color. Make it yours!

Example

```
<html>

  <body>

    <h1>Hello Avada!</h1>

  </body>

</html>
```

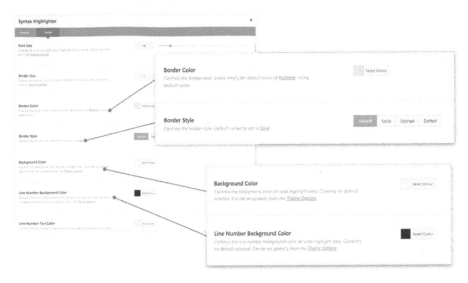

```html
<html>

  <body>

    <h1>Hello Avada!</h1>

  </body>

</html>


<html>

  <body>

    <h1>Hello Avada!</h1>

  </body>

</html>
```

Process to create a Syntax Highlighter

Step 1) Add HTML:

Example

A <div> containing HTML code:

```html
<div id="myDiv">
&lt;!DOCTYPE html&gt;<br>
&lt;html&gt;<br>
&lt;body&gt;<br>
<br>
&lt;h1&gt;Testing an HTML Syntax Highlighter&lt;/h2&gt;<br>
&lt;p&gt;Hello world!&lt;/p&gt;<br>
&lt;a href="https://www.w3schools.com"&gt;Back to School&lt;/a&gt;<br>
```

```
<br>
&lt;/body&gt;<br>
&lt;/html&gt;
</div>
```

Step 2) Add JavaScript:

Example

Create a function called "w3CodeColor" and call it, using the DIV element as a parameter:

```
w3CodeColor(document.getElementById("myDiv"));

function w3CodeColor(elmnt) {
  // click "Try it Yourself" to see the JavaScript...
}
```

Exception Handling Syntax

Exception handling syntax varies between programming languages, partly to cover semantic differences but largely to fit into each language's overall syntactic structure. Some languages do not call the relevant concept 'exception handling'; others may not have direct facilities for it, but can still provide means to implement it.

Most commonly, error handling uses a try...[catch...][finally...] block, and errors are created via a throw statement, but there is significant variation in naming and syntax.

Catalogue of Exception Handling Syntaxes

Ada

Exception declarations

```
Some_Error : exception;
```

Raising exceptions

```
raise Some_Error;

raise Some_Error with "Out of memory"; -- specific diagnostic message
```

Exception handling and propagation

```
with Ada.Exceptions, Ada.Text_IO;

procedure Foo is

  Some_Error : exception;

begin

  Do_Something_Interesting;
```

```
exception -- Start of exception handlers
 when Constraint_Error =>
   ... -- Handle constraint error
 when Storage_Error =>
   -- Propagate Storage_Error as a different exception with a useful message
   raise Some_Error with "Out of memory";
 when Error : others =>
   -- Handle all others
   Ada.Text_IO.Put("Exception: ");
   Ada.Text_IO.Put_Line(Ada.Exceptions.Exception_Name(Error));
   Ada.Text_IO.Put_Line(Ada.Exceptions.Exception_Message(Error));
end Foo;
```

Assembly Language

Most assembly languages will have a macro instruction or an interrupt address available for the particular system to intercept events such as illegal op codes, program check, data errors, overflow, divide by zero, and other such. IBM and Univac mainframes had the STXIT macro. Digital Equipment Corporation RT11 systems had trap vectors for program errors, i/o interrupts, and such. DOS has certain interrupt addresses. Microsoft Windows has specific module calls to trap program errors.

Bash

```
#!/usr/bin/env bash
#set -e provides another error mechanism
print_error(){
    echo "there was an error"
}
trap print_error exit #list signals to trap
tempfile=`mktemp`
trap "rm $tempfile" exit
./other.sh || echo warning: other failed
echo oops)
echo never printed
One can set a trap for multiple errors, responding to any signal with syntax like:
trap `echo Error at line ${LINENO}' ERR
```

Basic

An *On Error goto/gosub* structure is used in BASIC and is quite different from modern exception handling; in BASIC there is only one global handler whereas in modern exception handling, exception handlers are stacked.

```
ON ERROR GOTO handler
OPEN "Somefile.txt" FOR INPUT AS #1
CLOSE #1
PRINT "File opened successfully"
END


handler:
PRINT "File does not exist"
END ' RESUME may be used instead which returns control to original position.
```

C

The most common way to implement exception handling in standard C is to use setjmp/longjmp functions:

```
#include <setjmp.h>
#include <stdio.h>
#include <stdlib.h>


enum { SOME_EXCEPTION = 1 } exception;
jmp_buf state;


int main(void)
{
 if(!setjmp(state))            // try
 {
  if(/* something happened */)
  {
   exception = SOME_EXCEPTION;
   longjmp(state, 0);          // throw SOME_EXCEPTION
  }
 }
 else switch(exception)
```

```
    {
     case SOME_EXCEPTION:              // catch SOME_EXCEPTION
      puts("SOME_EXCEPTION caught");
      break;
     default:                  // catch ...
      puts("Some strange exception");
    }
    return EXIT_SUCCESS;
    }
```

Microsoft-specific

Two types exist:

- Structured Exception Handling (SEH)

- Vectored Exception Handling (VEH, introduced in Windows XP)

Example of SEH in C programming language:

```
int filterExpression (EXCEPTION_POINTERS* ep) {
  ep->ContextRecord->Eip += 8; // divide instruction may be encoded from 2 to
8 bytes
  return EXCEPTION_CONTINUE_EXECUTION;
}
int main(void) {
  static int zero;
  __try {
    zero = 1/zero;
    __asm {
     nop
     nop
     nop
     nop
     nop
     nop
     nop
    }
    printf ("Past the exception.\n");
```

```
  } __except (filterExpression (GetExceptionInformation())) {
    printf ("Handler called.\n");
  }
  return 0;
}
```

C#

```
public static void Main()
{
  try
  {
   // Code that could throw an exception
  }
  catch(System.Net.WebException ex)
  {
   // Process a WebException
  }
  catch(System.Exception)
  {
    // Process a System level CLR exception, that is not a System.Net.WebEx-
ception,
    // since the exception has not been given an identifier it cannot be ref-
erenced
  }
  catch
  {
   // Process a non-CLR exception
  }
  finally
  {
   // (optional) code that will *always* execute
  }
}
C++
```

```
#include <exception>
int main() {
  try {
    // do something (might throw an exception)
  }
  catch (const std::exception& e) {
    // handle exception e
  }
  catch (...) {
    // catches all exceptions, not already caught by a catch block before
    // can be used to catch exception of unknown or irrelevant type
  }
}
```

In C++, a *resource acquisition is initialization* technique can be used to clean up resources in exceptional situations. C++ intentionally does not support finally. The outer braces for the method are optional.

ColdFusion Markup Language (CFML)

Script Syntax

```
<cfscript>
try {
  //throw CF9+
  throw(type="TypeOfException", message="Oops", detail="xyz");
  // alternate throw syntax:
  throw "Oops"; // this equivalent to the "message" value in the above example
} catch (any e) {
  writeOutput("Error: " & e.message);
  rethrow; //CF9+
} finally { //CF9+
  writeOutput("I run even if no error");
}
</cfscript>
```

Adobe ColdFusion documentation

Tag Syntax

```
<cftry>

   code that may cause an exception

   <cfcatch ...>

     <cftry>

       First level of exception handling code

       <cfcatch ...>

         Second level of exception handling code

       </cfcatch>

       <cffinally>

           final code

        </cffinally>

     </cftry>

   </cfcatch>

 </cftry>
```

Adobe ColdFusion documentation

Railo-Lucee Specific Syntax

Added to the standard syntax above, CFML dialects of Railo and Lucee allow a retry statement.

This statement returns processing to the start of the prior try block.

CFScript example:

```
try {

   // code which could result in an exception


} catch (any e){

   retry;

}
```

Tag-syntax example:

```
<cftry>


   <!--- code which could result in an exception --->


   <cfcatch>
```

```
                  <cfretry>

    </cfcatch>

  </cftry>
```

D

```
import std.stdio; // for writefln()

int main() {

 try {

   // do something that might throw an exception

 }

 catch (FooException e) {

   // handle exceptions of type FooException

 }

 catch (Object o) {

   // handle any other exceptions

   writefln("Unhandled exception: ", o);

   return 1;

 }

 return 0;

}
```

In D, a finally clause or the resource acquisition is initialization technique can be used to clean up resources in exceptional situations.

Delphi

Exception declarations

```
type ECustom = class(Exception) // Exceptions are children of the class Ex-
ception.

 private

  FCustomData: SomeType;    // Exceptions may have custom extensions.

 public

  constructor CreateCustom(Data: SomeType); // Needs an implementation

  property CustomData: SomeType read FCustomData;

 end;
```

Raising exceptions

```
raise Exception.Create('Message');
```

```
raise Exception.CreateFmt('Message with values: %d, %d',[value1, value2]); //
See SysUtils.Format() for parameters.


raise ECustom.CreateCustom(X);
```

Exception handling and propagation

```
try // For finally.
 try // For except.
  ... // Code that may raise an exception.
 except
  on C:ECustom do
   begin
     ... // Handle ECustom.
     ... if Predicate(C.CustomData) then ...
   end;
  on S:ESomeOtherException do
   begin
     // Propagate as an other exception.
     raise EYetAnotherException.Create(S.Message);
   end;
  on E:Exception do
   begin
     ... // Handle other exceptions.
     raise; // Propagate.
   end;
 end;
finally
 // Code to execute whether or not an exception is raised (e.g., clean-up
code).
 end;
```

Erlang

```
try

% some dangerous code
```

```
catch
  throw:{someError, X} -> ok;   % handle an exception
  error:X -> ok;              % handle another exception
  _:_ -> ok                 % handle all exceptions
after
  % clean up
end
```

Haskell

Haskell does not have special syntax for exceptions. Instead, a try/catch/finally/etc. interface is provided by functions.

```
import Prelude hiding(catch)
import Control.Exception
instance Exception Int
instance Exception Double
main = do
  catch
    (catch
      (throw (42::Int))
      (\e-> print (0,e::Double)))
    (\e-> print (1,e::Int))
```

prints

(1,42)

in analogy with this C++

```
#include <iostream>
using namespace std;
int main()
{
  try
    {throw (int)42;}
  catch(double e)
    {cout << "(0," << e << ")" << endl;}
  catch(int e)
    {cout << "(1," << e << ")" << endl;}
}
```

Another example is

```
do {
  -- Statements in which errors might be thrown
} `catch` \ex -> do {
  -- Statements that execute in the event of an exception, with 'ex' bound to
the exception
}
```

In purely functional code, if only one error condition exists, the Maybe type may be sufficient, and is an instance of Haskell's Monad class by default. More complex error propagation can be achieved using the Error or ErrorT monads, for which similar functionality (using `catch`) is supported.

Java

```
try {
  // Normal execution path
  throw new EmptyStackException();
} catch (ExampleException ee) {
  // deal with the ExampleException
} finally {
  // This optional section is executed upon termination of any of the try or
catch blocks above,
  // except when System.exit() is called in "try" or "catch" blocks;
}
```

JavaScript

```
try {
  // Statements in which exceptions might be thrown
  throw 'error';
} catch(error) {
  // Statements that execute in the event of an exception
} finally {
  // Statements that execute afterward either way
}
```

Lisp

Common Lisp

```
(ignore-errors (/ 1 0))
```

```
(handler-case
  (progn
    (print "enter an expression")
    (eval (read)))
  (error (e) (print e)))


(unwind-protect
  (progn
    (print "enter an expression")
    (eval (read)))
  (print "This print will always be executed, similar to finally."))
```

Lua

Lua uses the pcall and xpcall functions, with xpcall taking a function to act as a catch block.

Predefined function

```
function foo(x)
  if x then
    return x
  else
    error "Not a true value"
  end
end


function attempt(arg)
  success, value = pcall(foo, arg)

  if not success then
    print("Error: " .. tostring(value))
  else
    print("Returned: " .. tostring(value))
  end
end
```

```
attempt("hello")
  -- Returned: hello

attempt(nil)
  -- Error: stdin:5: Not a true value

attempt({})
  -- Returned: table: 00809308


if foo(42) then print "Success" end
  -- Success
```

Anonymous Function

```
if pcall(
  function()
    -- Do something that might throw an error.
  end)
then
  print "No errors" -- Executed if the protected call was successful.
else
  print "Error encountered" -- Executed if the protected call failed.
end


print "Done" -- Will always be executed
```

Objective-C

```
Exception declarations
NSException *exception = [NSException exceptionWithName:@"myException"
              reason:@"whatever" userInfo:nil];


Raising exceptions
@throw exception;
```

Exception handling and propagation

```
@try {
  ...
}
@catch (SomeException *se) {
  // Handle a specific exception type.
  ...
}
@catch (NSException *ne) {
  // Handle general exceptions.
  ...


  // Propagate the exception so that it's handled at a higher level.
  @throw;
}
@catch (id ue) {
  // Catch all thrown objects.
  ...
}
@finally {
  // Perform cleanup, whether an exception occurred or not.
  ...
}
```

OCaml

```
exception MyException of string * int (* exceptions can carry a value *)
let _ =
 try
  raise (MyException ("not enough food", 2));
  print_endline "Not reached"
 with
 | MyException (s, i) ->
    Printf.printf "MyException: %s, %d\n" s i
```

```
| e -> (* catch all exceptions *)
    Printf.eprintf "Unexpected exception : %s" (Printexc.to_string e);
    (*If using Ocaml >= 3.11, it is possible to also print a backtrace: *)
    Printexc.print_backtrace stderr;
      (* Needs to beforehand enable backtrace recording with
        Printexc.record_backtrace true
      or by setting the environment variable OCAMLRUNPARAM="b1"*)
```

Perl 5

The Perl mechanism for exception handling uses die to throw an exception when wrapped inside an eval { ... }; block. After the eval, the special variable $@ contains the value passed from die. However, scoping issues can make doing this correctly quite ugly:

```
my ( $error, $failed );
{
  local $@;
  $failed = not eval {
    # Code that could throw an exception (using 'die')
    open(FILE, $file) || die "Could not open file: $!";
    while (<FILE>) {
      process_line($_);
    }
    close(FILE) || die "Could not close $file: $!";
    return 1;
  };
  $error = $@;
}


if ( $failed ) {
  warn "got error: $error";
}
```

Perl 5.005 added the ability to throw objects as well as strings. This allows better introspection and handling of types of exceptions.

```
eval {
  open(FILE, $file) || die MyException::File->new($!);
  while (<FILE>) {
```

```
  process_line($_);

 }

 close(FILE) || die MyException::File->new($!);

};

if ($@) {

 # The exception object is in $@

 if ($@->isa('MyException::File')) {

  # Handle file exception

 } else {

  # Generic exception handling

  # or re-throw with 'die $@'

 }

}
```

The __DIE__ pseudo-signal can be trapped to handle calls to die. This is not suitable for exception handling since it is global. However it can be used to convert string-based exceptions from third-party packages into objects.

```
local $SIG{__DIE__} = sub {

 my $err = shift;

 if ($err->isa('MyException')) {

  die $err; # re-throw

 } else {

  # Otherwise construct a MyException with $err as a string

  die MyException::Default->new($err);

 }

};
```

The forms shown above can sometimes fail if the global variable $@ is changed between when the exception is thrown and when it is checked in the if ($@) statement. This can happen in multi-threaded environments, or even in single-threaded environments when other code (typically called in the destruction of some object) resets the global variable before the checking code. The following example shows a way to avoid this problem. But at the cost of not being able to use return values:

```
eval {

 # Code that could throw an exception (using 'die') but does NOT use the re-
 turn statement;

 1;

} or do {
```

```
# Handle exception here. The exception string is in $@
};
```

Several modules in the Comprehensive Perl Archive Network (CPAN) expand on the basic mechanism:

- Error provides a set of exception classes and allows use of the try/throw/catch/finally syntax.

- TryCatch and Try::Tiny both allow use of try/catch/finally syntax instead of boilerplate to handle exceptions correctly.

- Exception::Class is a base class and class-maker for derived exception classes. It provides a full structured stack trace in $@->trace and $@->trace->as_string.

- Fatal overloads previously defined functions that return true/false e.g., open, close, read, write, etc. This allows built-in functions and others to be used as if they threw exceptions.

PHP

```
// Exception handling is only available in PHP versions 5 and greater.
try
{
 // Code that might throw an exception
 throw new Exception('Invalid URL.');
}
catch (FirstExceptionClass $exception)
{
 // Code that handles this exception
}
catch (SecondExceptionClass $exception)
{
 // Code that handles a different exception
}
finally
{
 // Perform cleanup, whether an exception occurred or not.
}
```

PowerBuilder

Exception handling is available in PowerBuilder versions 8.0 and above.

```
TRY

   // Normal execution path

CATCH (ExampleException ee)

   // deal with the ExampleException

FINALLY

   // This optional section is executed upon termination of any of the try or
catch blocks above

END TRY
```

PowerShell

Version 1.0

```
trap [Exception]

{

 # Statements that execute in the event of an exception

}

# Statements in which exceptions might be thrown
```

Version 2.0

```
Try {

   Import-Module ActiveDirectory

   }

Catch [Exception1] {

 # Statements that execute in the event of an exception, matching the excep-
tion

   }

Catch [Exception2],[Exception3etc] {

 # Statements that execute in the event of an exception, matching any of the
exceptions

   }

Catch {

 # Statements that execute in the event of an exception, not handled more
specifically

   }
```

Python

```
f = None

try:
```

```
    f = file("aFileName")
    f.write(could_make_error())
except IOError:
  print "Unable to open file"
except:   # catch all exceptions
  print "Unexpected error"
else:    # executed if no exceptions are raised
  print "File write completed successfully"
finally: # clean-up actions, always executed
  if f:
    f.close()
```

R

```
tryCatch({
  stop("Here an error is signaled")  # default S3-class is simpleError a sub-
class of error
  cat("This and the following lines are not executed because the error is
trapped before\n")
  stop( structure(simpleError("mySpecialError message"),class=c("specialEr-
ror","error","condition")) )
}
,specialError=function(e){
  cat("catches errors of class specialError\n")
}
,error=function(e){
  cat("catches the default error\n")
}
,finally={ cat("do some cleanup (e.g., setwd)\n") }
)
```

Rebol

```
REBOL [
  Title: "Exception and error handling examples"
]
```

```
; TRY a block; capturing an error! and converting to object!
if error? exception: try [1 / 0][probe disarm exception]


; ATTEMPT results in the value of the block or the value none on error
print attempt [divide 1 0]


; User generated exceptions can be any datatype!
example: func ["A function to throw an exception"
][
  throw "I'm a string! exception"
]
catch [example]


; User generated exceptions can also be named,
;  and functions can include additional run time attributes
sophisticated: func ["A function to throw a named error exception"
  [catch]
][
  throw/name make error! "I'm an error! exception" 'moniker
]
catch/name [sophisticated] 'moniker
```

Rexx

```
signal on halt;
 do a = 1
    say a
    do 100000 /* a delay */
    end
 end
 halt:
 say "The program was stopped by the user"
 exit
```

Ruby

```ruby
begin
 # Do something nifty
 raise SomeError, "This is the error message!" # Uh-oh!
rescue SomeError
 # This is executed when a SomeError exception
 # is raised
rescue AnotherError => error
 # Here, the exception object is referenced from the
 # `error' variable
rescue
 # This catches all exceptions derived from StandardError
 retry # This executes the begin section again
else
 # This is executed only if no exceptions were raised
ensure
 # This is always executed, exception or not
end
```

S-Lang

```
try
 {
  % code that might throw an exception
 }
 catch SomeError:
 {
  % code that handles this exception
 }
 catch SomeOtherError:
 {
  % code that handles this exception
 }
 finally  % optional block
```

```
{
  % This code will always get executed
}
```

New exceptions may be created using the new_exception function, e.g.,

```
new_exception ("MyIOError", IOError, "My I/O Error");
```

will create an exception called MyIOError as a subclass of IOError. Exceptions may be generated using the throw statement, which can throw arbitrary S-Lang objects.

Smalltalk

```
[ "code that might throw an exception" ]
   on: ExceptionClass
   do: [:ex | "code that handles exception" ].
```

The general mechanism is provided by the message on:do: Exceptions are just normal objects that subclass Error, you throw one by creating an instance and sending it a #signal message, e.g., MyException new signal. The handling mechanism (#on:do:) is again just a normal message implemented by BlockClosure. The thrown exception is passed as a parameter to the handling block closure, and can be queried, as well as potentially sending #resume to it, to allow execution flow to continue.

Swift

Exception handling is supported since Swift 2.

```
enum MyException : ErrorType {
  case Foo(String, Int)
}
func someFunc() throws {
  throw MyException.Foo("not enough food", 2)
}
do {
  try someFunc()
  print("Not reached")
} catch MyException.Foo(let s, let i) {
  print("MyException: \(s), \(i)")
} catch {
  print("Unexpected exception : \(error)")
}
```

Tcl

```
if { [ catch {
  foo
} err ] } {
  puts "Error: $err"
}
```

Since Tcl 8.6, there is also a try command:

```
try {
    someCommandWithExceptions
} on ok {res opt} {
    # handle normal case.
} trap ListPattern1 {err opt} {
    # handle exceptions with an errorcode matching ListPattern1
} trap ListPattern2 {err opt} {
    # ...
} on error {err opt} {
    # handle everything else.
} finally {
    # run whatever commands must run after the try-block.
}
```

VBScript

```
With New Try: On Error Resume Next
    'Do Something (Only one statement recommended)
.Catch :On Error GoTo 0: Select Case .Number
    Case 0 'This line is required in VBScript when using 'Case Else' clause.
      'No exception
    Case ERRORNUMBER
      'Handle exception
    Case Else
      'Unknown exception
End Select: End With
```

```
' *** Try Class ***
Class Try
  Private mstrDescription
  Private mlngHelpContext
  Private mstrHelpFile
  Private mlngNumber
  Private mstrSource

  Public Sub Catch()
    mstrDescription = Err.Description
    mlngHelpContext = Err.HelpContext
    mstrHelpFile = Err.HelpFile
    mlngNumber = Err.Number
    mstrSource = Err.Source
  End Sub

  Public Property Get Source()
    Source = mstrSource
  End Property

  Public Property Get Number()
    Number = mlngNumber
  End Property

  Public Property Get HelpFile()
    HelpFile = mstrHelpFile
  End Property

  Public Property Get HelpContext()
    HelpContext = mlngHelpContext
  End Property

  Public Property Get Description()
```

```
        Description = mstrDescription
    End Property
End Class
```

Visual Basic

```
With New Try: On Error Resume Next
    'Do Something (Only one statement recommended)
.Catch :On Error GoTo 0: Select Case .Number
    Case ERRORNUMBER
        'Handle exception
    Case Is <> 0
        'Unknown exception
End Select: End With


' *** Try Class ***
Private mstrDescription As String
Private mlngHelpContext As Long
Private mstrHelpFile   As String
Private mlngLastDllError As Long
Private mlngNumber     As Long
Private mstrSource     As String


Public Sub Catch()
   mstrDescription = Err.Description
   mlngHelpContext = Err.HelpContext
   mstrHelpFile = Err.HelpFile
   mlngLastDllError = Err.LastDllError
   mlngNumber = Err.Number
   mstrSource = Err.Source
End Sub


Public Property Get Source() As String
```

```
    Source = mstrSource
End Property


Public Property Get Number() As Long
  Number = mlngNumber
End Property


Public Property Get LastDllError() As Long
  LastDllError = mlngLastDllError
End Property


Public Property Get HelpFile() As String
  HelpFile = mstrHelpFile
End Property


Public Property Get HelpContext() As Long
  HelpContext = mlngHelpContext
End Property


Public Property Get Description() As String
  Description = mstrDescription
End Property
```

Visual Basic .NET

```
Try
  ` code to be executed here
Catch ex As Exception When condition
  ` Handle Exception when a specific condition is true
Catch ex As ExceptionType
  ` Handle Exception of a specified type (i.e. DivideByZeroException, Overflow-
Exception, etc.)
Catch ex As Exception
```

```
' Handle Exception (catch all exceptions of a type not previously specified)
Finally
  ' Cleanup, close connections, etc
  ' NB this code is always executed regardless of if an Exception was raised
or not!
End Try
```

Visual Prolog

```
try
  % Block to protect
catch TraceId do
  % Code to execute in the event of an exception; TraceId gives access to the
exception information
finally
  % Code will be executed regardles however the other parts behave
end try
```

X++

```
public static void Main(Args _args)
{
  try
  {
   // Code that could throw an exception
  }
  catch (Exception::Error) // Or any other exception type
  {
   // Process the error
  }
  catch
  {
   // Process any other exception type not handled previously
  }
```

```
    // Code here will execute as long as any exception is caught
}
```

Semantics

Semantics in IT is a term for the ways that data and commands are presented.

Semantics is a linguistic concept separate from the concept of syntax, which is also often related to attributes of computer programming languages. The idea of semantics is that the linguistic representations or symbols support logical outcomes, as a set of words and phrases signify ideas to both humans and machines.

In computer programming, a discussion of semantics may include the semantics of computer commands. Again, the semantic representation of words associated with controls, values and other corporate branding concepts, works on a logical basis. With that in mind, if a programmer uses words that don't make sense to the computer, this may be characterized as a "semantic error." Programmers may talk about "semantic structure" for either commands or elements of code that represent objects.

Other core issues with semantics involve the difference between machine language, which is not easily interpreted by humans, and upper-level programming languages that use common human semantics. These must then be translated down to machine language, often to a binary representation. That task of interpretation is at the core of how computers and humans work together on project outcomes.

Semantics in IT is a term for the ways that data and commands are presented.

Semantics is a linguistic concept separate from the concept of syntax, which is also often related to attributes of computer programming languages. The idea of semantics is that the linguistic representations or symbols support logical outcomes, as a set of words and phrases signify ideas to both humans and machines.

In general, semantics involves using specific words and labels. For example, a semantic network uses words to represent elements of a network. These types of semantics are geared more toward human audiences than toward a machine interpretation.

In computer programming, a discussion of semantics may include the semantics of computer commands. Again, the semantic representation of words associated with controls, values and other corporate branding concepts, works on a logical basis. With that in mind, if a programmer uses words that don't make sense to the computer, this may be characterized as a "semantic error." Programmers may talk about "semantic structure" for either commands or elements of code that represent objects.

Other core issues with semantics involve the difference between machine language, which is not easily interpreted by humans, and upper-level programming languages that use common human semantics. These must then be translated down to machine language, often to a binary representation. That task of interpretation is at the core of how computers and human's work together on project outcomes.

Semantic Domain

Formal semantics gives rules for translation from one domain (usually the program's abstract syntax) to another formally defined domain, the domain includes the state space and the space of functions/relations over the state:

- Operational semantics describes the effect of each statement on the state – usually giving the post-state as a function of the pre-state.

- Axiomatic Semantics usually defines a translation into logic formulae in some well defined logic language – the formulae describe, for each statement, the relation between the pre-state and the post-state of the executing the statement. This is usually given as a predicate transformer: a formula is true at the post-state if some syntactic transformation of it is true at the pre-state – or the other way around. Logic models are sometimes given over which these formulae are interpreted – the effect of a program in these models is the interpretation of the formulae – usually a relation.

- Denotational semantics defines a translation into some (partial) function space usually defined in set/category theory. The meaning of a program is a (partial) function/relation in that space.

We will briefly discuss below:

Operational Semantics

Operational semantics is an approach to the semantics of programming languages that uses the concept of an "abstract machine" that has a state and some primitive instructions or rules that cause the states to change. The machine is defined by specifying how the components of the state are changed by each of the instructions or rules. Computations are sequences of state transitions. The abstract machine is not meant to be a model of any realistic machine or machine language; it is meant to be simple enough so that the language can be unambiguously defined by simple rules for state transitions. The semantic description of a programming language specifies a translation into this operational model. Examples of this approach include the Vienna Definition Language used to define PL/I, which was the first method for defining the semantics of a programming language.

Approaches

Gordon Plotkin introduced the structural operational semantics, Robert Hieb and Matthias Felleisen the reduction contexts, and Gilles Kahn the natural semantics.

Small-step Semantics

Structural Operational Semantics

Structural operational semantics (also called structured operational semantics or small-step semantics) was introduced by Gordon Plotkin in (Plotkin81) as a logical means to define operational semantics. The basic idea behind SOS is to define the behavior of a program in terms of the behavior of its parts, thus providing a structural, i.e., syntax-oriented and inductive, view on operational semantics. An SOS specification defines the behavior of a program in terms of a (set of) transition relation(s). SOS specifications take the form of a set of inference rules that define the valid transitions of a composite piece of syntax in terms of the transitions of its components.

For a simple example, we consider part of the semantics of a simple programming language; proper illustrations are given in Plotkin81 and Hennessy90, and other textbooks. Let C_1, C_2 range over programs of the language, and let s range over states (e.g. functions from memory locations to values). If we have expressions (ranged over by E), values (V) and locations (L), then a memory update command would have semantics:

$$\frac{\langle E, s \rangle \Rightarrow V}{\langle L := E, s \rangle \rightarrow (s \uplus (L \mapsto V))}$$

Informally, the rule says that "if the expression E in state 8 reduces to value V, then the program L:=E will update the state s with the assignment L=V".

The semantics of sequencing can be given by the following three rules:

$$\frac{\langle C_1, s \rangle \rightarrow s'}{\langle C_1; C_2, s \rangle \rightarrow \langle C_2, s \rangle} \qquad \frac{\langle C_1, s \rangle \rightarrow \langle C_1', s' \rangle}{\langle C_1; C_2, s \rangle \rightarrow \langle C_1'; C_2, s' \rangle} \qquad \frac{}{\langle \text{skip}, s \rangle \rightarrow s'}$$

Informally, the first rule says that, if program in state C_1 finishes in state s', then the program $C_1; C_2$ in state s' will reduce to the program $C_1; C_2$ in state s'. (You can think of this as formalizing "You can run C_1, and then run C_2 using the resulting memory store.) The second rule says that if the program C_1 in state s can reduce to the program C_1' with state s', then the program $C_1; C_2$ in state s will reduce to the program $C_1; C_2$ in state s'. (You can think of this as formalizing the principle for an optimizing compiler: "You are allowed to transform C_1 as if it were stand-alone, even if it is just the first part of a program.") The semantics is structural, because the meaning of the sequential program $C_1; C_2$, is defined by the meaning of C_1 and the meaning of C_2.

If we also have Boolean expressions over the state, ranged over by B, then we can define the semantics of the while commond:

$$\frac{\langle B, s \rangle \Rightarrow \text{true}}{\langle \text{while } B \text{ do } C, s \rangle \rightarrow \langle C; \text{while } B \text{ do } C, s \rangle} \qquad \frac{\langle B, s \rangle \Rightarrow \text{false}}{\langle \text{while } B \text{ do } C, s \rangle \rightarrow s}$$

Such a definition allows formal analysis of the behavior of programs, permitting the study of relations between programs. Important relations include simulation preorders and bisimulation. These are especially useful in the context of concurrency theory.

Thanks to its intuitive look and easy-to-follow structure, SOS has gained great popularity and has become a de facto standard in defining operational semantics. As a sign of success, the original report (so-called Aarhus report) on SOS (Plotkin81) has attracted more than 1000 citations according to the CiteSeer, making it one of the most cited technical reports in Computer Science.

Reduction Semantics

Reduction semantics are an alternative presentation of operational semantics using so-called reduction contexts. The method was introduced by Robert Hieb and Matthias Felleisen in 1992 as a technique for formalizing an equational theory for control and state. For example, the grammar of a simple call-by-value lambda calculus and its contexts can be given as:

$$e = v \mid (e\ e) \mid x \qquad v = \lambda x.e \qquad C = [\ ] \mid (C\ e) \mid (v\ C)$$

The contexts C include a hole $[\ ]$ where a term can be plugged in. The shape of the contexts indicate where reduction can occur (i.e., a term can be plugged into a term). To describe a semantics for this language, axioms or reduction rules are provided:

$$(\lambda x.e)\ v \to e[x\ /\ v] \quad (\beta)$$

This single axiom is the beta rule from the lambda calculus. The reduction contexts show how this rule composes with more complicated terms. In particular, this rule can trigger for the argument position of an application like $((\lambda x.x\ \lambda x.x)\lambda x.(x\ x))$ because there is a context $([\ ]\ \lambda x.(x\ x))$ that matches the term. In this case, the contexts uniquely decompose terms so that only one reduction is possible at any given step. Extending the axiom to match the reduction contexts gives the *compatible closure*. Taking the reflexive, transitive closure of this relation gives the *reduction relation* for this language.

The technique is useful for the ease in which reduction contexts can model state or control constructs (e.g., continuations). In addition, reduction semantics have been used to model object-oriented languages, contract systems, and other language features.

Big-step Semantics

Natural Semantics

Big-step structural operational semantics is also known under the names natural semantics, relational semantics and evaluation semantics. Big-step operational semantics was introduced under the name *natural semantics* by Gilles Kahn when presenting Mini-ML, a pure dialect of the ML language.

One can view big-step definitions as definitions of functions, or more generally of relations, interpreting each language construct in an appropriate domain. Its intuitiveness makes it a popular choice for semantics specification in programming languages, but it has some drawbacks that make it inconvenient or impossible to use in many situations, such as languages with control-intensive features or concurrency.

A big-step semantics describes in a divide-and-conquer manner how final evaluation results of language constructs can be obtained by combining the evaluation results of their syntactic counterparts (subexpressions, substatements, etc.).

Comparison

There are a number of distinctions between small-step and big-step semantics that influence whether one or the other forms a more suitable basis for specifying the semantics of a programming language.

Big-step semantics have the advantage of often being simpler (needing fewer inference rules) and often directly correspond to an efficient implementation of an interpreter for the language (hence Kahn calling them "natural".) Both can lead to simpler proofs, for example when proving the preservation of correctness under some program transformation.

The main disadvantage of big-step semantics is that non-terminating (diverging) computations do not have an inference tree, making it impossible to state and prove properties about such computations.

Small-step semantics give more control of the details and order of evaluation. In the case of instrumented operational semantics, this allows the operational semantics to track and the semanticist to state and prove more accurate theorems about the run-time behaviour of the language. These properties make small-step semantics more convenient when proving type soundness of a type system against an operational semantics.

Denotational Semantics

In computer science, denotational semantics (initially known as mathematical semantics or Scott–Strachey semantics) is an approach of formalizing the meanings of programming languages by constructing mathematical objects (called *denotations*) that describe the meanings of expressions from the languages. Other approaches to providing formal semantics of programming languages include axiomatic semantics and operational semantics.

Broadly speaking, denotational semantics is concerned with finding mathematical objects called domains that represent what programs do. For example, programs (or program phrases) might be represented by partial functions or by games between the environment and the system.

An important tenet of denotational semantics is that *semantics should be compositional*: the denotation of a program phrase should be built out of the denotations of its subphrases.

Denotations of Recursive Programs

Denotational semantics are given to a program phrase as a function from an environment (that has the values of its free variables) to its denotation. For example, the phrase n*m produces a denotation when provided with an environment that has binding for its two free variables: n and m. If in the environment n has the value 3 and m has the value 5, then the denotation is 15.

A function can be modeled as denoting a set of ordered pairs where each ordered pair in the set consists of two parts:

(1) an argument for the function and

(2) the value of the function for that argument. For example, the set of order pairs {[0 1] [4 3]}

is the denotation of a function with value 1 for argument 0, value 3 for the argument 4, and is otherwise undefined.

The problem to be solved is to provide denotations for recursive programs that are defined in terms of themselves such as the definition of the factorial function as

```
factorial ≡ λ(n) if (n==0) then 1 else n*factorial(n-1).
```

A solution is to build up the denotation by approximation. The factorial function is a total function from N to N (defined everywhere in its domain), but we model it as a partial function. At the beginning, we start with the empty function (an empty set). Next, we add the ordered pair [0 1] to the function to result in another partial function that better approximates the factorial function. Afterwards, we add yet another ordered pair [1 1] to create an even better approximation.

It is instructive to think of this chain of iteration as F^0, F^1, F^2, ... where F^i indicates i-many applications of F.

- $F^0(\{\})$ is the totally undefined partial function $\{\}$.

- $F^1(\{\})$ is the function $\{[0\ 1]\}$ that is defined at 0, to be 1, and undefined elsewhere.

- $F^5(\{\})$ is the function $\{[0\ 1]\ [1\ 1]\ [2\ 2]\ [3\ 6]\ [4\ 24]\}$.

This iterative process builds a sequence of partial functions from N to N. Partial functions form a chain-complete partial order using $\subseteq$ as the ordering. Furthermore, this iterative process of better approximations of the factorial function forms an expansive (also called progressive) mapping because each $F^i \le F^{i+1}$ using $\subseteq$ as the ordering. So by a fixed-point theorem (specifically Bourbaki–Witt theorem), there exists a fixed point for this iterative process.

In this case, the fixed point is the least upper bound of this chain, which is the full factorial function, which can be expressed as the direct limit

$$\bigsqcup_{i \in N} F^i(\{\}).$$

Here, the symbol "$\sqcup$" is the directed join (of directed sets), meaning "least upper bound". The directed join is essentially the join of directed sets.

Denotational Semantics of Non-deterministic Programs

The concept of power domains has been developed to give a denotational semantics to non-deterministic sequential programs. Writing P for a power-domain constructor, the domain $P(D)$ is the domain of non-deterministic computations of type denoted by D.

There are difficulties with fairness and unboundedness in domain-theoretic models of non-determinism.

Denotational Semantics of Concurrency

Many researchers have argued that the domain-theoretic models given above do not suffice for the more general case of concurrent computation. For this reason various new models have been introduced. In the early 1980s, people began using the style of denotational semantics to give semantics for concurrent languages. Examples include Will Clinger's work with the actor model; Glynn Winskel's work with event structures and petri nets; and the work by Francez, Hoare, Lehmann, and de Roever (1979) on trace semantics for CSP. All these lines of inquiry remain under investigation (e.g. the various denotational models for CSP).

Recently, Winskel and others have proposed the category of profunctors as a domain theory for concurrency.

Denotational Semantics of State

State (such as a heap) and simple imperative features can be straightforwardly modeled in the denotational semantics. All the textbooks below have the details. The key idea is to consider a command as a partial function on some domain of states. The denotation of "x:=3" is then the function that takes a state to the state with 3 assigned to x. The sequencing operator ";" is denoted by composition of functions. Fixed-point constructions are then used to give a semantics to looping constructs, such as "while".

Things become more difficult in modelling programs with local variables. One approach is to no longer work with domains, but instead to interpret types as functors from some category of worlds to a category of domains. Programs are then denoted by natural continuous functions between these functors.

Denotations of Data Types

Many programming languages allow users to define recursive data types. For example, the type of lists of numbers can be specified by

```
datatype list = Cons of nat * list | Empty
```

This section deals only with functional data structures that cannot change. Conventional imperative programming languages would typically allow the elements of such a recursive list to be changed.

For another example: the type of denotations of the untyped lambda calculus is

datatype $D = D$ of $(D \to D)$

The problem of *solving domain equations* is concerned with finding domains that model these kinds of datatypes. One approach, roughly speaking, is to consider the collection of all domains as a domain itself, and then solve the recursive definition there. The textbooks below give more details.

Polymorphic data types are data types that are defined with a parameter. For example, the type of α lists is defined by

```
datatype α list = Cons of α * α list | Empty
```

Lists of natural numbers, then, are of type nat list, while lists of strings are of type string list.

Some researchers have developed domain theoretic models of polymorphism. Other researchers have also modeled parametric polymorphism within constructive set theories.

A recent research area has involved denotational semantics for object and class based programming languages.

Denotational Semantics for Programs of Restricted Complexity

Following the development of programming languages based on linear logic, denotational semantics have been given to languages for linear usage (see e.g. proof nets, coherence spaces) and also polynomial time complexity.

Denotational Semantics of Sequentiality

The problem of full abstraction for the sequential programming language PCF was, for a long time, a big open question in denotational semantics. The difficulty with PCF is that it is a very sequential language. For example, there is no way to define the parallel-or function in PCF. It is for this reason that the approach using domains, as introduced above, yields a denotational semantics that is not fully abstract.

This open question was mostly resolved in the 1990s with the development of game semantics and also with techniques involving logical relations.

Denotational Semantics as Source-to-source Translation

It is often useful to translate one programming language into another. For example, a concurrent programming language might be translated into a process calculus; a high-level programming language might be translated into byte-code. (Indeed, conventional denotational semantics can be seen as the interpretation of programming languages into the internal language of the category of domains.)

In this context, notions from denotational semantics, such as full abstraction, help to satisfy security concerns.

Abstraction

It is often considered important to connect denotational semantics with operational semantics. This is especially important when the denotational semantics is rather mathematical and abstract, and the operational semantics is more concrete or closer to the computational intuitions. The following properties of a denotational semantics are often of interest:

1. Syntax independence: The denotations of programs should not involve the syntax of the source language.

2. Soundness: All observably distinct programs have distinct denotations.

3. Full abstraction: Two programs have the same denotations precisely when they are observationally equivalent. For semantics in the traditional style, full abstraction may be understood roughly as the requirement that "operational equivalence coincides with denotational

equality". For denotational semantics in more intensional models, such as the actor model and process calculi, there are different notions of equivalence within each model, and so the concept of full abstraction is a matter of debate, and harder to pin down. Also the mathematical structure of operational semantics and denotational semantics can become very close.

Additional desirable properties we may wish to hold between operational and denotational semantics are:

1. Constructivism: Constructivism is concerned with whether domain elements can be shown to exist by constructive methods.

2. Independence of denotational and operational semantics: The denotational semantics should be formalized using mathematical structures that are independent of the operational semantics of a programming language; However, the underlying concepts can be closely related.

3. Full completeness or definability: Every morphism of the semantic model should be the denotation of a program.

Compositionality

An important aspect of denotational semantics of programming languages is compositionality, by which the denotation of a program is constructed from denotations of its parts. For example, consider the expression "7 + 4". Compositionality in this case is to provide a meaning for "7 + 4" in terms of the meanings of "7", "4" and "+".

A basic denotational semantics in domain theory is compositional because it is given as follows. We start by considering program fragments, i.e. programs with free variables. A *typing context* assigns a type to each free variable. For instance, in the expression $(x + y)$ might be considered in a typing context $(x{:}nat, y{:}nat)$. We now give a denotational semantics to program fragments, using the following scheme.

1. We begin by describing the meaning of the types of our language: the meaning of each type must be a domain. We write $[\![\tau]\!]$ for the domain denoting the type τ. For instance, the meaning of type nat should be the domain of natural numbers: $[\![nat]\!] = N_\bot$.

2. From the meaning of types we derive a meaning for typing contexts. We set $[\![\, x_1{:}\,\tau_1, ..., x_n{:}\tau_n]\!] = [\![\tau_1]\!] \times ... \times [\![\tau_n]\!]$. For instance, $[\![x{:}nat, y{:}nat]\!] = N_\bot \times N_\bot$. As a special case, the meaning of the empty typing context, with no variables, is the domain with one element, denoted 1.

3. Finally, we must give a meaning to each program-fragment-in-typing-context. Suppose that P is a program fragment of type σ, in typing context Γ, often written $\Gamma \vdash P{:}\sigma$. Then the meaning of this program-in-typing-context must be a continuous function $[\![\Gamma \vdash P{:}\sigma]\!] : [\![\Gamma]\!] \to [\![\sigma]\!]$. For instance, $[\![\vdash 7{:}nat]\!] : 1 \to N_\bot$ is the constantly "7" function, while $[\![x{:}nat, y{:}nat \vdash x{+}y{:}nat]\!] : N_\bot \times N_\bot \to N_\bot$ is the function that adds two numbers.

Now, the meaning of the compound expression $(7{+}4)$ is determined by composing the three functions $[\![\vdash 7{:}nat]\!] : 1 \to N_\bot$, $[\![\vdash 4{:}nat]\!] : 1 \to N_\bot$, and $[\![x{:}nat, y{:}nat \vdash x{+}y{:}nat]\!] : N_\bot \times N_\bot \to N_\bot$.

In fact, this is a general scheme for compositional denotational semantics. There is nothing specific about domains and continuous functions here. One can work with a different category instead. For example, in game semantics, the category of games has games as objects and strategies as morphisms: we can interpret types as games, and programs as strategies. For a simple language without general recursion, we can make do with the category of sets and functions. For a language with side-effects, we can work in the Kleisli category for a monad. For a language with state, we can work in a functor category. Milner has advocated modelling location and interaction by working in a category with interfaces as objects and *bigraphs* as morphisms.

Semantics versus Implementation

According to Dana Scott :

It is not necessary for the semantics to determine an implementation, but it should provide criteria for showing that an implementation is correct.

According to Clinger:

Usually, however, the formal semantics of a conventional sequential programming language may itself be interpreted to provide an (inefficient) implementation of the language. A formal semantics need not always provide such an implementation, though, and to believe that semantics must provide an implementation leads to confusion about the formal semantics of concurrent languages. Such confusion is painfully evident when the presence of unbounded nondeterminism in a programming language's semantics is said to imply that the programming language cannot be implemented.

Connections to other Areas of Computer Science

Some work in denotational semantics has interpreted types as domains in the sense of domain theory, which can be seen as a branch of model theory, leading to connections with type theory and category theory. Within computer science, there are connections with abstract interpretation, program verification, and model checking.

Axiomatic Semantics

Axiomatic semantics are semantic expressions of the relationships inherent in a piece of code. These expressions can be helpful in describing how some piece of software works.

An interesting thing about axiomatic semantics as contrasted to other types of expressions is that they are fairly agnostic of specific results and conditions. Rather, axiomatic semantics describe the way that a system works. One way to think of this is using the root word, axiom, which implies some broader truism about a system. For example, an axiomatic semantical statement about a certain function would describe what it is meant to do, what sort of argument it takes, and what sort of result it returns. This would not require knowledge of the actual variables involved.

Axiomatic semantics has many applications, such as:

- Program verifiers
- Symbolic execution tools for bug hunting
- Software validation tools
- Malware detection
- Automatic test generation

It is also used for proving the correctness of algorithms or hardware descriptions, "extended static checking (e.g., checking array bounds), and documenting programs and interfaces.

Example

An example program that computes the sum of the first hundred numbers: $\sum 1 \leq m \leq 100m$.

> S := 0;
>
> N := 1;

while ¬(N = 101) do

> S := S + N;
>
> N := N + 1;

We can see that the commands S := 0; N := 1; initialize the values in the locations. so we add comments as follows;

> S := 0;
>
> {S = 0}
>
> N := 1;
>
> {N = 1}
>
> while ¬(N = 101) do
>
>> S := S + N;
>>
>> N := N + 1;

We can also add the comment after the execution of the while loop meaning that S will have the required value.

> S := 0;
>
> {S = 0}
>
> N := 1;

$\{N = 1\}$

while $\neg(N = 101)$ do

    $S := S + N;$

    $N := N + 1;$

$\{N = 101 \wedge S = \sum 1 \leq m \leq 100m.$

Inside the while loop we add comment on both N and S: N ranges from 1 to 101 and S represents the partial sum. This comment express the key relationship between the value at location S and the value at location N.

    $S := 0;$

    $\{S = 0\}$

    $N := 1;$

    $\{N = 1\}$

    while $\neg(N = 101)$ do

        $\{1 \leq N < 101 \wedge S = \sum 1 \leq m < N^m\}$

        $S := S + N;$

        $\{1 \leq N < 101 \wedge S = \sum 1 \leq m \leq N^m\}$

        $N := N + 1;$

    $\{N = 101 \wedge S = \sum 1 \leq m \leq 100^m\}$

The assertion $S = \sum 1 \leq m \leq N^m\}$ is called an invariant of the while-loop because it remains true under each iteration of the loop.

Action Semantics

Action Semantics is a hybrid of denotational and operational semantics.

As in denotational semantics, inductively-defined semantic functions map phrases to their denotations, only here, the denotations are so-called actions. The notation for actions is itself defined operationally.

Action Semantics avoids the use of higher-order functions expressed in λ-notation.

The universe of pure mathematical functions is so distant from that of (most) programming languages that the representation of programming concepts in it is often excessively complex. The foundations of reflexive Scott-domains and higher-order functions are unfamiliar and inaccessible to many programmers (although the idea of functions that take other functions as arguments, and perhaps also return functions as results, is not difficult in itself).

Action semantics provides a rich action notation with a direct operational interpretation

The universe of actions involves not only control and data flow, but also scopes of bindings, effects on storage, and interactive processes, allowing a simple and direct representation of many programming concepts.

Computed values are given by actions, and the action combination 'A1 then A2 ' passes all the values given by A1 to A2 . For example, assuming evaluate : Exp → Action, the value computed by evaluate E1 is the one tested by the action 'given true' below:

> evaluate cond(E1 , E2 , E3) =
>
>> evaluate E1 then
>>
>> (given true then evaluate E2
>>
>>> otherwise evaluate E3)

Bindings are implicitly propagated to the sub-actions of most actions, and can always be referred to, as illustrated below:

> evaluate I = give the val bound to I

Effects on storage implicitly follow the flow of control:

> evaluate assign(E1 , E2) =
>
>> evaluate E1 and evaluate E2
>>
>> then update(the loc#1 , the val#2)

Concurrent processes are represented by agents that perform separate actions, with asynchronous message-passing.

Three kinds of first-order entities:

- Data: Basic mathematical values.
- Yielders: Expressions that evaluate to data using current information.
- Actions: Dynamic, computational entities that model operational behavior.

Data and Sorts

Data manipulated by a programming language

- Integers
- Cells
- Booleans

- Tuples
- Maps

Classification of Data

Data classified according to how far it tends to be propagated during action performance.

Transient

Tuples of data given as the immediate results of action performance. Use them or lose them.

Scoped

Data consisting of bindings of tokens (identifiers) to data as in environments.

Stable

Stable data model memory as values stored in cells (locations); may be altered by explicit actions only.

Actions are also classified this way

Data Specification

module TruthValues

   exports

    sort TruthValue

    operations

     true : TruthValue

     false : TruthValue

     not _ : TruthValue → TruthValue

     both(_,_) : TruthValue,TruthValue → TruthValue

     either(_,_) : TruthValue,TruthValue → TruthValue

     _ is _ : TruthValue,TruthValue → TruthValue

    end exports

    equations

     ...

   end TruthValues

   module Integers

     imports TruthValues

     exports

      sort Integer

Operations

  0 : Integer

  1 : Integer

  10 : Integer

  successor : Integer → Integer

  predecessor : Integer → Integer

  sum(_,_) : Integer, Integer → Integer

  difference(_,_) : Integer, Integer → Integer

  product(_,_) : Integer, Integer → Integer

  integer-quotient(_,_) : Integer,Integer → Integer

  _ is _: Integer, Integer → TruthValue

  _ is less than _ : Integer,Integer → TruthValue

  _ is greater than _ : Integer, Integer →

                    TruthValue

end exports

equations

...

end Integers

Sort Operations (A Lattice)

Join (union) of two sorts S1 and S2: S1 | S2. Meet (intersection) of sorts S1 and S2: S1 & S2. Bottom element: nothing.

Yielders

Current information (maintained implicitly)

- The given transients,

- The received bindings, and

- The current state of the storage.

Yielders are terms that evaluate to data dependent on the current information.

the given S : Data → Yielder

  Yield the transient data given to an action, provided it agrees with the sort S.

the given S # n : Datum, PosInteger → Yielder

  Yield the nth item in tuple of transient data given to action, provided it agrees with sort S.

the _ bound to _ : Data, Token → Yielder

  Yield the object bound to an identifier denoted by Token in current bindings, after verifying that its type is sort specified as Data.

the _ stored in _ : Data, Yielder → Yielder

  Yield value of sort Data stored in memory location denoted by the cell yielded by second argument.

Precedence

Highest:Prefix (right-to-left)

    Infix (left-to-right)

Lowest: Outfix

Actions

- When performed, actions accept the data passed to them as the current information
  - o   The given transients,
  - o   The received bindings, and
  - o   The current state of storage.

to give new transients, produce new bindings, and/or update the state of the storage.

An action performance may

  - o   Complete (terminate normally),
  - o   Fail (terminate abnormally), or
  - o   Diverge (not terminate at all).

Facets of Action Semantics

Actions are classified into facets, depending on the main type of information processed.

- Functional Facet: actions that process transient information.

- Imperative Facet: actions that affect memory.

- Declarative Facet: actions that process scoped information.

- Basic Facet: actions that principally specify flow of control.

Functional and Basic Facets

Primitive functional action give Y Give value obtained by evaluating the yielder Y

Action combinators are used to define control flow as well as to manage the movement of information between actions.

combinator : Action, Action → Action

A1 and then A2

   Perform the first action and then perform the second.

   Dashed line shows control flow:

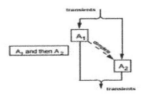

Flow lines from the top to the bottom of the diagram show the behavior of the transients.

Concatenation: Join the data flow lines

A1 and A2

   Allows the performance of the two actions to be interleaved.

   No control dependency in diagram,

   so actions can be performed collaterally.

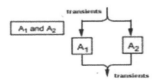

A1 then A2

Perform the first action using the transients given to the combined action and then perform the second action using the transients given by the first action.

The transients given by the combined action are the transients given by the second action.

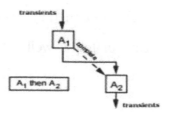

Example

give sum(the given Integer#1,

the given Integer#2)

and

give (the given Integer#1 is the given Integer#2

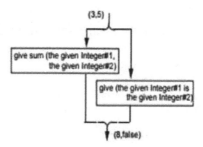

Imperative Facet

Imperative facet deals with storage:

- Allocating memory locations.
- Updating the contents of locations.
- Fetching values from memory.
- Deallocating memory locations.

Any action may alter the state of a cell, and such a modification remains in effect until some other action modifies the cell again.

Current storage is a finite mapping from cells to the sort (Storable | undefined).

Imperative Yielder

the S stored in Y : Data, Yielder → Yielder

  Yield the value of sort S stored in the cell yielded by Y.

Primitive Imperative Actions

allocate a cell

  Find an unused cell, storing undefined in it, and give cell as the transient of action.

store Y1 in Y2

  Update the cell yielded by Y2 to contain the Storable yielded by Y1.

The imperative facet has no special action combinators, but any action has the potential of altering storage.

Suppose that one location, denoted by $cell_1$, has been allocated and currently contains the value undefined. Also assume that the next cell to be allocated will be $cell_2$.

	Initial storage:	$cell_1$	undefined
store 77 in $cell_1$		$cell_1$	77
and then			
allocate a cell		$cell_1$	77
		$cell_2$	undefined
then			
store 15 in the given Cell		$cell_1$	77
		$cell_2$	15
and then			
store product (the Integer stored in $cell_1$, the Integer stored in $cell_2$) in cell1		$cell_1$	1155
		$cell_2$	15

Module for Imperative Features

Module Imperative imports Integers, Maps exports

  sort Storable = Integer

  sort Storage =

        map [Cell to (Storable | undefined)]

sort Cell

operations

  cell1 : Cell

  allocate a cell : Action

store _ in _ : Yielder, Yielder → Action

the _ stored in _ : Storable, Yielder → Yielder

end exports

equations

...

end Imperative

References

- Milner, Robin (2009). The Space and Motion of Communicating Agents. Cambridge University Press. ISBN 978-0-521-73833-0

- Compiler-design-syntax-analysis: tutorialspoint.com, Retrieved 15 June 2018

- Felleisen, M.; Hieb, R. "The Revised Report on the Syntactic Theories of Sequential Control and State". Theoretical Computer Science. doi:10.1016/0304-3975(92)90014-7

- Syntax-highlighter: avada.theme-fusion.com, Retrieved 11 July 2018

- Axiomatic-semantics-17804: techopedia.com, Retrieved 11 June 2018

- Nissim Francez, C. A. R. Hoare, Daniel Lehmann, and Willem-Paul de Roever. "Semantics of nondeterminism, concurrency, and communication", Journal of Computer and System Sciences. December 1979

- Semantics-computing-687: techopedia.com, Retrieved 08 April 2018

- Levy, Paul Blain (2007). "Amb Breaks Well-Pointedness, Ground Amb Doesn't". Electr. Notes Theor. Comput. Sci. 173: 221–239. doi:10.1016/j.entcs.2007.02.036

- Operational-semantics, dictionaries-thesauruses-pictures-and-press-releases: encyclopedia.com, Retrieved 28 May 2018

Data Types

A classification or categorization of data which enables a compiler or interpreter to know how a programmer intends to use the data is a data type. This chapter has been carefully written to provide an easy understanding of the varied data types such as primitive data type, machine data type, Boolean data type, numeric data type, etc.

A data type, in programming, is a classification that specifies which type of value a variable has and what type of mathematical, relational or logical operations can be applied to it without causing an error. A string, for example, is a data type that is used to classify text and an integer is a data type used to classify whole numbers.

Data Type	Used for	Example
String	Alphanumeric characters	hello world, Alice, Bob123
Integer	Whole numbers	7, 12, 999
Float (floating point)	Number with a decimal point	3.15, 9.06, 00.13
Character	Encoding text numerically	97 (in ASCII, 97 is a lower case 'a')
Boolean	Representing logical values	TRUE, FALSE

The data type defines which operations can safely be performed to create, transform and use the variable in another computation. When a program language requires a variable to only be used in ways that respect its data type, that language is said to be strongly typed. This prevents errors, because while it is logical to ask the computer to multiply a float by an integer (1.5 x 5), it is illogical to ask the computer to multiply a float by a string (1.5 x Alice). When a programming language allows a variable of one data type to be used as if it were a value of another data type, the language is said to be weakly typed.

Technically, the concept of a strongly typed or weakly typed programming language is a fallacy. In every programming language, all values of a variable have a static type -- but the type might be one whose values are classified into one or more classes. And while some classes specify how the data type's value will be compiled or interpreted, there are other classes whose values are not marked with their class until run-time. The extent to which a programming language discourages or prevents type error is known as type safety.

C Data Type

In C programming, variables or memory locations should be declared before it can be used. Similarly, a function also needs to be declared before use.

Data types in C

1. Fundamental Data Types

- Integer types
- Floating type
- Character type.

2. Derived Data Types

- Arrays
- Pointers
- Structures
- Enumeration.

int - Integer data types

Integers are whole numbers that can have both positive and negative values but no decimal values.

Example: 0, -5, 10.

In C programming, keyword int is used for declaring integer variable. For example:

```
int id;
```

Here, id is a variable of type integer.

You can declare multiple variable at once in C programming. For example:

```
int id, age;
```

The size of int is either 2 bytes(In older PC's) or 4 bytes. If you consider an integer having size of 4 byte(equal to 32 bits), it can take 2^{32} distinct states as: $-2^{31}, -2^{31}+1, ...,-2, -1, 0, 1, 2, ..., 2^{31}-2, 2^{31}-1$. If you try to store larger number than $2^{31}-1$, i.e,+2147483647 and smaller number than -2^{31}, i.e, -2147483648, program will not run correctly.

Similarly, int of 2 bytes, it can take 2^{16} distinct states from -2^{15} to $2^{15}-1$.

float - Floating Types

Floating type variables can hold real numbers such as: 2.34, -9.382, 5.0 etc. You can declare a floating point variable in C by using either float or double keyword. For example:

```
float accountBalance;
```

```
double bookPrice;
```

Here, both accountBalance and bookPrice are floating type variables.

In C, floating values can be represented in exponential form as well. For example:

```
float normalizationFactor = 22.442e2;
```

Difference between Float and Double

The size of float (single precision float data type) is 4 bytes. And the size of double (double precision float data type) is 8 bytes. Floating point variables has a precision of 6 digits whereas the precision of double is 14 digits.

char - Character Types

Keyword char is used for declaring character type variables. For example:

```
char test = 'h';
```

Here, test is a character variable. The value of test is ‹h›.

The size of character variable is 1 byte.

C Qualifiers

Qualifiers alters the meaning of base data types to yield a new data type.

Size qualifiers

Size qualifiers alters the size of a basic type. There are two size qualifiers, long and short. For example:

```
long double i;
```

The size of double is 8 bytes. However, when long keyword is used, that variable becomes 10 bytes.

There is another keyword short which can be used if you previously know the value of a variable will always be a small number.

Sign Qualifiers

Integers and floating point variables can hold both negative and positive values. However, if a variable needs to hold positive value only, unsigned data types are used. For example:

```
// unsigned variables cannot hold negative value

unsigned int positiveInteger;
```

There is another qualifier signed which can hold both negative and positive only. However, it is not necessary to define variable signed since a variable is signed by default.

An integer variable of 4 bytes can hold data from -2^{31} to $2^{31}-1$. However, if the variable is defined as unsigned, it can hold data from 0 to $2^{32}-1$.

It is important to note that, sign qualifiers can be applied to int and char types only.

Constant Qualifiers

An identifier can be declared as a constant. To do so const keyword is used.

```
const int cost = 20;
```

The value of cost cannot be changed in the program.

Volatile Qualifiers

A variable should be declared volatile whenever its value can be changed by some external sources outside the program. Keyword volatile is used for creating volatile variables.

C++ Data Type

All variables use data-type during declaration to restrict the type of data to be stored. Therefore, we can say that data types are used to tell the variables the type of data it can store.

Whenever a variable is defined in C++, the compiler allocates some memory for that variable based on the data-type with which it is declared. Every data type requires different amount of memory.

Data types in C++ is mainly divided into two types:

1. Primitive Data Types: These data types are built-in or predefined data types and can be used directly by the user to declare variables. example: int, char , float, bool etc. Primitive data types available in C++ are:

    *   Integer

    *   Character

    *   Boolean

    *   Floating Point

    *   Double Floating Point

    *   Valueless or Void

    *   Wide Character.

2. Abstract or user defined data type: These data types are defined by user itself. Like, defining a class in C++ or a structure.

    *   Integer: Keyword used for integer data types is int. Integers typically requires 4 bytes of memory space and ranges from -2147483648 to 2147483647.

    *   Character: Character data type is used for storing characters. Keyword used for character data type is char. Characters typically requires 1 byte of memory space and ranges from -128 to 127 or 0 to 255.

    *   Boolean: Boolean data type is used for storing boolean or logical values. A boolean variable can store either *true* or *false*. Keyword used for boolean data type is bool.

    *   Floating Point: Floating Point data type is used for storing single precision floating point values or decimal values. Keyword used for floating point data type is float. Float

variables typically requires 4 byte of memory space.

- Double Floating Point: Double Floating Point data type is used for storing double precision floating point values or decimal values. Keyword used for double floating point data type is double. Double variables typically requires 8 byte of memory space.

- void: Void means without any value. void datatype represents a valueless entity. Void data type is used for those function which does not returns a value.

- Wide Character: Wide character data type is also a character data type but this data type has size greater than the normal 8-bit datatype. Represented by wchar_t. It is generally 2 or 4 bytes long.

Datatype modifiers: As the name implies, datatype modifiers are used with the built-in data types to modify the length of data that a particular data type can hold. Data type modifiers available in C++ are:

- Signed

- Unsigned

- Short

- Long.

Below table summarizes the modified size and range of built-in datatypes when combined with the type modifiers:

Data Type	Size (In Bytes)	Range
short int	2	-32,768 to 32,767
unsigned short int	2	0 to 65,535
unsigned int	4	0 to 4,294,967,295
int	4	-2,147,483,648 to 2,147,483,647
long int	8	-2,147,483,648 to 2,147,483,647
unsigned long int	4	0 to 4,294,967,295
long long int	8	$-(2^{63})$ to $(2^{63})-1$
unsigned long long int	8	0 to 18,446,744,073,709,551,615
signed char	1	-128 to 127
unsigned char	1	0 to 255
float	4	
double	8	
long double	12	
wchar_t	2 or 4	1 wide character

Note : Above values may vary from compiler to compiler. In above example, we have considered GCC 64 bit.

We can display the size of all the data types by using the size of ( ) function and passing the keyword of the datatype as argument to this function as shown below:

```cpp
// C++ program to sizes of data types
#include<iostream>
using namespace std;


int main()
{
    cout << «Size of char : « << sizeof(char)
      << « byte» << endl;
    cout << «Size of int : « << sizeof(int)
      << « bytes» << endl;
    cout << «Size of short int : « << sizeof(short int)
      << « bytes» << endl;
    cout << «Size of long int : « << sizeof(long int)
       << « bytes» << endl;
    cout << «Size of signed long int : « << sizeof(signed long int)
       << « bytes» << endl;
    cout << «Size of unsigned long int : « << sizeof(unsigned long int)
       << « bytes» << endl;
    cout << «Size of float : « << sizeof(float)
       << « bytes» <<endl;
    cout << «Size of double : « << sizeof(double)
       << « bytes» << endl;
    cout << «Size of wchar_t : « << sizeof(wchar_t)
       << « bytes» <<endl;


    return 0;
}
```

```
Size of char : 1 byte

Size of int : 4 bytes

Size of short int : 2 bytes

Size of long int : 8 bytes

Size of signed long int : 8 bytes

Size of unsigned long int : 8 bytes

Size of float : 4 bytes

Size of double : 8 bytes

Size of wchar_t : 4 bytes
```

Python Data Type

Python has five standard data types but this programming language does not make use of any keyword to specify a particular data type, rather Python is intelligent enough to understand a given data type automatically.

- Numbers
- String
- List
- Tuple
- Dictionary.

Here, Number specifies all types of numbers including decimal numbers and string represents a sequence of characters with a length of 1 or more characters. For now, let's proceed with these two data types and skip List, Tuple, and Dictionary, which are advanced data types in Python.

Primitive Data Type

A primitive data type is either a data type that is built into a programming language, or one that could be characterized as a basic structure for building more sophisticated data types. Programmers will often be immediately familiar with the primitive data types used in coding, which do not involve more sophisticated data sets for effective representation.

Examples of primitive data types include integers, floating point numbers and individual characters in text. Each of these primitive data types is an example of something that doesn't require a large amount of data for representation. Characters simply correspond to a single reference point in an ASCII chart. Integers are numbers that do not need complex identifiers such as exponents and decimal points. Boolean values require only a binary choice between two possible values.

Other data types may or may not be primitive, depending on the design of a programming language or system. One common example is strings. A string variable is a collection of characters put together into a single dynamic variable. Programming languages work on strings to amend them as necessary. In this case, if a string is built into a program or has a particular kind of support, it could be called a primitive data type. However, it does not share some of the basic design elements of the primitive data types.

Other specific explanations of primitive data types include the idea that a primitive data type cannot be broken down into a simpler data type. Others explain primitive data types by contrasting them with user-defined classes, more sophisticated classes that are created by users, whereas primitive data types have already been created by the platform or interface that the programmer or developer is using. These explanations help to explain why one specific type of variable may be considered a primitive data type in one language but not in another. Other experts may contrast primitive data types with derived data types, which are created using collections of primitive data types. As a result, they can be broken down into more basic elements than the primitive data types.

The categories of primitive types include:

- Character types
- Date/time types
- Large object types
- Numeric types
- Logical types
- ANY type.

Character Types

In the current internationalized marketplace, it is particularly vital to be conscious of the encoding you use with character or text type data. EGL provides a variety of encoding types for single-byte, double-byte, and multibyte characters. Note that you can also refer to subsets of these character types as substrings.

Table: Primitive character types

Primitive	Size	Limits	Data type
CHAR	1 byte	CHAR(32767)	Single-byte characters using local code page encoding
DBCHAR	2 bytes	DBCHAR(16383)	Double-byte characters using local code page encoding (cannot contain single-byte characters)

Primitive	Size	Limits	Data type
MBCHAR	1 or 2 bytes	MBCHAR(32767)	MBCS data. Double byte characters are recognized because the lead byte belongs to a reserved set. Specify length in single bytes.
STRING	varies	For Java™, the maximum supported by a Java Virtual Machine. For JavaScript, the maximum supported by a browser. For COBOL, 32,767 characters.	Unicode (UTF-16 encoding) characters.
UNICODE	2 bytes	UNICODE(16383)	Unicode (UTF-16 encoding) characters.
HEX	4 bits	HEX(65534)	Hexadecimal digits 0-9 and A-F.

You can specify a STRING with a specific number of characters, in which case it is a limited-length string, or you can declare a variable-length string by omitting the length specification, as in the following examples:

```
myLimitedString STRING(25);

myVarString STRING;
```

In the above example, myLimitedString is different from a CHAR(25) variable because STRINGs contain Unicode data while CHARs contain data in the native character set. Limited-length strings are most commonly used to map to the SQL VARCHAR type.

Escape Sequences for Strings

The following table shows the escape sequences you must use to place certain special characters in a string.

Table: Escape sequences for strings

Escape sequence	Character name
\"	Double quotation mark
\\	Backslash
\t	Tab
\r	Carriage return
\f	Line feed
\n	Newline
\b	Backspace

The following example includes the newline character:

```
var1 String = "This is a string \n that will appear on two lines."
```

Compatibility Considerations

Table: Compatibility considerations

Platform	Issue
JavaScript generation	The following types are supported: ANY, BIGINT, BIN (but only in the absence of decimal places), Boolean, DataItem, DATE, DECIMAL, Delegate, Dictionary, FLOAT, INT, NUM, NUMBER, SMALLFLOAT, SMALLINT, STRING (but only in the absence of a size limit) , TIME, TIMESTAMP, NUM, MONEY, Service parts, Interface parts, External types (stereotype JavaScript), arrays of supported types, and non-structured Basic, Exception, and SQL Record parts.
	The following types are not supported: ArrayDictionary, BIN (with decimal places), BLOB, CHAR, CLOB, DBCHAR, HEX, INTERVAL, MBCHAR, NUMC, STRING (with a size limit), PACF, UNICODE, and structured Record parts.

Date/Time Types

As a rule, EGL separates date information from presentation format.

Table: Primitive date/time types

Primitive	Size	Data format
DATE	8 digits	Gregorian yyyyMMdd
INTERVAL	1 to 21 digits	Based on mask
TIME	6 digits	HHmmss
TIMESTAMP	1 to 20 digits	Based on mask

The following considerations apply to date/time types:

- EGL always stores DATE values in Gregorian form, using eight digits in the format yyyyMMdd (four-digit year, two digits each for month and day). However, during input and output, EGL uses a parsing format or a display format and the Java™ version of the International Components for Unicode libraries (ICU4J) to perform the necessary date conversions. If a Thai application asks a user to type in a date from the Buddhist calendar, EGL still stores that date in eight-digit Gregorian form (with the help of ICU4J).

- EGL always stores TIME values in the form HHmmss. If you need a time value that includes milliseconds, you must use a TIMESTAMP variable.

- Though EGL stores a variable based on TIMESTAMP as yyyyMMddHHmmss by default, you can specify a different mask when you declare the variable, as in the following example:

  myTS timestamp("yyyyMMdd").

Compatibility

Table: Compatibility considerations for date/time types:

Platform	Issue
iSeries COBOL	If a DATE type variable corresponds to an SQL column that is defined as DATE in the SQL database, the date format of the data in the database must match the format specified by the iSeries QDATFMT system variable.
JavaScript generation	Rich UI does not support the Interval type. For other details, see *Rich UI date and time support*.
z/OS COBOL	If a DATE type variable corresponds to an SQL column that is defined as DATE in the SQL database, the date format of the data in the database must match the format specified by the Default Long System Gregorian Date Format for the national language options module.

Large Object Types

The large object types BLOB and CLOB let you create variables to hold up to 2GB of unformatted data.

Table: Primitive large object types

Primitive	Size	Data type
BLOB	1 byte to 2GB	Binary
CLOB	1 byte to 2GB	Character

Compatibility

Table: Compatibility considerations for large object types

Platform	Issue
COBOL generation	Large object types BLOB and CLOB are not supported for COBOL generation.
JavaScript generation	The following types are supported: ANY, BIGINT, BIN (but only in the absence of decimal places), Boolean, DataItem, DATE, DECIMAL, Delegate, Dictionary, FLOAT, INT, NUM, NUMBER, SMALLFLOAT, SMALLINT, STRING (but only in the absence of a size limit) , TIME, TIMESTAMP, NUM, MONEY, Service parts, Interface parts, External types (stereotype JavaScript), arrays of supported types, and non-structured Basic, Exception, and SQL Record parts. The following types are not supported: ArrayDictionary, BIN (with decimal places), BLOB, CHAR, CLOB, DBCHAR, HEX, INTERVAL, MBCHAR, NUMC, STRING (with a size limit), PACF, UNICODE, and structured Record parts.

Numeric Types

EGL provides a variety of numeric data types. Some of the numeric types (such as BIGINT or FLOAT) automatically indicate the length and decimal places. For other numeric types (such as BIN or DECIMAL), you must specify the length and (if appropriate) the number of decimal places, as in the following example:

```
truckMileage BIN(9,2);          // 9 digits, two decimal places

DataItem zipCode INT

 { validValues = [00000,99999]}; // 5 digits only

myZipCode zipcode;
```

EGL allocates storage for truckMileage and myZipCode, but not for the zipCode data item, which is only a model.

Table: EGL primitive numeric types

Primitive	Size	Specify length	Decimals	Data type	DB2 equivalent
BIGINT	18 digits (8 bytes)	N	N	binary	BIGINT
BIN	4, 9, or 18 digits (2, 4, or 8 bytes)	Y	Y	binary	n/a
DECIMAL	18 or 31 digits COBOL 32 digits JAVA	Y	Y	packed decimal characters	DECIMAL
FLOAT	18 digits (8 bytes)	N	Y	double-precision floating point	FLOAT
INT	9 digits (4 bytes)	N	N	binary	INTEGER
MONEY	18 or 31 digits COBOL 32 digits JAVA	Y	Y	packed decimal characters	DECIMAL
NUM	31 digits	Y	Y	numeric characters (zoned decimal)	NUMERIC
NUMC*	18 digits	Y	Y	numeric characters (zoned decimal)	NUMERIC
PACF*	18 digits	Y	Y	packed decimal characters	DECIMAL
S M A L L - FLOAT	9 digits (4 bytes)	N	Y	single- precision floating point	REAL
SMALLINT	4 digits (2 bytes)	N	N	binary	SMALLINT

*NUMC and PACF available only in VisualAge Generator compatibility mode.

The following considerations apply to numeric types:

1. All maximum lengths given in digits are approximate—for example, the maximum value you can store in two bytes while keeping one bit available for a sign is +32,767 or -32,768. You can safely store any four digit number in two bytes, so the table shows the maximum length as 4 digits.

2. The three sizes of BIN (4, 9, and 18 digits) correspond to SMALLINT, INT, and BIGINT respectively, and are the only permitted sizes for BIN variables. The difference between a variable declared as BIN(4,2) and one declared as INT is that the BIN variable has two

decimal places. An INT variable has no decimal places.

3. You can store a 32-digit number in a DECIMAL or MONEY variable in Java™. In COBOL, the maximum length is either 18 or 31 digits, depending on the value of the **maxNumer-icDigits** build descriptor option. Also, 31 digits are the maximum for DB/2.

4. In EGL-generated Java programs, the value of a FLOAT variable ranges from 4.9e-324 to 1.7976931348623157e308. In EGL-generated COBOL programs on z/OS®, the value ranges from 5.4e-79 to 7.2e+75. In EGL-generated COBOL programs on iSeries®, the value ranges from 2.225074e-308 to 1.797693e+308.

5. In EGL-generated Java programs, the value of a SMALLFLOAT ranges from 3.40282347e+38 to 1.40239846e-45. In EGL-generated COBOL programs on z/OS, the value ranges from from 5.4e-79 to 7.2e+75. In EGL-generated COBOL programs on iSeries, the value ranges from 1.175494e-38 to 3.402823e+38. Note that the range of values on z/OS is the same for both FLOAT and SMALLFLOAT. The difference between the two types is in the size of the mantissa (also called the significand): 6 hexadecimal digits for the SMALLFLOAT (at least 7 decimal digits) and 14 hexadecimal digits for the FLOAT (at least 17 decimal digits).

6. MONEY is identical to DECIMAL except that, when you output a variable based on MON-EY, EGL uses the strLib.defaultMoneyFormat system variable to determine the output format. By default this format has two decimal places and includes a currency symbol.

7. EGL supports the NUMC and PACF types so you can work with files and databases from older applications. In new development, use variables and fields based on BIN or an equivalent integer type (BIGINT, INT, or SMALLINT), or on the DECIMAL type; calculations are more efficient with those variable types. You get the greatest efficiency by using four-digit BIN variables with no decimal places (the equivalent of the SMALLINT type).

8. Other efficiency considerations include the following points:

    • In calculations, assignments, and comparisons, NUM fields that have no decimal places are more efficient than those that do have decimal places.

    • For code generated in Java, calculations with DECIMAL, NUM, NUMC, and PACF fields are equally efficient. For code generated in COBOL, however, these distinctions apply:

        ◦ Calculations with NUM fields are more efficient than calculations with NUMC fields.

        ◦ Calculations with DECIMAL fields are more efficient than calculations with PACF fields.

9. If you are new to mainframe computing, you might not recognize two common types of numeric variables in COBOL: zoned decimal and packed decimal. If you work with these types, your EGL data types must match the format and sign configuration of the data these types contain. Here is a quick overview:

- EBCDIC represents ordinary positive numbers 0-9 with hex characters F0-F9 (for example, 150 translates to F1F5F0). COBOL also supports "zoned" data types that allow signs (in EGL these are NUM and NUMC). The rightmost hex digit carries the sign for the whole number, with a D replacing the F for a negative number. Thus F1F5D0 translates to -150. In the case of NUMC, a C replaces the F for a positive number, rendering positive 150 as F1F5C0.

- The repeated F characters may seem redundant to those unfamiliar with EBCDIC. Packed decimal data types (represented in EGL by DECIMAL, MONEY, and PACF) eliminate the redundancy. The packed decimal version of -150 is 150D. Positive 150 is 150, except in the PACF format, where it would be 150F.

Compatibility Considerations

Table: Compatibility considerations

Platform	Issue
JavaScript generation	The following types are supported: ANY, BIGINT, BIN (but only in the absence of decimal places), Boolean, DataItem, DATE, DECIMAL, Delegate, Dictionary, FLOAT, INT, NUM, NUMBER, SMALLFLOAT, SMALLINT, STRING (but only in the absence of a size limit) , TIME, TIMESTAMP, NUM, MONEY, Service parts, Interface parts, External types (stereotype JavaScript), arrays of supported types, and non-structured Basic, Exception, and SQL Record parts. The following types are not supported: ArrayDictionary, BIN (with decimal places), BLOB, CHAR, CLOB, DBCHAR, HEX, INTERVAL, MBCHAR, NUMC, STRING (with a size limit), PACF, UNICODE, and structured Record parts.

Logical Types

There is only a single logical data type, the BOOLEAN. The BOOLEAN type recognizes the following STRING values as "literals":

- TRUE
- YES
- FALSE
- NO

Table: Primitive logical types

Primitive	Size	Data type
BOOLEAN	1 byte	EGL evaluates a BOOLEAN type variable as either TRUE or FALSE, and also recognizes the values YES (same as TRUE) and NO (same as FALSE) as Boolean literals.

ANY Types

The special EGL data type ANY lets you create a variable whose data type is not fixed. When you assign a value to an ANY type variable, EGL knows the type of that value at run time, but not at development or generation time.

You can assign an INT value to an ANY type variable at one point in your program, and assign a STRING or HEX value to the same variable at a later time.

You cannot use an ANY type variable in a numeric expression unless you use the **as** operator to cast the variable as a numeric type, as in the following example:

```
myInt INT = 42;

myAny ANY = myInt;

myInt = myAny as INT + 38;
```

ANY, like the BLOB, CLOB, and array types, is a reference type rather than a value type. This means that the variable contains a reference to an area of reserved memory rather than containing a value.

Compatibility Considerations

Table: Compatibility considerations

Platform	Issue
JavaScript generation	The following types are supported: ANY, BIGINT, BIN (but only in the absence of decimal places), Boolean, DataItem, DATE, DECIMAL, Delegate, Dictionary, FLOAT, INT, NUM, NUMBER, SMALLFLOAT, SMALLINT, STRING (but only in the absence of a size limit) , TIME, TIMESTAMP, NUM, MONEY, Service parts, Interface parts, External types (stereotype JavaScript), arrays of supported types, and non-structured Basic, Exception, and SQL Record parts.
	The following types are not supported: ArrayDictionary, BIN (with decimal places), BLOB, CHAR, CLOB, DBCHAR, HEX, INTERVAL, MBCHAR, NUMC, STRING (with a size limit), PACF, UNICODE, and structured Record parts.

Machine Data Type

Machine data is digital information created by the activity of computers, mobile phones, embedded systems and other networked devices. Such data became more prevalent as technologies such as radio frequency identification (RFID) and telematics advanced. More recently, machine data has gained further attention as use of the Internet of Things, Hadoopand other big data management technologies has grown.

Application, server and business process logs, call detail records and sensor data are prime examples of machine data. Internet clickstream data and website activity logs also factor into discussions of machine data.

Combining machine data with other enterprise data types for analysis is expected to provide new views and insight on business activities and operations. For example, some large industrial manufacturers are analyzing machine data on the performance of field equipment in near-real-time, together with historical performance data, to better understand service problems and to try to predict equipment maintenance issues before machines break down.

Other examples of applications that center on the use of machine data include setups for monitoring oil and gas pipelines, natural disaster warning systems based on feeds from marine sensors, forecasting systems that take data from satellites and weather stations to help predict weather in small geographic areas, and a building energy management system that analyzes HVAC and elevator data to improve efficiency. Further use cases are likely to arise as emerging machine learning applications begin to mature.

The following are common types of machine data:

- Sensors

  Sensors are devices that detect physical phenomena such as light and sound and turn it into streams of data. For example, video of a street corner or temperature readings from a part in a machine.

- Calculations

  Data that is calculated from other data. For example, an algorithm that calculates a risk estimate for an investment based on market data.

- Predictions

  Algorithms and artificial intelligence that attempt to predict the future. For example, a robot that attempts to predict the near future direction of pedestrians as it walks down the street.

- Automation

  Automated tasks that create data such as events, controls or commands. For example, a manufacturing control system may issue commands to a conveyor belt and create a status log.

- Metadata

  Data about other data such as a timestamp that is added to event data.

- Decisions & Interpretations

  Machine decisions such as an algorithm that decides to approve a customer's application for credit.

- Transactions

  Machines may generate transactions that have commercial and legal significance for the organization that owns the machine. For example, a machine may decide to execute a stock trade for a financial institution based on rules in an algorithm.

Boolean Data Type

The Boolean data type can be one of two values, either True or False. We use Booleans in programming to make comparisons and to control the flow of the program.

Booleans represent the truth values that are associated with the logic branch of mathematics, which informs algorithms in computer science. Named for the mathematician George Boole, the word Boolean always begins with a capitalized B. The values `True` and `False` will also always be with a capital T and F respectively, as they are special values in Python.

Comparison Operators

In programming, comparison operators are used to compare values and evaluate down to a single Boolean value of either True or False.

The table below shows Boolean comparison operators.

Operator	What it means
==	Equal to
!=	Not equal to
<	Less than
>	Greater than
<=	Less than or equal to
>=	Greater than or equal to

To understand how these operators work, let's assign two integers to two variables in a Python program:

```
x = 5
y = 8
```

We know that in this example, since x has the value of 5, it is less than y which has the value of 8.

Using those two variables and their associated values, let's go through the operators from the table above. In our program, we'll ask Python to print out whether each comparison operator evaluates to either True or False. To help us and other humans better understand this output, we'll have Python also print a string to show us what it's evaluating.

```
x = 5
y = 8


print("x == y:", x == y)
print("x != y:", x != y)
```

```
print("x < y:", x < y)

print("x > y:", x > y)

print("x <= y:", x <= y)

print("x >= y:", x >= y)


Output

x == y: False

x != y: True

x < y: True

x > y: False

x <= y: True

x >= y: False
```

Following mathematical logic, in each of the expressions above, Python has evaluated:

- Is 5 (x) equal to 8 (y)? False

- Is 5 not equal to 8? True

- Is 5 less than 8? True

- Is 5 greater than 8? False

- Is 5 less than or equal to 8? True

- Is 5 not less than or equal to 8? False

Although we used integers here, we could substitute them with float values.

Strings can also be used with Boolean operators. They are case-sensitive unless you employ an additional string method.

We can look at how strings are compared in practice:

```
Sammy = "Sammy"

sammy = "sammy"

print("Sammy == sammy: ", Sammy == sammy)


Output

Sammy == sammy: False
```

The string "Sammy" above is not equal to the string "sammy", because they are not exactly the same; one starts with an upper-case S and the other with a lower-case s. But, if we add another variable that is assigned the value of "Sammy", then they will evaluate to equal:

```
Sammy = "Sammy"

sammy = "sammy"

also_Sammy = "Sammy"


print("Sammy == sammy: ", Sammy == sammy)

print("Sammy == also_Sammy", Sammy == also_Sammy)


Output

Sammy == sammy: False

Sammy == also_Sammy: True
```

You can also use the other comparison operators including > and < to compare two strings. Python will compare these strings lexicographically using the ASCII values of the characters.

We can also evaluate Boolean values with comparison operators:

```
t = True
f = False


print("t != f: ", t != f)


Output

t != f: True
```

The above code block evaluated that True is not equal to False.

Note the difference between the two operators = and ==.

```
x = y  # Sets x equal to y

x == y # Evaluates whether x is equal to y
```

The first, = is the assignment operator, which will set one value equal to another. The second, == is a comparison operator which will evaluate whether two values are equal.

Logical Operators

There are three logical operators that are used to compare values. They evaluate expressions down to Boolean values, returning either True or False. These operators are and, or, and not and are defined in the table below.

Operator	What it means	What it looks like
and	True if both are true	x and y
or	True if at least one is true	x or y
not	True only if false	not x

Logical operators are typically used to evaluate whether two or more expressions are true or not true. For example, they can be used to determine if the grade is passing **and** that the student is registered in the course, and if both cases are true then the student will be assigned a grade in the system.

To understand how logical operators work, let's evaluate three expressions:

```
print((9 > 7) and (2 < 4)) # Both original expressions are True

print((8 == 8) or (6 != 6)) # One original expression is True

print(not(3 <= 1))     # The original expression is False


Output

True

True

True
```

In the first case, print((9 > 7) and (2 < 4)), both 9 > 7 and 2 < 4 needed to evaluate to True since the and operator was being used.

In the second case, print((8 == 8) or (6 != 6)), since 8 == 8 evaluated to True, it did not make a difference that 6 != 6 evaluates to False because the or operator was used. If we had used the andoperator, this would evaluate to False.

In the third case, print(not(3 <= 1)), the not operator negates the False value that 3 <=1 returns.

Let's substitute floats for integers and aim for False evaluations:

```
print((-0.2 > 1.4) and (0.8 < 3.1)) # One original expression is False

print((7.5 == 8.9) or (9.2 != 9.2)) # Both original expressions are False

print(not(-5.7 <= 0.3))     # The original expression is True
```

In the example above,

- and must have at least one False expression evaluate to False,

- or must have both expressions evaluate to False, and

- not must have its inner expression be True for the new expression to evaluate to False.

If the results seem unclear to you, we'll go through some truth tables to get you up to speed.

You can also write compound statements using and, or, and not:

```
not((-0.2 > 1.4) and ((0.8 < 3.1) or (0.1 == 0.1)))
```

Let's look at the inner-most expression first: (0.8 < 3.1) or (0.1 == 0.1). This expression evaluates to True because both mathematical statements are True.

Now, we can take the returned value True and combine it with the next inner expression: (-0.2 > 1.4) and (True). This example returns False because the mathematical statement -0.2 > 1.4 is False, and (False) and (True) returns False.

Finally, we have the outer expression: not(False), which evaluates to True, so the final returned value if we print this statement out is:

```
Output

True
```

The logical operators and, or, and not evaluate expressions and return Boolean values.

Truth Tables

There is a lot to learn about the logic branch of mathematics, but we can selectively learn some of it to improve our algorithmic thinking when programming.

Below are truth tables for the comparison operator ==, and each of the logic operators and, or, and not. While you may be able to reason them out, it can also be helpful to work to memorize them as that can make your programming decision-making process quicker.

== Truth Table

x	==	y	Returns
True	==	True	True
True	==	False	False
False	==	True	False
False	==	False	True

And Truth Table

x	and	y	Returns
True	and	True	True
True	and	False	False
False	and	True	False
False	and	False	False

Or Truth Table

x	or	y	Returns
True	or	True	True
True	or	False	True
False	or	True	True
False	or	False	False

Not Truth Table

not	x	Returns
not	True	False
not	False	True

Truth tables are common mathematical tables used in logic, and are useful to memorize or keep in mind when constructing algorithms (instructions) in computer programming.

Using Boolean Operators for Flow Control

To control the stream and outcomes of a program in the form of flow control statements, we can use a condition followed by a clause.

A condition evaluates down to a Boolean value of True or False, presenting a point where a decision is made in the program. That is, a condition would tell us if something evaluates to True or False.

The clause is the block of code that follows the condition and dictates the outcome of the program. That is, it is the do this part of the construction "If x is True, then do this."

The code block below shows an example of comparison operators working in tandem with conditional statements to control the flow of a Python program:

```python
if grade >= 65:          # Condition

    print("Passing grade")   # Clause


else:

    print("Failing grade")
```

This program will evaluate whether each student's grade is passing or failing. In the case of a student with a grade of 83, the first statement will evaluate to True, and the print statement of Passing grade will be triggered. In the case of a student with a grade of 59, the first statement will evaluate to False, so the program will move on to execute the print statement tied to the else expression: Failing grade.

Because every single object in Python can be evaluated to True or False, the PEP 8 Style Guide recommends against comparing a value to True or False because it is less readable and will frequently return an unexpected Boolean. That is, you should avoid using if sammy == True: in your programs. Instead, compare sammy to another non-Boolean value that will return a Boolean.

Boolean operators present conditions that can be used to decide the eventual outcome of a program through flow control statements.

Numeric Data Type

Numeric data types are numbers stored in database columns. These data types are typically grouped by:

- Exact numeric types, values where the precision and scale need to be preserved. The exact numeric types are BIGINT, DECIMAL, INTEGER, NUMERIC, NUMBER, and MONEY.

- Approximate numeric types, values where the precision needs to be preserved and the scale can be floating. The approximate numeric types are DOUBLE PRECISION, FLOAT, and REAL.

Integer Data Type

The INTEGER data type is a 32-bit integer. The shorthand name of the data type is INT. Numbers of the INTEGER type are within the range from -2^{32} to $2^{32} - 1$, that is, from -2,147,483,648 to 2,147,483,647.

Integer Example:

```
CREATE TABLE CUSTOMER (

  CUST_NO INTEGER NOT NULL,

  CUSTOMER VARCHAR(25) NOT NULL,

  CONTACT_FIRST VARCHAR(15),

  CONTACT_LAST VARCHAR(20),

   PRIMARY KEY (CUST_NO) )
```

The INTEGER data type stores whole numbers that range from -2,147,483,647 to 2,147,483,647 for 9 or 10 digits of precision.

The number 2,147,483,648 is a reserved value and cannot be used. The INTEGER value is stored as a signed binary integer and is typically used to store counts, quantities, and so on.

Arithmetic operations and sort comparisons are performed more efficiently on integer data than on float or decimal data. INTEGER columns, however, cannot store absolute values beyond $(2^{31}-1)$. If a data value lies outside the numeric range of INTEGER, the database server does not store the value.

INTEGER data types require 4 bytes of storage per value.

Floating Point Data Type

Floating-point data types are stored in the IEEE SINGLE and DOUBLE precision formats. Both formats have a sign bit field, an exponent field, and a fraction field. The fields represent floating-point numbers in the following manner:

```
Floating-Point Number = <sign> 1.<fraction field> x 2 (<exponent field> - bias)
```

- Sign bit field

  The sign bit field is the most significant bit of the floating-point number. The sign bit is 0 for positive numbers and 1 for negative numbers.

- Fraction field

  The fraction field contains the fractional part of a normalized number. Normalized numbers are greater than or equal to 1 and less than 2. Since all normalized numbers are of the form 1.XXXXXXX, the 1 becomes implicit and is not stored in memory. The bits in the fraction field are the bits to the right of the binary point, and they represent negative powers of 2.

- For example:

  ```
  0.011 (binary) = 2⁻² + 2⁻³ = 0.25 + 0.125 = 0.375
  ```

- Exponent field

  The exponent field contains a biased exponent; that is, a constant bias is subtracted from the number in the exponent field to yield the actual exponent. (The bias makes negative exponents possible.)

- If both the exponent field and the fraction field are zero, the floating-point number is zero.

- NaN

  A NaN (Not a Number) is a special value that is used when the result of an operation is undefined. For example, dividing a number by zero results in a NaN.

Float Data Type

The FLOAT data type is stored in the IEEE single-precision format which is 32 bits long. The most significant bit is the sign bit, the next 8 most significant bits are the exponent field, and the remaining 23 bits are the fraction field. The bias of the exponent is 127. The range of single-precision format values is from 1.18×10^{-38} to 3.4×10^{38}. The floating-point number is precise to 6 decimal digits.

```
31   30            23 22                                0

S    Exp. + Bias      Fraction

0    000 0000 0  000 0000 0000 0000 0000 0000 = 0.0
0    011 1111 1  000 0000 0000 0000 0000 0000 = 1.0
1    011 1111 1  011 0000 0000 0000 0000 0000 = -1.375
1    111 1111 1  111 1111 1111 1111 1111 1111 = NaN
```

Double

The DOUBLE data type is stored in the IEEE double-precision format which is 64 bits long. The most significant bit is the sign bit, the next 11 most significant bits are the exponent field, and the remaining 52 bits are the fractional field. The bias of the exponent is 1023. The range of single precision format values is from 2.23×10^{-308} to 1.8×10^{308}. The floating-point number is precise to 15 decimal digits.

```
63    62                52 51                                    0
 ┌───┬──────────────────┬──────────────────────────────────────┐
 │   │                  │                                       │
 │ S │ Exp. + Bias      │ Fraction                              │
 └───┴──────────────────┴──────────────────────────────────────┘


 0    000 0000 0000 0000 0000 ... 0000 0000 0000 = 0.0

 0    011 1111 1111 0000 0000 ... 0000 0000 0000 = 1.0

 1    011 1111 1110 0110 0000 ... 0000 0000 0000 = -0.6875

 1    111 1111 1111 1111 1111 ... 1111 1111 1111 = NaN
```

Limitations

- No thousands-separator commas.

- No support for loading exceptional values, meaning Not a Number (NaN) values and infinities.

The syntax of floating-point values is the same as the syntax of fixed-point values augmented by an optional trailing exponent specification.

The optional decimal point can be followed by zero or more decimal digits if there is at least one decimal digit before the decimal point. The the optional decimal point can be followed by one or more decimal digits if there are no decimal digits before the decimal point. If there is no explicit decimal point, the system assumes a decimal point immediately following the last decimal digit. You can specify a comma as a separator by using it like the decimal point.

The optional power of 10 exponent is e (lowercase or uppercase), with an optional sign and a mandatory sequence of decimal digits.

The following table describes the floating-point precision and representation:

Table: Floating-point precision and representation

Type	Real	Double
Representation	4-byte IEEE floating point	8-byte IEEE floating point
Approx. largest normalized value	±3.40e+38	±1.79e+308
Approx. smallest normalized value	±1.18e-38	±3.40e-308
Approx. smallest denormalized value	±7.01e-46	±2.50e-324

The following conditions result in system errors:

- Overflow

  The field exceeds the largest representable value (maximum exponent and maximum significand).

- Underflow

  The number is too small to approximate in the denormalized range.

Fixed Point Data Type

Fixed-point data type helps us to know what happens in the hardware. In the other words when an algorithm is represented in floating-point domain, all of the variables have 64 bits(in MATLAB programming). So all of the operations are done with large number of bits. We know that it is impossible to implement an algorithm with large number of flip flops. Because large number of flip flops need a larger area, and more power consumption. In order to solve this problem the algorithm should be converted to the fixed-point domain. In the fixed-point domain a pair (W,F) is considered for each of the parameters in the algorithm, where W is the word length of the parameters and F is the fractional length of the parameters. It is obvious that larger W and F results in a better performance and lower bit error rate (BER) but the design needs a large silicon area. On the other hand smaller W and F result in a larger BER but less area. So we should choose suitable values of (W,F) for each parameter in the algorithm. For this reason a simulation should be ran for the algorithm to get the dynamic range of the parameters. Simulation results indicate the dynamic range of the variables and the number of bits for W and F, which are used to represent the variables with the desired precision.

A fixed-point data type is characterized by the word length in bits, the position of the binary point, and whether it is signed or unsigned. The position of the binary point is the means by which fixed-point values are scaled and interpreted.

For example, a binary representation of a generalized fixed-point number (either signed or unsigned) is shown below:

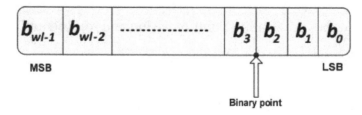

Where:

b_i is the ith binary digit,

wl is the word length in bits,

b_{wl-1} is the location of the most significant, or highest, bit (MSB),

b_0 is the location of the least significant, or lowest, bit (LSB).

The binary point is shown three places to the left of the LSB. In this example, therefore, the number is said to have three fractional bits, or a fraction length of three.

Fixed-Point data types can be either signed or unsigned. Signed binary fixed-point numbers are typically represented in one of these ways:

- Sign/magnitude
- One's complement
- Two's complement.

Two's complement is the most common representation of signed fixed-point numbers and is the only representation used by Fixed-point Toolbox in MATLAB.

Fixed-point numbers can be encoded according to the following scheme:

$$\mathrm{Re}\, al - value = 2^{-fractional-length} \times store\, \mathrm{int}\, eger$$

where store integer the raw binary number, in which the binary point assumed to be at the far right of the word.

Conversion of an algorithm from floating-point domain to fixed-point domain can be done through the MATLAB fixed-point toolbox.

Fixed-Point Toolbox provides fixed-point data types in MATLAB and enables algorithm development by providing fixed-point arithmetic. Fixed-Point Toolbox enables you to create the following types of objects:

- fi — Defines a fixed-point numeric object in the MATLAB workspace. Each fi object is composed of value data, a fimath object, and a numerictype object.

- fimath — Governs how overloaded arithmetic operators work with fi objects

- fipref — Defines the display, logging, and data type override preferences of fi objects

- numerictype — Defines the data type and scaling attributes of fi objects

- quantizer — Quantizes data sets.

Normally complicated algorithms have many variables so the number of fixed-point objects grows significantly. Moreover, in some cases a long time simulation is needed to obtain the BER curves of the algorithm. In the above cases fixed-point simulation with MATLAB fixed-point toolbox needs a large amount of memory, time, and CPU usage and in most of the cases it will crash.

In order to solve the above problem a simple method for floating-point to fixed-point conversion is proposed in this tutorial. Simulation results with this method and simulation results with the MATLAB fixed-point toolbox are the same, but the simulation with the proposed method is significantly faster than the other. For example one iteration of K-Best algorithm simulation with

MATLAB fixed-point toolbox, takes 237 seconds but simulation with the proposed method, needs only 36 seconds.

Floating-point to Fixed-point conversion

In order to convert a floating-point value to the corresponding fixed-point vlaue use the following steps.

Consider a floating-point variable, a :

- Step 1: Calculate $b = a \times 2^F$, where F is the fractional length of the variable. Note that b is represented in decimal.

- Step 2: Round the value of b to the nearest integer value. For example:

  $round\,(3.56) = 4$

  $round\,(-1.9) = -2$

  $round\,(-1.5) = -2$

- Step 3: Convert b from decimal to binary representation and name the new variable c .

- Step 4: Now, we assume that c , needs n bits to represent the value of b in binary. On the other hand we obtain the values of W and F, from the simulation. So the value of W should be equal or larger than n . If Small value is chosen for W, we should truncate c . If W is larger than $n, (W - n)$ zero-bits add to the leftmost of c .

Now consider the simulation is ran carefully and suitable values of (W,F) are obtained. It means that W is equal or larger than n . So (W- n) zero are added to leftmost of c . Then we select F bits of c from position 0 to F-1 as the fractional part of the fixed-point variable. Therefore the conversion from floating-point to fixed-point is finished by finding the position of binary point in c . In order to verify the result, we can do the same conversion with MATLAB fixed-point toolbox. The results of both methods are the same, but the proposed method is faster. Because in MATLAB method we should call a large number of fixed-point functions and fixed-point objects, which are time consuming and they need a large memory.

In each case the operation is done through the both methods and shown that the results are the same.

Note:

- In the following examples "Method 1" shows the MATLAB fixed-point toolbox and "Method 2" shows the above method.

- The dot in the binary representation is used to separate the fractional part and the integer part of the variable. But it isn't a part of the variable.

Example:

This example shows that the value of (W,F) should choose carefully from the simulation (according to the dynamic range of variables).

Method 1:

$$fi\,(3.613,1,7,4) = 3.625 \quad \xrightarrow{\text{convert to binary with bin()}} \quad 011.1010$$

$$fi\,(3.613,1,10,7) = 3.6094 \quad \xrightarrow{\text{convert to binary with bin()}} \quad 011.1001110$$

$$fi(3.613,1,15,12) = 3.613 \quad \xrightarrow{\text{convert to binary with bin()}} \quad 011.100111001111$$

Example:

This example shows the conversion of a floating-point value to fixed-point value and then find the corresponding binary value and finally shows the conversion of a binary value to corresponding real-value by.

Method 1:

$$fi(3.613,1,15,12) = 3.613 \quad \xrightarrow{\text{convert to binary with bin()}} \quad 011.100111001111 \quad (W,F) = (15,12)$$

$$(011100111001111)_b = (14799)_d \quad \xrightarrow{\text{convert to decimal by(1)}} \quad 14799 \times 2^{-12} = 3.613$$

Example

This example shows conversion of a floating-point value to corresponding fixed-point value in two methods. Both positive and negative values are covered in this example.

$$a = 3.013 \;\; (W,F) = (8,3)$$

Method 1:

$$fi(3.013,1,8,3) = 3.00 \quad \xrightarrow{\text{convert to binary with bin()}} \quad 00011.000$$

Method 2:

Step 1: $b = a \times 2^{F}$ $\;3.013 \times 2^{+3} = 24.1040$

Step 2: $round\,(24.1040) \quad 24$

Step 3: $c = dec\,2bin(b) = 11000$

Step 4: $c = 00011.000$

Example:

$$a = 9.51432\;,\;(W,F) = (12,7)$$

Method 1:

$$fi = (9.51432,1,12,7) = 9.5156 \quad \xrightarrow{\text{convert to binary with bin()}} \quad 01001.1000010$$

Method 2:

Step 1: $b = a \times 2^{F}$ $\;9.51432 \times 2^{+7} = 1217.8329$

Step 2: $round\,(1217.8329) = 1218$

Step 3: $c = dec2bin\,(b) = 010011000010$

Step 4: $c = 01001.1000010$

Example:

$$a = -9.0514 \; , \; (W,F) = (14,9)$$

Method 1:

$$fi\,(-9.0514\,,1,14,9) = -9.0508 \quad \xrightarrow{\text{convert to binary with bin()}} \quad 10110.111100110$$

Method 2:

Step 1: $b = a \times 2^{F} = -9.0514 \times 2^{+9} = \text{-}4634.3$

Step 2: $round\,(\text{-}4634.3) = -4634$

Step 3: $c = dec2bin\,(b) = 10110111100110$

Step 4: $c = 10110.111100110$

Example: Multiplication 1

This example shows the conversion of a floating-point multiplication to fixed-point multiplication. In order to perform this conversion:

1st : Each of operands are converted to fixed-point only by step 1 and step 2.

2nd : Perform the multiplication with new values.

3rd : Apply the step 3 and step 4 on the multiplication result.

$$a = 3.613, \; (W,F) = (8,4) \quad , \quad b = 2, \; (W,F) = (5,2)$$

Note: (W,F) for the result of multiplication is (13,6).

Method 1:

$$d = fi(3.613,1,8,4) = 3.625 \quad , \quad e = fi\,(2,1,5,2) = 2$$

$$mult = d \times e\,7.25 \quad \xrightarrow{\text{convert to binary with bin()}} \quad c = 0000111.010000$$

Note that if the multiplication is performed before fixed-point conversion, the result will be different with the above result. It is better to perform fixed-point conversion for each operand, then perform the operation.

Method 2:

Step 1: $d = a \times 2^{F} = 3.613 \times 2^{+4} = 57.808$

Step 2: $round\,(57.808) = 58$

Step 1: $e = b \times 2^F = 2 \times 2^{+2} = 8$

Step 2: $round\ (8) = 8$

$c = a \times b$

$mult = round\ (d) \times round\ (e) = 58 \times 8 = 464$

Step 3: $c = dec2bin(mult) = 0111010000$

Step 4: $c = 0000111.010000$

Example: Multiplication 2

$$a = 2.13,\ (W,F) = (8,5) \quad , \quad b = 3.2456,\ (W,F) = (12,9)$$

Note: (W,F) for the result of multiplication is $(20,14)$.

Method 1:

$$d = fi(2.13,1,8,5) = 2.125 \quad , \quad e = fi(3.2456,1,12,9) = 3.2461$$

$$mult = d \times e = 6.8979 \xrightarrow{\text{convert to binary with bin()}} c = 000110.11100101111000$$

Method 2:

Step 1: $d = a \times 2^F = 2.13 \times 2^{+5} = 68.16$

Step 2: $round(68.16) = 68$

Step 1: $e = b \times 2^F = 3.2456 \times 2^{+9} = 1661.7472$

Step 2: $round(1662) = 1662$

$c = a \times b$

$mult = round\ (d) \times ound\ (e) = 68 \times 1662 = 113016$

Step 3: $c = dec2bin(mult) = 011011100101111000$

Step 4: $c = 000110.11100101111000$

Composite Data Type

A composite data type is a data type that contains more than one value. It is declared as a normal variable but contains a predefined number of values.

Pos

A simple example of a composite data type is the data type pos. It contains three numerical values (x, y and z).

The declaration looks like a simple variable:

```
VAR pos pos1;
```

Assigning all values is done like with an array:

```
pos1 := [600, 100, 800];
```

The different components have names instead of numbers. The components in pos are named x, y and z. The value in one component is identified with the variable name, a point and the component name:

```
pos1.z := 850;
```

Orient

The data type orient specifies the orientation of the tool. The orientation is specified by four numerical values, named q1, q2, q3 and q4.

```
VAR orient orient1 := [1, 0, 0, 0];
```

```
TPWrite "The value of q1 is " \Num:=orient1.q1;
```

Pose

A data type can be composed of other composite data types. An example of this is the data type pose, which consists of one pos named trans and one orient named rot.

```
VAR pose pose1 := [[600, 100, 800], [1, 0, 0, 0]];
```

```
VAR pos pos1 := [650, 100, 850];
```

```
VAR orient orient1;
```

```
pose1.pos := pos1;
```

```
orient1 := pose1.rot;
```

```
pose1.pos.z := 875;
```

Robtarget

robtarget is too complex a data type.

robtarget consists of four parts:

Data type	Name	Description
pos	trans	x, y and z coordinates
orient	rot	Orientation
confdata	robconf	Specifies robot axes angles
extjoint	extax	Specifies positions for up to 6 additional axes. The value is set to 9E9 where no additional axis is used.

```
VAR robtarget p10 := [ [600, -100, 800], [0.707170, 0, 0.707170, 0], [0, 0, 0,
0], [ 9E9, 9E9, 9E9, 9E9, 9E9, 9E9] ];

! Increase the x coordinate with 50

p10.trans.x := p10.trans.x + 50;
```

Structure Types

There is no single data type comprising all structures. Instead, each definition of a structure represents a unique data type, even if two structures define identical elements in the same order. However, if you create two or more instances of the same structure, Visual Basic considers them to be of the same data type.

Tuples

A tuple is a lightweight structure that contains two or more fields whose types are predefined. Tuples are supported starting with Visual Basic 2017. Tuples are most commonly used to return multiple values from a single method call without having to pass arguments by reference or packaging the returned fields in a more heavy-weight class or structure

Arrays

You've seen one array type already: remember that Strings are one-dimensional arrays of characters. Java represents the String "Frodo Baggins!" like this.

F	r	o	d	o		B	a	g	g	i	n	g	!

You can access bits of the string by giving their position in the array. In computer science, you generally start counting array positions at 0. Suppose we set,

> String name = "Frodo Baggins!";

in the Java code. Then name = 'F', the first character in the array. Another nice thing you can do is slice out substrings; for example, name.substring(0, 5) is "Frodo". If you're reading carefully, you should be thinking that something is wrong here, because name is really the position of the space; but you always specify the slice from start to end + 1, so the substring doesn't actually wind up having the space. The most common mistakes with arrays involve trying to get an element before the start or after the end of the array, like,

> char error1 = name[-1];

or

> char error2 = name;

Both of these assignments attempt to look outside the bounds of the array for data, which is generally a bad idea, since we have no idea what's there. These mistakes will usually generate run-time errors.

You can make arrays of anything, including integers, characters, doubles, and other arrays. Here's an array declaration that works to draw Polygons in a Java applet; the first point is at x, y, the second at x, y, etc. Java's drawPolygon methods sort out the coordinates for point 1 (x_coords, y_coords), through however many points you have asked for.

/* define an array of integers called x_coords, and set it up with 4 numbers;

     to close the polygon, you need to include the first point at the end */

int [] x_coords = {0, 50, 50, 0, 0};

int [] y_coords = {0, 0, 50, 50, 0};

page.drawPolygon(xcrds, ycrds, 5);

You access individual members of the array by using their subscripts (positions) in the array. The first position is 0, so y_coords would be 50 in the example above.

To do string matching in Java, you pretty much have to use arrays:

/* define a function named Match that returns an integer giving the position

     of the first match for char c in String str */

int Match(String str, char c)

{

/* length of the string we're searching; we need to be sure that

     we don't fall off the end */

int length;

/* counter for our position in the array */

int j = 0;

/* get the length of the String str */

length = length(str);

/* check every position in the string, from start to end, until

     there's a match */

while (j < length)

{

     /* compare the letter at position j in the String to the

          char c we're looking for

```
        if (str[j] == c)

        /* if there's a match, we can quit and send back

                        our current position */

                return j;

        /* increment the position counter by 1;

                this only happens if we haven't found a match yet */

        j++;

    }

        /* if we have gotten to this point, the character we're looking

                for isn't there, so we return a weird value */

        return −1;

    }
```

Remember that the most insidious problem with arrays is wandering off their ends by mistake. In the above code, j must be greater than −1 and less than the length of the string. (Satisfy yourself that this really checks every letter in the string without walking off the end.) If the value we return is −1, then str[-1] is not defined! (Neither is str[length].) So if we call this routine from our main program, we'd say:

```
    int position;

    String name = "Socrates";

    char [] letters = {'x', 'r', 'q', 'n', 'y', 'c', 's'};

    int letterpos = 0;

    /* loop over the letters in the letters array */

    while (letterpos < 7)

    {

        /* search for current letter in the String name */

        position = Match(name, letters[letterpos]);

        /* if we found a valid match, then we can look it up in the String array*/

        if (position > -1)

                System.out.println(name[position] + " found at " + position);
```

```
/* but if the position is −1, then the character doesn't match */

else

        System.out.println("No match found for " + ch1 + " in " + name);

/* increment the position counter to check for the next letter */

letterpos++;

}
```

Classes

Often, arrays are a bit limited. Every array has to contain the same type of data. It's generally nice for the programmer to be able to define certain particular data types. In Java, you do this by defining classes. For example, you can define a new class for an x, y point by gluing two integers together. This code describes another kind of composite type, defined by the program.

```
public class Point

{

    int x;

    int y;

}
```

We call the variables inside the class definition (x and y, here) the class variables, because they must be accessed through the class.

What might you want to do with Points? You might want to move them, or rotate them, or draw lines between them. The methods that operate on Points also get defined as part of the Point class. This idea of grouping data of a particular type with the methods allowed to work on the data is a key feature of object-oriented programming, because it tends to make code more modular and more portable.

For starters, we'd like to initialize Points. We can do this by writing a constructor for them. The constructor is a special method in your class. It has no return type (basically, it's sending back a new instance of class Point). It must have the exact same name as the class. In our example, it takes 2 parameters, an integer for the x position and another integer for the y position. We'll also include a routine to move points around by a certain x and y distance.

```
public class Point

{

    int x;

    int y
```

```
        Point(int init_x, int init_y)

            {

                    x = init_x;

                    y = init_y;

        }

        void MovePoint(int dx, int dy)

        {

                    x += dx;

                    y += dy;

        }

        }
```

Now, we can include this class in a project, initialize 2 new points in our main function, and move them by saying:

```
        public static void main (String [] args)

        {

                Point p1 = new Point(1,2);

                Point p2 = new Point(5,9);

                p1.MovePoint(5,3); //now p1 is at (6,5)

                p2.MovePoint(-3,1); //now p2 is at (2,10)

        }
```

If you look at this code carefully, you can see that p1 and p2 are just the names of two different Point-type variables. The class Point defines what a Point is and does. p1 and p2 are objects (particular examples) of type Point. The class is the blueprint for a type; it defines what kinds of variables the type holds and what methods can work on these variables. The object is a particular instance of that type, with actual values assigned to its variables.

Your drawing space is defined using an object called page, of class Graphics. This means that when you use the drawing methods in the Graphics class, you had to call them via the page object, as below.

import java.applet.*;

import java.awt.*;

```
public class Class1 extends Applet

{

        public void paint(Graphics page)

{

                setBackground(Color.white);

                /* all of these methods are defined in class Graphics and are called

                        via the page object */

                page.drawOval(60,70,100,50);

                page.setColor(Color.blue);

                page.fillOval(60,70,10,50);

                page.setColor(Color.red);

                page.drawRect(0,0,50,50);

                page.drawString("Happy Birthday!");

        }

}
```

Most interesting programming problems can be broken down into logical chunks of data that fall nicely into a class structure. The program then consists of managing the behavior of these objects. For example, if you were writing a game to play checkers, you might start by defining one class for a checker (to keep track of color, x position, and y position), and another for the 8x8 game board, maybe as a 2D array with each cell holding a checker, or nothing. Then you could write methods in the game board class to check the legality of each move, make players take turns, and decide when the game is over.

Matrices

In Ptolemy II, arrays are ordered sets of tokens. Ptolemy II also supports matrices, which are more specialized than arrays. They contain only certain primitive types, currently *boolean, complex, double, fixedpoint, int,* and *long.* Currently *float, short* and *unsignedByte* matrices are not supported. Matrices cannot contain arbitrary tokens, so they cannot, for example, contain matrices. They are intended for data intensive computations. Matrices are specified with square brackets, using commas to separate row elements and semicolons to separate rows. E.g., "[1, 2, 3; 4, 5, 5+1]" gives a two by three integer matrix (2 rows and 3 columns). Note that an array or matrix element can be given by an expression. A row vector can be given as "[1, 2, 3]" and a column vector as "[1; 2; 3]". Some MATLAB-style array constructors are supported. For example, "[1:2:9]" gives an array of odd numbers from 1 to 9, and is equivalent to "[1, 3, 5, 7, 9]." Similarly, "[1:2:9; 2:2:10]" is equivalent to "[1, 3, 5, 7, 9; 2, 4, 6, 8, 10]." In the syntax "[p:q:r]", p is the first element, q is the step between elements, and *r* is an upper bound on the last element. That is, the matrix will not contain an element larger than *r*. If a matrix with mixed types is specified, then the elements will be converted to a common type, if possible. Thus, for example, "[1.0, 1]" is equivalent to "[1.0, 1.0]," but "[1.0, 1L]" is illegal (because there is no common type to which both elements can be converted losslessly).

Reference to elements of matrices have the form "*matrix(n, m)*" or "*name(n, m)*" where *name* is the name of a matrix variable in scope, *n* is the row index, and *m* is the column index. Index numbers start with zero, as in Java, not 1, as in MATLAB. For example,

```
>> [1, 2; 3, 4](0,0)

1

>> a = [1, 2; 3, 4]

[1, 2; 3, 4]

>> a(1,1)

4
```

Matrix multiplication works as expected. For example, as seen in the expression evaluator,

```
>> [1, 2; 3, 4]*[2, 2; 2, 2]

[6, 6; 14, 14]
```

Of course, if the dimensions of the matrix don't match, then you will get an error message. To do element wise multiplication, use the multipyElements() function. Matrix addition and subtraction are element wise, as expected, but the division operator is not supported. Element wise division can be accomplished with the divideElements() function, and multiplication by a matrix inverse can be accomplished using the inverse() function. A matrix can be raised to an *int*, *short* or *unsignedByte* power, which is equivalent to multiplying it by itself some number of times. For instance,

```
>> [3, 0; 0, 3]\^3

[27, 0; 0, 27]
```

A matrix can also be multiplied or divided by a scalar, as follows:

```
>> [3, 0; 0, 3]*3

[9, 0; 0, 9]
```

A matrix can be added to a scalar. It can also be subtracted from a scalar, or have a scalar subtracted from it. For instance,

```
>> 1-[3, 0; 0, 3]
```

```
[-2, 1; 1, -2]
```

A matrix can be checked for equality with another matrix as follows:

```
>> [3, 0; 0, 3]!=[3, 0; 0, 6]

true

>> [3, 0; 0, 3]==[3, 0; 0, 3]

true
```

For other comparisons of matrices, use the compare() function. As with scalars, testing for equality using the == or != operators tests the values, independent of type. For example,

```
>> [1, 2]==[1.0, 2.0]

true
```

To get type-specific equality tests, use the equals() method, as in the following examples:

```
>> [1, 2].equals([1.0, 2.0])

false

>> [1.0, 2.0].equals([1.0, 2.0])

true
```

Records

A record token is a composite type containing named fields, where each field has a value. The value of each field can have a distinct type. Records are delimited by curly braces, with each field given a name. For example, "{a=1, b=''foo''}" is a record with two fields, named "a" and "b", with values 1 (an integer) and "foo" (a string), respectively. The value of a field can be an arbitrary expression, and records can be nested (a field of a record token may be a record token).

Ordered records behave similarly to normal records except that they preserve the original ordering of the labels rather than alphabetizing them. Ordered records are delimited using square brackets rather than curly braces. For example, [b="foo", a=1] is an ordered record token in which ‹b› will remain the first label.

Fields may be accessed using the period operator. For example,

```
{a=1,b=2}.a
```

yields 1. You can optionally write this as if it were a method call:

```
{a=1,b=2}.a()
```

The arithmetic operators +, -, *, /, and % can be applied to records. If the records do not have identical fields, then the operator is applied only to the fields that match, and the result contains only the fields that match. Thus, for example,

```
{foodCost=40, hotelCost=100} + {foodCost=20, taxiCost=20}
```

yields the result

```
{foodCost=60}
```

You can think of an operation as a set intersection, where the operation specifies how to merge the values of the intersecting fields. You can also form an intersection without applying an operation. In this case, using the intersect() function, you form a record that has only the common fields of two specified records, with the values taken from the first record. For example,

```
>> intersect({a=1, c=2}, {a=3, b=4})
```

```
{a=1}
```

Records can be joined (think of a set union) without any operation being applied by using the merge() function. This function takes two arguments, both of which are record tokens. If the two record tokens have common fields, then the field value from the first record is used. For example,

```
merge({a=1, b=2}, {a=3, c=3})
```

yields the result {a=1, b=2, c=3}.

Records can be compared, as in the following examples:

```
>> {a=1, b=2}!={a=1, b=2}
```

```
false
```

```
>> {a=1, b=2}!={a=1, c=2}
```

```
true
```

Note that two records are equal only if they have the same field labels and the values match. As with scalars, the values match irrespective of type. For example:

```
>> {a=1, b=2}=={a=1.0, b=2.0+0.0i}
```

```
true
```

The order of the fields is irrelevant for normal (unordered) records. Hence

```
>> {a=1, b=2}=={b=2, a=1}
```

```
true
```

Moreover, normal record fields are reported in alphabetical order, irrespective of the order in which they are defined. For example,

```
>> {b=2, a=1}
```

```
{a=1, b=2}
```

Equality comparisons for ordered records respect the original order of the fields. For example,

```
>> [a=1, b=2]==[b=2, a=1]

false
```

Additionally, ordered record fields are always reported in the order in which they are defined. For example,

```
>> [b=2, a=1]

[b=2, a=1]
```

To get type-specific equality tests, use the equals() method, as in the following examples:

```
>> {a=1, b=2}.equals({a=1.0, b=2.0+0.0i})

false

>> {a=1, b=2}.equals({b=2, a=1})

true
```

Finally, You can create an empty record using the emptyRecord() function:

```
>> emptyRecord()

{}
```

Enumerated Data Type

Enumerated type is a user-defined data type used in computer programming to map a set of names to numeric values. Enumerated data type variables can only have values that are previously declared. In other words, they work with a finite list of values.

Enumerated data types help make the code more self-documenting and prevent programmers from writing illogical code on values of enumerators. Enumerated data also hides unnecessary details from programmers.

Enumerator names usually behave as constants in programming languages, although they are identifiers in most ways. A variable assigned as enumerated type can have any of the enumerators as value.

In certain languages, enumerator data types many be built into the language. Many programming languages permit users to define new enumerated types and certain programming languages also define the ordering that needs to be followed for the members associated with enumerated data types. The enumerators are unique, but certain programming languages do permit the enumerator to be listed twice in the declaration of the type.

Example

For example, if you need a column to only have values 'Email', 'SMS' and 'Phone', you can do this by first defining an enumerated type:

```
CREATE TYPE e_contact_method AS ENUM (

  'Email',

  'Sms',

  'Phone')
```

Then associate the enum to the column that needs to have a fixed set of values.

```
CREATE TABLE contact_method_info (

  contact_name text,

  contact_method e_contact_method,

  value text

)
```

Using enums

```
INSERT INTO contact_method_info

VALUES ('Jeff', 'Email', 'jeff@mail.com')


# select * from contact_method_info;

 contact_name | contact_method |    value

--------------+----------------+---------------

 Jeff    | Email     | jeff@mail.com

(1 row)
```

You cannot insert a value for the contact*method column thats not in e*contact_method enum.

```
# INSERT INTO contact_method_info VALUES ('Jeff', 'Fax', '4563456');

ERROR: invalid input value for enum e_contact_method: "Fax"

LINE 1: INSERT INTO contact_method_info VALUES ('Jeff', 'Fax', '4563...

Viewing/Modifying enum values

You can view the list of values in an enum:

# select t.typname, e.enumlabel

  from pg_type t, pg_enum e
```

```
where t.oid = e.enumtypid;


 typname     | enumlabel

------------------+-----------

e_contact_method | Email

e_contact_method | Sms

e_contact_method | Phone

(3 rows)
```

You can append values to existing enums:

```
ALTER TYPE e_contact_method

 ADD VALUE 'Facebook' AFTER 'Phone';


# select t.typname, e.enumlabel from pg_type t, pg_enum e

 where t.oid = e.enumtypid;

  typname    | enumlabel

------------------+-----------

e_contact_method | Email

e_contact_method | Sms

e_contact_method | Phone

e_contact_method | Facebook

(4 rows)
```

Values can be added anywhere in between as enums have a sort order which is the order in which the value was inserted, and it is preserved.

```
ALTER TYPE e_contact_method

 ADD VALUE 'Twitter' BEFORE 'Sms';


# select t.typname, e.enumlabel, e.enumsortorder from pg_type t, pg_enum e

 where t.oid = e.enumtypid order by e.enumsortorder;

  typname    | enumlabel | enumsortorder
```

```
------------------+----------+---------------
e_contact_method | Email    |        1
e_contact_method | Twitter  |       1.5
e_contact_method | Sms      |        2
e_contact_method | Phone    |        3
e_contact_method | Facebook |        4
(5 rows)
```

At the time of this writing, Postgres does not provide a way to remove values from enums.

Pascal and syntactically similar languages

Pascal

In Pascal, an enumerated type can be implicitly declared by listing the values in a parenthesised list:

```
var
    suit: (clubs, diamonds, hearts, spades);
```

The declaration will often appear in a type synonym declaration, such that it can be used for multiple variables:

```
type
    cardsuit = (clubs, diamonds, hearts, spades);
    card = record
        suit: cardsuit;
        value: 1 .. 13;
        end;
var
  hand: array [ 1 .. 13 ] of card;
  trump: cardsuit;
```

The order in which the enumeration values are given matters. An enumerated type is an ordinal type, and the pred and succ functions will give the prior or next value of the enumeration, and ord can convert enumeration values to their integer representation. Standard Pascal does not offer a conversion from arithmetic types to enumerations, however. Extended Pascal offers this functionality via an extended succ function. Some other Pascal dialects allow it via type-casts. Some modern descendants of Pascal, such as Modula-3, provide a special conversion syntax using a method called VAL; Modula-3 also treats BOOLEAN and CHAR as special pre-defined enumerated types and uses ORD and VAL for standard ASCII decoding and encoding.

Pascal style languages also allow enumeration to be used as array index:

```
var

  suitcount: array [cardsuit] of integer;
```

Ada

In Ada, the use of "=" was replaced with "is" leaving the definition quite similar:

```
type Cardsuit is (clubs, diamonds, hearts, spades);
```

In addition to `Pred`, `Succ`, `Val` and `Pos` Ada also supports simple string conversions via `Image` and `Value`.

Similar to C-style languages Ada allows the internal representation of the enumeration to be specified:

```
for Cardsuit use

  (clubs => 1, diamonds => 2, hearts => 4, spades => 8);
```

Unlike C-style languages Ada also allows the number of bits of the enumeration to be specified:

```
for Cardsuit'Size use 4; -- 4 bits
```

Additionally, one can use enumerations as indexes for arrays, like in Pascal, but there are attributes defined for enumerations,

```
      Shuffle : constant array(Cardsuit) of Cardsuit :=

      (Clubs => Cardsuit'Succ(Clubs), -- see attributes of enumerations
'First, 'Last, 'Succ, 'Pred

    Diamonds => Hearts, --an explicit value

      Hearts => Cardsuit'Last, --first enumeration value of type Cardsuit
e.g., clubs

      Spades => Cardsuit'First --last enumeration value of type Cardsuit
e.g., spades

      );
```

Like Modula-3 Ada treats Boolean and Character as special pre-defined (in package "Standard") enumerated types. Unlike Modula-3 one can also define own character types:

```
type Cards is ('7', '8', '9', 'J', 'Q', 'K', 'A');
```

C and syntactically similar languages

C

The original K&R dialect of the programming language C had no enumerated types. They were added in the ANSI standard for C, which became ANSI C (sometimes termed C89). In C, enumerations are created by explicit definitions (the enum keyword by itself does not cause allocation of storage) which use the enum keyword and are reminiscent of struct and union definitions:

```
enum cardsuit {

   Clubs,

   Diamonds,

   Hearts,

   Spades

};


struct card {

   enum cardsuit suit;

   short int value;

} hand;

enum cardsuit trump;
```

C exposes the integer representation of enumeration values directly to the programmer. Integers and enum values can be mixed freely, and all arithmetic operations on enum values are permitted. It is even possible for an enum variable to hold an integer that does not represent any of the enumeration values. In fact, according to the language definition, the above code will define Clubs, Diamonds, Hearts, and Spades as constants of type int, which will only be converted (silently) to enum cardsuit if they are stored in a variable of that type.

C also allows the programmer to choose the values of the enumeration constants explicitly, even without type. For example,

```
enum cardsuit {

   Clubs   = 1,

   Diamonds = 2,

   Hearts   = 4,

   Spades   = 8

};
```

could be used to define a type that allows mathematical sets of suits to be represented as an `enum cardsuit` by bitwise logic operations.

Swift

In C, enumerations assign related names to a set of integer values. In Swift, enumerations are much more flexible and need not provide a value for each case of the enumeration. If a value (termed a raw value) is provided for each enumeration case, the value can be a string, a character, or a value of any integer or floating-point type.

Alternatively, enumeration cases can specify associated values of any type to be stored along with each different case value, much as unions or variants do in other languages. One can define a common set of related cases as part of one enumeration, each of which has a different set of values of appropriate types associated with it.

In Swift, enumerations are a first-class type. They adopt many features traditionally supported only by classes, such as computed properties to provide additional information about the enumeration's current value, and instance methods to provide functionality related to the values the enumeration represents. Enumerations can also define initializers to provide an initial case value and can be extended to expand their functionality beyond their original implementation; and can conform to protocols to provide standard functionality.

```
enum CardSuit {

    case clubs

    case diamonds

    case hearts

    case spades

}
```

Unlike C and Objective-C, Swift enumeration cases are not assigned a default integer value when they are created. In the CardSuit example above, clubs, diamonds, hearts, and spades do not implicitly equal 0, 1, 2 and 3. Instead, the different enumeration cases are fully-fledged values in their own right, with an explicitly-defined type of CardSuit.

Multiple cases can appear on a single line, separated by commas:

```
enum CardSuit {

    case clubs, diamonds, hearts, spades

}
```

When working with enumerations that store integer or string raw values, one doesn't need to explicitly assign a raw value for each case because Swift will automatically assign the values.

For instance, when integers are used for raw values, the implicit value for each case is one more than the previous case. If the first case doesn't have a value set, its value is 0.

The enumeration below is a refinement of the earlier Planet enumeration, with integer raw values to represent each planet's order from the sun:

```
enum Planet: Int {

    case mercury = 1, venus, earth, mars, jupiter, saturn, uranus, neptune

}
```

In the example above, Planet.mercury has an explicit raw value of 1, Planet.venus has an implicit raw value of 2, and so on.

Perl

Dynamically typed languages in the syntactic tradition of C (e.g., Perl or JavaScript) do not, in general, provide enumerations. But in Perl programming the same result can be obtained with the shorthand strings list and hashes (possibly slices):

```
my @enum = qw(Clubs Diamonds Hearts Spades);

my( %set1, %set2 );

@set1{@enum} = ();       # all cleared

@set2{@enum} = (1) x @enum; # all set to 1

$set1{Clubs} ...       # false

$set2{Diamonds} ...      # true
```

Perl 6

Perl 6 does provide enumerations. There are multiple ways to declare enumerations in Perl 6, all creating a back-end Map.

```
enum Cat <sphynx siamese bengal shorthair other>; # Using "quote-words"

enum Cat ('sphynx', 'siamese', 'bengal', 'shorthair', 'other'); # Using
a list

enum Cat (sphynx => 0, siamese => 1, bengal => 2, shorthair => 3, other =>
4); # Using Pair constructors

enum Cat (:sphynx(0), :siamese(1), :bengal(2), shorthair(3), :other(4));
# Another way of using Pairs, you can also use `:0sphynx`
```

C#

Enumerated types in the C# programming language preserve most of the "small integer" semantics of C's enums. Some arithmetic operations are not defined for enums, but an enum value can be explicitly converted to an integer and back again, and an enum variable can have values that were not declared by the enum definition. For example, given,

```
enum Cardsuit { Clubs, Diamonds, Spades, Hearts };
```

the expressions `CardSuit.Diamonds+1` and `CardSuit.Hearts - CardSuit.Clubs` are allowed directly (because it may make sense to step through the sequence of values or ask how many steps there are between two values), but `CardSuit.Hearts*CardSuit.Spades` is deemed to make less sense and is only allowed if the values are first converted to integers.

C# also provides the C-like feature of being able to define specific integer values for enumerations. By doing this it is possible to perform binary operations on enumerations, thus treating enumeration values as sets of flags. These flags can be tested using binary operations or with the Enum type's builtin 'HasFlag' method.

The enumeration definition defines names for the selected integer values and is syntactic sugar, as it is possible to assign to an enum variable other integer values that are not in the scope of the enum definition.

C++

C++ has enumeration types that are directly inherited from C's and work mostly like these, except that an enumeration is a real type in C++, giving added compile-time checking. Also (as with structs), the C++ enum keyword is automatically combined with a typedef, so that instead of naming the type enum name, simply name it name. This can be simulated in C using a typedef: typedef enum {Value1, Value2} name;

C++11 provides a second, type-safe enumeration type that is not implicitly converted to an integer type. It allows io streaming to be defined for that type. Additionally the enumerations do not leak, so they have to be used with Enumeration Type::enumeration. This is specified by the phrase "enum class". For example:

```
enum class Color
```

The *underlying type* is an implementation-defined integral type that is large enough to hold all enumerated values (it doesn't have to be the smallest possible type!). In C++ you can specify the underlying type directly. That allows "forward declarations" of enumerations:

```
enum class Color : long {Red, Green, Blue}; // must fit in size and memory
layout the type 'long'

enum class Shapes : char; // forward declaration. If later there are val-
ues defined that don't fit in 'char' it is an error.
```

Go

Go uses the iota keyword to create enumerated constants.

```
type ByteSize float64


const (
```

```
    _           = iota // ignore first value by assigning to blank identifier

    KB ByteSize = 1 << (10 * iota)

    MB

    GB

)
```

Java

The J2SE version 5.0 of the Java programming language added enumerated types whose declaration syntax is similar to that of C:

```
enum Cardsuit { CLUBS, DIAMONDS, SPADES, HEARTS };

...

Cardsuit trump;
```

The Java type system, however, treats enumerations as a type separate from integers, and inter-mixing of enum and integer values is not allowed. In fact, an enum type in Java is actually a special compiler-generated class rather than an arithmetic type, and enum values behave as global pre-generated instances of that class. Enum types can have instance methods and a constructor (the arguments of which can be specified separately for each enum value). All enum types implicitly extend the Enum abstract class. An enum type cannot be instantiated directly.

Internally, each enum value contains an integer, corresponding to the order in which they are declared in the source code, starting from 0. The programmer cannot set a custom integer for an enum value directly, but one can define overloaded constructors that can then assign arbitrary values to self-defined members of the enum class. Defining getters allows then access to those self-defined members. The internal integer can be obtained from an enum value using the ordinal() method, and the list of enum values of an enumeration type can be obtained in order using the values() method. It is generally discouraged for programmers to convert enums to integers and vice versa. Enumerated types are Comparable, using the internal integer; as a result, they can be sorted.

The Java standard library provides utility classes to use with enumerations. The EnumSet class implements a Set of enum values; it is implemented as a bit array, which makes it very compact and as efficient as explicit bit manipulation, but safer. The EnumMap class implements a Map of enum values to object. It is implemented as an array, with the integer value of the enum value serving as the index.

TypeScript

A helpful addition to the standard set of datatypes from JavaScript is the 'enum'. Like languages like C#, an enum is a way of giving more friendly names to sets of numeric values.

```
enum Color {Red, Green, Blue};
```

```
var c: Color = Color.Green;
```

By default, enums begin numbering their members starting at 0. This can be changed by manually setting the value of one its members. For example, the prior example can start at 1 instead of 0:

```
enum Color {Red = 1, Green, Blue};

var c: Color = Color.Green;

Or, even manually set all the values in the enum:

enum Color {Red = 1, Green = 2, Blue = 4};

var c: Color = Color.Green;
```

A handy feature of enums is that you can also go from a numeric value to the name of that value in the enum. For example, if we had the value 2 but weren't sure which that mapped to in the Color enum above, we could look up the corresponding name:

```
enum Color {Red = 1, Green, Blue};

var colorName: string = Color;


alert(colorName);
```

Python

An enum module was added to the Python standard library in version 3.4.

```
from enum import Enum

class Cards(Enum):

    clubs = 1

    diamonds = 2

    hearts = 3

    spades = 4
```

There is also a functional API for creating enumerations with automatically generated indices (starting with one):

```
Cards = Enum('Cards', ['clubs', 'diamonds', 'hearts', 'spades'])
```

Python enumerations do not enforce semantic correctness (a meaningless comparison to an incompatible enumeration always returns False rather than raising a TypeError):

```
>>> Color = Enum('Color', ['red', 'green', 'blue'])

>>> Shape = Enum('Shape', ['circle', 'triangle', 'square', 'hexagon'])
```

```
>>> def has_vertices(shape):

...     return shape != Shape.circle

...

>>> has_vertices(Color.green)

True
```

Fortran

Fortran only has enumerated types for interoperability with C; hence, the semantics is similar to C and, as in C, the enum values are just integers and no further type check is done. The C example from above can be written in Fortran as,

```
enum, bind( C )

  enumerator :: CLUBS = 1, DIAMONDS = 2, HEARTS = 4, SPADES = 8

end enum
```

Visual Basic/VBA

Enumerated datatypes in Visual Basic (up to version 6) and VBA are automatically assigned the "Long" datatype and also become a datatype themselves:

```
'Zero-based

Enum CardSuit

  Clubs

  Diamonds

  Hearts

  Spades

End Enum


Sub EnumExample()

  Dim suit As CardSuit

  suit = Diamonds

  MsgBox suit

End Sub
```

Example Code in vb.Net

```
Enum CardSuit
```

```
        Clubs

        Diamonds

        Hearts

        Spades

    End Enum


    Sub EnumExample()

        Dim suit As CardSuit

        suit = CardSuit.Diamonds

        MessageBox.show(suit)

    End Sub
```

Algebraic Data Type in Functional Programming

In functional programming languages in the ML lineage (e.g., Standard ML (SML), OCaml, and Haskell), an algebraic data type with only nullary constructors can be used to implement an enumerated type. For example (in the syntax of SML signatures):

```
    datatype cardsuit = Clubs | Diamonds | Hearts | Spades

    type card = { suit: cardsuit; value: int }

    val hand : card list

    val trump : cardsuit
```

In these languages the small-integer representation is completely hidden from the programmer, if indeed such a representation is employed by the implementation. However, Haskell has the Enum type class which a type can derive or implement to get a mapping between the type and Int.

Lisp

Common Lisp uses the member type specifier, e.g.,

```
    (deftype cardsuit ()

    `(member club diamond heart spade))
```

that states that object is of type cardsuit if it is #'eql to club, diamond, heart or spade. The member type specifier is not valid as a Common Lisp Object System (CLOS) parameter specializer, however. Instead, (eql atom), which is the equivalent to (member atom) may be used (that is, only one member of the set may be specified with an eql type specifier, however, it may be used as a

CLOS parameter specializer.) In other words, to define methods to cover an enumerated type, a method must be defined for each specific element of that type.

```
Additionally,

(deftype finite-element-set-type (&rest elements)

  `(member ,@elements))
```

may be used to define arbitrary enumerated types at runtime. For instance

```
(finite-element-set-type club diamond heart spade)
```

would refer to a type equivalent to the prior definition of cardsuit, as of course would simply have been using

```
(member club diamond heart spade)
```

but may be less confusing with the function #'member for stylistic reasons.

Databases

Some databases support enumerated types directly. MySQL provides an enumerated type ENUM with allowable values specified as strings when a table is created. The values are stored as numeric indices with the empty string stored as 0, the first string value stored as 1, the second string value stored as 2, etc. Values can be stored and retrieved as numeric indexes or string values.

XML Schema

XML Schema supports enumerated types through the enumeration facet used for constraining most primitive datatypes such as strings.

```
<xs:element name="cardsuit">

 <xs:simpleType>

  <xs:restriction base="xs:string">

   <xs:enumeration value="Clubs"/>

   <xs:enumeration value="Diamonds"/>

   <xs:enumeration value="Hearts"/>

   <xs:enumeration value="Spades"/>

  </xs:restriction>

 </xs:simpleType>

</xs:element>
```

Abstract Data Type

Abstract Data type (ADT) is a type (or class) for objects whose behavior is defined by a set of value and a set of operations.

The definition of ADT only mentions what operations are to be performed but not how these operations will be implemented. It does not specify how data will be organized in memory and what algorithms will be used for implementing the operations. It is called "abstract" because it gives an implementation independent view. The process of providing only the essentials and hiding the details is known as abstraction.

The user of data type need not know that data type is implemented, for example, we have been using int, float, char data types only with the knowledge with values that can take and operations that can be performed on them without any idea of how these types are implemented. So a user only needs to know what a data type can do but not how it will do it. We can think of ADT as a black box, which hides the inner structure and design of the data type. Now we'll define three ADTs namely List ADT, Stack ADT, Queue ADT.

List ADT

A list contains elements of same type arranged in sequential order and following operations can be performed on the list.

- get() – Return an element from the list at any given position.

- insert() – Insert an element at any position of the list.

- remove() – Remove the first occurrence of any element from a non-empty list.

- removeAt() – Remove the element at a specified location from a non-empty list.

- replace() – Replace an element at any position by another element.

- size() – Return the number of elements in the list.

- isEmpty() – Return true if the list is empty, otherwise return false.

- isFull() – Return true if the list is full, otherwise return false.

Stack ADT

A Stack contains elements of same type arranged in sequential order. All operations takes place at a single end that is top of the stack and following operations can be performed:

- push() – Insert an element at one end of the stack called top.

- pop() – Remove and return the element at the top of the stack, if it is not empty.

- peek() – Return the element at the top of the stack without removing it, if the stack is not empty.

- size() – Return the number of elements in the stack.

- isEmpty() – Return true if the stack is empty, otherwise return false.

- isFull() – Return true if the stack is full, otherwise return false.

Queue ADT

A Queue contains elements of same type arranged in sequential order. Operations takes place at both ends, insertion is done at end and deletion is done at front. Following operations can be performed:

- enqueue() – Insert an element at the end of the queue.

- dequeue() – Remove and return the first element of queue, if the queue is not empty.

- peek() – Return the element of the queue without removing it, if the queue is not empty.

- size() – Return the number of elements in the queue.

- isEmpty() – Return true if the queue is empty, otherwise return false.

- isFull() – Return true if the queue is full, otherwise return false.

From these definitions, we can clearly see that the definitions do not specify how these ADTs will be represented and how the operations will be carried out. There can be different ways to implement an ADT, for example, the List ADT can be implemented using arrays, or singly linked list or doubly linked list. Similarly, stack ADT and Queue ADT can be implemented using arrays or linked lists.

The Relationships

In addition to looking at a *set*, a container where no relationship is assumed to exist between the objects, we will also look at the following binary relationships:

- Linear ordering,

- Hierarchical ordering,

- Partial ordering,

- Equivalence relationship, and

- Adjacency relationship.

The Standard Template Library (STL) uses the concept of a *strict weak*. A different relationship which may hold between objects is a *metric*, that is, two objects are related by the distance between the objects.

In some cases, namely the linear ordering, there will be numerous abstract data structures each which will specialize by emphasizing specific operations. In a sense, these relationships and specializations form a relationship of abstract data types as is shown in figure. In some cases, the abstract data structures provide further required functionality as a result of relationship, and in others, there is a specialization based on a focus on specific operations at the expense of others.

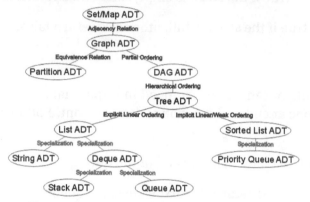

Figure: The structure of abstract data structures

Abstract data types based on these relations may be accessed via the left-hand menu; however, we will continue with a discussion on general containers including:

- The operations which can be performed on a container,

- General operations regarding objects stored in the container,

- How relationships may be defined either locally or globally,

- How relationships may be defined either implicitly through a function or explicitly by the programmer,

- The concept of an associate container: a key-object association where the relationship applies to the key,

- The uniqueness of objects within a container, and

- Implementations of abstract data structures in the Standard Template Library.

Finally, while mathematical objects such as matrices appear to have properties similar to containers, a discussion of why these are fundamentally different from ADTs is given.

Operation on Containers

A data structure or container is meant to store data and while there are many operations may be specific to a particular relationship, there are some operations which can be considered to be relevant to any container class.

There are some basic operations which are performed on the containers themselves including:

- Creating a container,

- Destroying a container,

- Making a copy of a container,

- Splitting a container into two or more containers,

- Taking the union of two containers (*merging* the containers), and
- Taking the intersection of two containers (the common objects).

The first three operations apply to all containers.

Operations on Objects in Containers

Given a container, there are a number of operations which one may wish to perform on that container regardless of any relationship which holds between the objects, including:

- Accessing the number of objects in the container,
- Determining if the container is empty,
- Inserting a new object into the container,
- Determining if an object is in the container (membership),
- Removing an object from the container, and
- Removing all objects from (*clearing*) the container.

We will see that the most efficient data structure, the *hash table*, is only applicable only when there is no relationship of interest; however, often the container will store objects which have a relationship which we may also require information.

Implicit versus Explicit Relations

An implicit relation is one where the relation depends on the objects in question: the integers 3, 5, 9, 13, 27 are implicitly ordered based on their values. The characters in the string "Hello world" are also ordered; however, their order is explicitly defined by the programmer. Students may be implicitly partitioned based on their academic program, but an image may be partitioned first on characteristics and then those partitioned may be explicitly merged. For example, figure below shows how an image can be partitioned based on characteristics and then those partitions recognized to be from the same structure are merged.

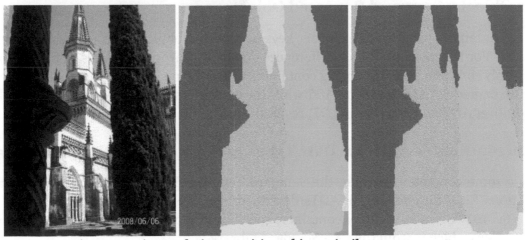

Figure: An image being partitioned into similar components

Locally Defined Relationships versus Globally Defined Relationships

A relationship may be globally defined if there exists a function `bool R( x, y )` which returns whether or not the two objects satisfy a relationship. For example, integers and real numbers have a globally defined relationship. Other relationships are locally defined in that only a few specific relations are stated and other restrictions must be deduced from those local relationships. For example, a file system only stores local sub-directories: `usr` is a sub-directory of the root directory, `local` is a sub-directory of `usr`, but the file system does not record that `local` is a sub-directory of the root—this must be deduced by examining the local relationships. The same holds true for the hierarchy of subclasses in Java: `ThreadDeath` is a subclass of `Error`, `Error` is a subclass of `Throwable`, and `Throwable` is a subclass of `Object`; however, it must be deduced that, for example, `ThreadDeath` is a subclass of both `Throwable` and `Object`.

Object Containers versus Associative Containers

A container may either be used to store objects which are related or to store (key, object) pairs where the keys are related and the object is associated with the key. For example:

- A simple lexical analyzer of C++ may use a stack of characters to match parentheses, brackets, and braces; and

- A string is a container which also stores characters without any association; however,

- Student records may be stored linearly based on a value such as a student identification number; and

- A parser of C++ may store information such as type (`int`, `double`, *etc*) and even value for constant variables in a hash table for fast reference.

As any object container, with very few modifications, can be made into an associative container, The one common occasion where the name of a the object container has a different name from the corresponding associative container is the case which the objects have no relation: these are referred to as the *Set ADT* and the *Map ADT*, respectively.

Unique Objects/Keys and Repeated Objects/Keys

Whether a container stores unique objects/keys or repeated objects/keys is again an implementation detail. For the most part, such differences do not appear in the names of the abstract data types, the only common exception being containers where the objects have no relation: the unique variants are named *Set ADT* and *Map ADT* while the containers allowing repeated objects/keys are named *Multiset ADT* and *Multimap ADT*, respectively.

Implementations of Abstract Data Types in the Standard Template Library

To provide some concrete examples, the Standard Template Library (STL) provides default implementations for a number of the ADTs described here. The implemented containers are described in figure which also includes containers specific to the SGI implementation of the STL and the `string` class which is from the C++ Standard Library.

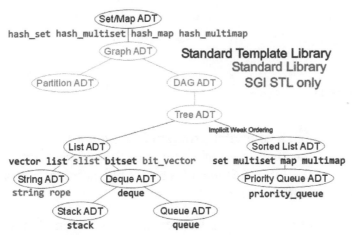

Figure: Implementations of the various ADTs in the C++ STL

One may note that there are multiple implementations for the same classes. These are summarized in table below.

Table: Properties of the various C++ STL containers

	Object Container	Associative Container
Unique Objects/Keys	set hash_set	map hash_map
Repeated Objects/Keys	multiset hash_multiset	multimap hash_multimap

The containers `bitset` and `bit_vector` are designed specifically to store bits. The container `vector` is based on a dynamically resizing two-ended array while `list` and `slist` are based on doubly and singly linked lists, respectively.

Note that the STL assumes a weak ordering.

References

- Bloch, Joshua (2008). Effective Java (Second ed.). Upper Saddle River, N.J.: Addison-Wesley. p. 158. ISBN 978-0-321-35668-0.

- Computer-programming-data-types: tutorialspoint.com, Retrieved 28 May 2018

- Primitive-data-type-29494: techopedia.com, Retrieved 09 July 2018

- Machine-data: internetofthingsagenda.techtarget.com, Retrieved 11 June 2018

- Understanding-boolean-logic-in-python-3: digitalocean.com, Retrieved 26 July 2018

- Floating-Point-Data-Types: trimble.com, Retrieved 28 April 2018

- Enumerated-type-23976: techopedia.com, Retrieved 28 April 2018

Type Systems

The set of rules through which a computer program is assigned its type on the basis of its property is called type system. The chapter closely examines the different type systems to provide an extensive understanding of the subject. It includes topics like nominal type system, structural type system, duck typing, strong and weak typing, etc.

Type systems are the biggest point of variation across programming languages. Even languages that look similar are often greatly different when it comes to their type systems.

A *type system* is a set of types and *type constructors* (arrays, classes, etc.) along with the rules that govern whether or not a program is legal with respect to types (i.e., type checking). A *type constructor* is a mechanism for creating a new type.

For example, ARRAY is a type constructor since when we apply it to an index type and an element type it creates a new type: an array type. class in C++ is another example of a type constructor: it takes the name of the superclass, the names and types of the fields, and creates a new class type.

C++ and Java have similar syntax and control structures. They even have a similar set of types (classes, arrays, etc.). However, they differ greatly with respect to the rules that determine whether or not a program is legal with respect to types. As an extreme example, one can do this in C++ but not in Java:

```
int x = (int) "Hello";
```

In other words, Java's type rules do not allow the above statement but C++'s type rules do allow it.

Why do different languages use different type systems? The reason for this is that there s no one *perfect* type system. Each type system has its strengths and weaknesses. Thus, different languages use different type systems because they have different priorities. A language designed for writing operating systems is not appropriate for programming the web; thus they will use different type systems. When designing a type system for a language, the language designer needs to balance the tradeoffs between execution efficiency, expressiveness, safety, simplicity, etc.

Thus, a good understanding of type systems is crucial for understanding how to best exploit programming languages.

Need for a Type System

Some older languages and all machine assembly languages do not have a notion of type. A program simply operates on memory, which consists of bytes or words. An assembly language may distinguish between "integers" and "floats", but that is primarily so that the machine knows whether it should use the floating point unit or the integer unit to perform a calculation. In this type-less world, there is no type checking. There is nothing to prevent a program from reading a random word in memory and treating it as an address or a string or an integer or a float or an instruction.

The ability to grab a random word from memory and interpret it as if it were a specific kind of value (e.g., integer) is not useful most of the time even though it may be useful sometimes (e.g., when writing low-level code such as device drivers). Thus even assembly language programmers use conventions and practices to organize their program's memory. For example, a particular block of memory may (by convention) be treated as an array of integers and another block a sequence of instructions. In other words, even in a type-less world, programmers try to impose some type structure upon their data. However, in a type-less world, there is no automatic mechanism for enforcing the types. In other words, a programmer could mistakenly write and run code that makes no sense with respect to types (e.g., adding 1 to an instruction). This mistake may manifest itself as a crash when the program is run or may silently corrupt values and thus the program produces an incorrect answer. To avoid these kinds of problems, most languages today have a rich type system. Such a type system has types and rules that try to prevent such problems. Some researchers have also proposed typed assembly languages recently; these would impose some kinds of type checking on assembly language programs!

The rules in a given type system allows some programs and disallows other programs. For example, unlike assembly language, one cannot write a program in Java that grabs a random word from memory and treats it as if it were an integer. Thus, every type system represents a *tradeoff between expressiveness and safety*. A type system whose rules reject all programs is completely safe but inexpressive: the compiler will immediately reject all programs and thus also all the "unsafe" programs. A type system whose rules accept all programs (e.g., assembly language) is very expressive but unsafe (someone may write a program that writes random words all over memory).

Types and Type Checking

We have been talking about types and type checking but have not defined it formally. We will now use a notion of types from theory that is very helpful in understanding how types work.

A *type* is a set of values.

A `boolean` type is the set that contains `True` and `False`. An `integer` type is the set that contains all integers from `minint` to `maxint` (where `minint` and `maxint` may be defined by the type system itself, as in Java, or by the underlying hardware, as in C). A `float` type contains all floating point values. An integer array of length 2 is the set that contains all length-2 sequences of integers. A `string` type is the set that contains all strings. For some types the set may be enumerable (i.e., we can write down all the members of the set, such as `True` and `False`). For other types type set may not be enumerable or at least be very hard to enumerate (e.g., `String`).

When we declare a variable to be of a particular type, we are effectively restricting the set of values that the variable can hold. For example, if we declare a variable to be of type `Boolean`, (i) we can only put `True` or `False` into the variable; and (ii) when we read the contents of the variable it must be either `True` or `False`.

Now that we have defined what a type is, we can define what it means to do type checking.

Type checking checks and enforces the rules of the type system to prevent type errors from happening. A *type error* happens when an expression produces a value outside the set of values it is supposed to have.

For example, consider the following assignment in MYSTERY syntax:

```
VAR s:String;

s := 1234;
```

Since s has type `String`, it can only hold values of type `String`. Thus, the expression on the right-hand-side of the assignment must be of type `String`. However, the expression evaluates to the value `1234` which does not belong to the set of values in `String`. Thus the above is a type error.

Consider another example:

```
VAR b: Byte;

b := 12345;
```

Since `b` has type `Byte`, it can only hold values from -128 to 127. Since the expression on the right-hand-side evaluates to a value that does not belong to the set of values in `Byte`, this is also a type error.

Strong type checking prevents all type errors from happening. The checking may happen at compile time or at run time or partly at compile time and partly at run time.

A *strongly-typed language* is one that uses strong type checking. Definition: *Weak type checking* does not prevent type errors from happening. Definition: A *weakly-typed language* is one that uses weak type checking.

If you use a weakly-typed language, it is up to your discipline to make sure that you do not have type errors in your program. Many languages use something in the middle: they catch many type errors but let some through.

Dimensions of type Checking

The type checking may be:

- Strong, weak, or something in between.

- At compile time, run time, or something in between.

Strong type checking catches all type errors. Thus, it provides the greatest amount of safety: programmers that write code in a strongly-typed language do not have to worry about many kinds of bugs. For example, when a program in a strongly-typed language dereferences an integer pointer (`int *`), we know for sure that if the dereference completes successfully it will produce an integer. On the other hand, strong type checking can be overly restrictive in some cases. Let's suppose you need to write a device driver and that the device's registers are mapped to some fixed known location in memory. When writing this driver you will need to grab data at the fixed locations in memory and treat them as if they were integers or whatever (depending on what the device specification says). A strongly typed language will not allow you to do this. Thus, for some applications, strong typing may be just right whereas for others, strong typing may be too restrictive. To get most of the benefits of strong typing while avoiding most of its disadvantages, some languages use a combination of the two.

If a language performs any type checking, it may perform it at compile time or at run time or partly at compile time and partly at run time. Consider the following code fragment:

```
VAR b: Byte; VAR x: INTEGER;

b := x;
```

The assignment to b may or may not be a type error. If x happens to have a value between -128 and 127 (which is the set of values in the set for byte), the assignment won't cause a type error; if x has a value outside the range -128 to 127 then the assignment will cause a type error. If the language is strongly typed and does type checking only at compile time, then it will reject the above program (because it may cause a type error when the program runs). If the language is strongly typed and does type checking at run time, then it will all allow the program to run but it till check at run time to make sure that a type error does not happen. In other words, if the language does type checking at run time, the compiler may transform the assignment above into:

```
IF (x < -128 OR x > 127) abort(); ELSE b := x;
```

Effectively, the compiler wraps a run-time check around the assignment to make sure that it does not cause a type error.

The above example also demonstrates the relative strengths and weaknesses of compile- time and run-time type checking:

- Compile-time type checking finds bugs sooner than run-time type checking.

- Run-time type checking is more expressive since it rejects fewer programs than compile-time type checking.

- Run-time type checking may slow down the program since it introduces checks that must be performed at run time.

Since there is no one clear winner between compile-time checking and run-time checking most modern languages do a bit of both. Java, for example, checks for many errors at compile times and for others at run time.

Things to Check During Type Checking

Assume that we have the following assignment and need to check whether or not the assignment is type correct (i.e., does not have a type error):

```
VAR l: Tl; VAR r: Tr;

...

l := r;
```

When type checking happens at run time, we just need to check that the actual value of r is in the set of values that lcan hold. When type checking happens exclusively at compile time, there are two possible rules that one could use:

1. Tl = Tr. In other words, the types of the left and right hand side must be *equal*

2. Set for Tr is a subset of the set for Tl. If all the values in the set for Tr belong to the set for Tl, then the assignment will always succeed. For example, consider the code fragment:

```
VAR b: Byte; VAR x:
INTEGER;

x := b;
```

Since the set of values in Byteis a subset of the set of values in INTEGER, the above assignment will never result in a type error.

We will assume the type checking rule: *the left and right hand sides of an assignment must be of equal types and the actual parameter passed to a procedure must have the same type as the corresponding formal parameter.* Option(2) actually forms the foundation of object-oriented languages!

Type Equality

When are two types equal? Based on the notion of types we have discussed above, one answer is:

Two types, T1 and T2, are equal if the set of values in T1 is the same as the set of values in T2

While the above definition makes good sense, it is not constructive: in other words, since the set of values in many types is unbounded (e.g., String) one cannot simply enumerate the sets of values and compare them. We need a definition that can be applied (as an algorithm) to determine when two types are equal.

Modula-3's definition of when two types are equal gives us a hint for what an algorithm should look like:

"Two types are the same if their definitions become the same when expanded; that is, when all constant expressions are replaced by their values and all type names are replaced by their definitions. In the case of recursive types, the expansion is the infinite limit of the partial expansions" [Systems Programming in Modula-3, Nelson 1991]

Let's see what this definition means.

Types INTEGER and INTEGER are equal because they are the same when expanded (there is nothing to expand here since INTEGER is a primitive type).

Types BOOLEAN and BOOLEAN are equal because they are the same when expanded (once again there is nothing to expand).

Types BOOLEAN and INTEGER are not equal because they are not the same when expanded.

Now consider these more interesting types:

```
TYPE A = ARRAY [1 TO 10] OF INTEGER; TYPE I =
INTEGER;

TYPE B = ARRAY [1 TO 10] OF INTEGER; TYPE C =
ARRAY [1 TO 10] OF I;
```

(The `TYPE` declarations declare a new name for a type, much like what `typedef`

accomplishes in C and C++).

Types A and B are equal because their expanded definitions are the same (both are `ARRAY [1 TO 10] OF INTEGER`). Types A and C are also equal because their expanded definitions are the same. Note that when expanding C's definition, we have to expand I with `INTEGER`.

How about these types:

```
TYPE T1 = RECORD val: INTEGER; next: REF T1; END; TYPE T2
= RECORD val: INTEGER; next: REF T2; END;
```

(REF T1 means pointer to T1, which in C/C++ notation you would write as T1*). These two types are infinite so you cannot expand out their definitions and compare. The key insight when comparing such types is that one can assume that two types are equal unless one finds a counter example. The way to implement this as follows: whenever the type equality mechanism encounters the same pair of types that it has encountered in the past, it assumes that they are the same. For example, the compiler will go through these steps in order to answer is-type-equals(T1,T2):

1. If both T1 and T2 are both records, examine their fields. Since both have the same number of fields, assume that the types are equal. The remaining steps try to find a contradiction to this.

2. Compare the first field of T1 to the first field of T2. Since both have the same name and same type, we have not yet found a reason why T1 and T2 must be not equal.

3. Since the second field of T1 and the second field of T2 have the same name, compare their type (i.e., is-type-equals(REF T1, REF T2)).

4. Since both types are REF types (i.e., pointer types) compare their referent types (i.e., is-type-equal(T1,T2)). Recall that we are assuming at this point that T1 and T2 are equal so there is nothing to do here.

Since there is nothing else left to check and we have not found any reason to believe that

T1 and T2 are different, they must be equal.

Here is a pair of types that are not equal:

```
TYPE T11 = RECORD val: INTEGER; next: REF T11; c: CHAR; END;

TYPE T21 = RECORD val: INTEGER; next: REF T21; c: INTEGER; END;
```

We will compare the third fields of the two types and find them to be not equal (CHAR is not equal to INTEGER). Thus, we have found a reason why T11 and T21 should not be considered equal.

Modula-3's type equality mechanism is called *structural type equality* since it looks at the structure of types to figure out if two types are the same. While structural equality makes a lot of sense, some language designers do not like it. For example, consider the two records:

```
TYPE Student = RECORD id: INTEGER; name: String; END; TYPE Course
= RECORD id: INTEGER; name: String; END;
```

The programmer has declared two types, Studentand Course, and they happen to have the same fields with the same types. As far as structural equality is concerned, these two types are equal. Consider the following code:

```
PROCEDURE registerForCourse(s: Student; c: Course) = … VAR aStudent:
Student;

VAR aCourse: Course;

…

registerForCourse(aCourse, aStudent)
```

The code first declares a procedure (registerForCourse) that takes a student and a course and then calls the procedure. Unfortunately, the code passes the arguments in the wrong order. The compiler will not flag the error since the types still match up according to structural equality. In other words, structural type equality may be too liberal in some cases. It is worth noting here that the above is a contrived example; in practice it is unlikely that two unrelated types will end up with exactly the same structure.

Nonetheless, many languages use an alternative to structural type equality: *name type equality*.

The idea behind name type equality is as follows: every time a program uses a type constructor the language automatically generates a unique name for the type. Another way to think of it is: every time a program creates a new type, the language automatically gives it a unique name. Two types are equal if they have the same name. Note that this name has nothing to do with the programmer-given name of the type (e.g., the Student and Course type names in the example above). Thus the term name type equality is often confusing to students of programming languages.

Let's now see some examples of name type equality:

```
TYPE Student = RECORD id: INTEGER; name: String; END; TYPE Course =
RECORD id: INTEGER; name: String; END;
```

These two types are different because each use of "RECORD" creates a new type name: the Student record and Course record thus have different names. However, if Student and Course were defined as follows, they would be equal types:

```
TYPE T = RECORD id: INTEGER; name: String; END;

TYPE Student = T; TYPE Course = T;
```

(TYPE is not considered to be a type constructor here since it does not create a new type; it just gives a new name for an existing type).

How about INTEGER and INTEGER? INTEGER is not a type constructor; thus, all uses of INTEGER have the same name. Thus all uses of the INTEGER type refer to the same type.

While structural type equality can be too liberal, name type equality can be too restrictive. For example, consider the following code fragment:

```
VAR a: ARRAY [1 TO 10] OF INTEGER;

PROCEDURE p(f: ARRAY[1 TO 10] OF INTEGER) = … BEGIN

  p(a);

END;
```

The above call to p will not succeed with name type equality since the two uses of ARRAY (for the declarations of a and f respectively) yield different types. In a language that uses name type equality, one would have to rewrite the above as:

```
TYPE T = ARRAY [1 TO 10] OF INTEGER; VAR a: T;

PROCEDURE p(f: T) = … BEGIN

  p(a);

END;
```

The above succeeds since there is just one use of the type constructor ARRAY.

In reality, most languages use a combination of name and structural equality. For example, Modula-3 uses structural equality for all types except when a programmer requests otherwise (using a special keyword BRANDED). C, C++, and Java use name type equality for all types other than arrays, which use structural type equality. Here is what Java's language definition says about type equality for its reference types (i.e., arrays, classes, and interfaces):

Two reference types are the same run-time type if:

They are both class or both interface types, are loaded by the same class loader, and have the same binary name, in which case they are sometimes said to be the same run-time class or the same run-time interface.

They are both array types, and their component types are the same run-time type(§10). [The Java Language Specification, 2nd Edition]

In other words, class and interface types must have the same name (a "binary name" is a fully qualified name such that each class/interface in a program has a unique name).

Arrays, on the other hand, use structural equality because one looks at the element type of the array to determine equality.

Implications of Type Equality Mechanisms

The issue of what type equality a language uses can have an impact on the kinds of programs that one can write in a language. In this section, I'll describe an example situation that is problematic for name equality but not for structural equality. While this example situation is described in terms of distributed computing, it represents a more general phenomenon that occurs whenever two programs communicate or if a program needs to read or write typed data to a file (e.g., a database application).

Consider two programs, P1 and P2, which communicate with each other. P2 exports the following routine that P1 can call:

```
PROCEDURE calledByP1(x: INTEGER) = ...
```

In a type-safe environment, we would like the communication to avoid type errors. In this case, we need to make sure that P1 passes an integer to calledByP1. This situation is different from a normal procedure call in that the caller and callee are in separate programs.

As long as P1 and P2 communicate only with primitive types, it is not a problem. Now let's suppose we want a richer form of communication. In that case P2 might contain:

```
TYPE R = RECORD x: INTEGER; y: INTEGER; END;

PROCEDURE calledByP1b(a: R) = ...
```

P1 can try to call this as follows:

```
TYPE P1R = RECORD x: INTEGER; y: INTEGER; END; VAR r: P1R;

BEGIN

   (* Assume that r is initialized with some data *) calledByP1b(r);

END;
```

Does this call work? Well, it depends on whether the language uses structural type equality or name type equality. If the language uses structural type equality, P1R and R are equal and thus P1 can call calledByP1b with r. If the language uses name equality, P1R and R are not equal types: they are created using two distinct applications of a type constructor. With name equality there is no clean way of fixing this problem: since P1 and P2 are different programs, they cannot share the same RECORD. In other words, with name equality, there is no clean way of making the above solution work.

A language that has name type equality can try to fix the above in one of two ways: it can relax name type equality for the types that are likely to be used in inter-program communication (perhaps this related to the reason why C and C++ use structural equality for array types). Or it can incorporate some other mechanisms involving run-time checking; this is what Java does.

In conclusion, Type systems are a large and fundamental part of modern programming languages. A type system has two parts: a set of types and a set of rules for checking consistent uses of the types. In this chapter we focused on a simple set of rules that use type equality only. Later on we will look at rules that look at other forms of type compatibility. We identified two kinds of type equality mechanisms: name type equality and structural type equality. Since there are strengths and weaknesses of both mechanisms, there is no one clear winner: different languages use different mechanisms and even within a language some types may use one mechanism and other types the other mechanism. Understanding these issues will give you a clear sense of how to work with the type system of a language rather than against the type system of the language.

Specialized Type Systems

Dependent Type System

Dependent types are types that depend on elements of other types. An example is the type A^n of vectors of length n with components of type A. Another example is the type $A^{m \times n}$ of m × n-matrices. We say that the type A^n depends on the number n, or that A^n is a family of types indexed by the number n. Yet another example is the type of trees of a certain height. With dependent types we can also define the type of height-balanced trees of a certain height, that is, trees where the height of subtrees differ by at most one.

In computer science and logic, a dependent type is a type whose definition depends on a value. A "pair of integers" is a type. A "pair of integers where the second is greater than the first" is a dependent type because of the dependence on the value. It is an overlapping feature of type theory and type systems. In intuitionistic type theory, dependent types are used to encode logic's quantifiers like "for all" and "there exists". In functional programming languages like Agda, ATS, Coq, F*, Epigram, Idris, and Shen, dependent types prevent bugs by allowing extremely expressive types.

Two common examples of dependent types are dependent functions and dependent pairs. A dependent function's return type may depend on the *value* (not just type) of an argument. A function that takes a positive integer "n" may return an array of length "n". (Note that this is different from polymorphism and generic programming, both of which include the type as an argument.) A dependent pair may have a second value that depends on the first. It can be used to encode a pair of integers where the second one is greater than the first.

Dependent types add complexity to a type system. Deciding the equality of dependent types in a program may require computations. If arbitrary values are allowed in dependent types, then deciding type equality may involve deciding whether two arbitrary programs produce the same result; hence type checking may become undecidable.

Π Type

Loosely speaking, dependent types are similar to the type of an indexed family of sets. More formally, given a type $A : \mathcal{U}$ in a universe of types $\mathcal{U}$, one may have a family of types $B : A \to \mathcal{U}$, which assigns to each term $a : A$ a type $B(a):$. We say that the type $B(a)$ varies with a.

A function whose type of return value varies with its argument (i.e. there is no fixed codomain) is a dependent function and the type of this function is called dependent product type, pi-type or dependent function type. For this example, the dependent function type is typically written as,

$$\prod_{x:A} B(x)$$

or

$$\prod_{x:A} B(x).$$

If $B : A \to \mathcal{U}$ is a constant function, the corresponding dependent product type is equivalent to an ordinary function type. That is, $\prod_{x:A} B$ is judgmentally equal to $A \to B$ when B does not depend on x.

The name 'pi-type' comes from the idea that these may be viewed as a Cartesian product of types. Pi-types can also be understood as models of universal quantifiers.

For example, if we write $\text{Vec}(\mathbb{R}, n)$ for n-tuples of real numbers, then $\prod_{n:\mathbb{N}} \text{Vec}(\mathbb{R}, n)$ would be the type of a function which, given a natural number n, returns a tuple of real numbers of size n. The usual function space arises as a special case when the range type does not actually depend on the input. E.g. $\prod_{n:\mathbb{N}} \mathbb{R}$ is the type of functions from natural numbers to the real numbers, which is written as $\mathbb{N} \to \mathbb{R}$ in typed lambda calculus.

Σ type

The dual of the dependent product type is the dependent pair type, dependent sum type, sigma-type, or (confusingly) dependent product type. Sigma-types can also be understood as existential quantifiers. Continuing the above example, if, in the universe of types $\mathcal{U}$, there is a type $A : \mathcal{U}$ and a family of types $B : A \to \mathcal{U}$, then there is a dependent pair type.,

$$\sum_{x:A} B(x)$$

The dependent pair type captures the idea of an ordered pair where the type of the second term is dependent on the value of the first. If,

$$(a,b) : \sum_{x:A} B(x)$$

then $a : A$ and $b : B(a)$. If B is a constant function, then the dependent pair type becomes (is judgementally equal to) the product type, that is, an ordinary Cartesian product $A \times B$.

Example as Existential Quantification

Let $A : \mathcal{U}$ be some type, and let $B : A \to \mathcal{U}$. By the Curry–Howard correspondence, B can be interpreted as a logical predicate on terms of A. For a given $a : A$, whether the type $B(a)$ is inhabited indicates whether a satisfies this predicate. The correspondence can be extended to existential quantification and dependent pairs: the proposition $\exists a \in A B(a)$ is true if and only if the type $\sum_{a:A} B(a)$ is inhabited.

For example, $n : \mathbb{N}$ is less than or equal to $m : \mathbb{N}$ if and only if there exists another natural number $k : \mathbb{N}$ such that $m + k = n$. In logic, this statement is codified by existential quantification:

$$m \leq n \Leftrightarrow \exists k \in \mathbb{N}\, m + k = n.$$

This proposition corresponds to the dependent pair type:

$$\sum_{k : \mathbb{N}} m + k = n.$$

That is, a proof of the statement that m is less than n is a pair that contains both a number k, which is the difference between m and n, and a proof of the equality $m + k = n$.

Systems of the Lambda Cube

Henk Barendregt developed the lambda cube as a means of classifying type systems along three axes. The eight corners of the resulting cube-shaped diagram each correspond to a type system, with simply typed lambda calculus in the least expressive corner, and calculus of constructions in the most expressive. The three axes of the cube correspond to three different augmentations of the simply typed lambda calculus: the addition of dependent types, the addition of polymorphism, and the addition of higher kinded type constructors (functions from types to types, for example). The lambda cube is generalized further by pure type systems.

First Order Dependent Type Theory

The system $\lambda\Pi$ of pure first order dependent types, corresponding to the logical framework LF, is obtained by generalising the function space type of the simply typed lambda calculus to the dependent product type.

Second Order Dependent Type Theory

The system $\lambda\Pi 2$ of second order dependent types is obtained from $\lambda\Pi$ by allowing quantification over type constructors. In this theory the dependent product operator subsumes both the $\rightarrow$ operator of simply typed lambda calculus and the $\forall$ binder of System F.

Higher Order Dependently Typed Polymorphic Lambda Calculus

The higher order system $\lambda\Pi\omega$ extends $\lambda\Pi 2$ to all four forms of abstraction from the lambda cube: functions from terms to terms, types to types, terms to types and types to terms. The system corresponds to the calculus of constructions whose derivative, the calculus of inductive constructions is the underlying system of the Coq proof assistant.

Simultaneous Programming Language and Logic

The Curry–Howard correspondence implies that types can be constructed that express arbitrarily complex mathematical properties. If the user can supply a constructive proof that a type is *inhabited* (i.e., that a value of that type exists) then a compiler can check the proof and convert it into executable computer code that computes the value by carrying out the construction. The proof checking feature makes dependently typed languages closely related to proof assistants. The code-generation aspect provides a powerful approach to formal program verification and proof-carrying code, since the code is derived directly from a mechanically verified mathematical proof.

Substructural Type System

Substructural type systems are a family of type systems analogous to substructural logics where one or more of the structural rules are absent or only allowed under controlled circumstances. Such systems are useful for constraining access to system resources such as files, locks and memory by keeping track of changes of state that occur and preventing invalid states.

Different Substructural Type Systems

Several type systems have emerged by discarding some of the structural rules of exchange, weakening, and contraction:

	exchange	weakening	contraction	use
linear	allowed	—	—	exactly once
affine	allowed	allowed	—	at most once
relevant	allowed	—	allowed	at least once
ordered	—	—	—	exactly once in order

- Linear type systems (allow exchange, but neither weakening nor contraction): Every variable is used exactly once.

- Affine type systems (allow exchange and weakening, but not contraction): Every variable is used at most once.

- Relevant type systems (allow exchange and contraction, but not weakening): Every variable is used at least once.

- Ordered type systems (discard exchange, contraction, and weakening): Every variable is used exactly once in the order it was introduced.

The explanation for affine type systems is best understood if rephrased as "every *occurrence* of a variable is used at most once".

Linear Type Systems

Linear types corresponds to linear logic and ensures that objects are used exactly once, allowing the system to safely deallocate an object after its use.

The Clean programming language makes use of uniqueness types (a variant of linear types) to help support concurrency, input/output, and in-place update of arrays.

Linear type systems allow references but not aliases. To enforce this, a reference goes out of scope after appearing on the right-hand side of an assignment, thus ensuring that only one reference to any object exists at once. Note that passing a reference as an argument to a function is a form of assignment, as the function parameter will be assigned the value inside the function, and therefore such use of a reference also causes it to go out of scope.

A linear type system is similar to C++'s unique_ptr class, which behaves like a pointer but can only be moved (i.e. not copied) in an assignment. Although the linearity constraint is checked at compile time, dereferencing an invalidated unique_ptr causes undefined behavior at run-time.

The single-reference property makes linear type systems suitable as programming languages for quantum computation, as it reflects the no-cloning theorem of quantum states. From the category theory point of view, no-cloning is a statement that there is no diagonal functor which could duplicate states; similarly, from the combinator point of view, there is no K-combinator which can destroy states. From the lambda calculus point of view, a variable x can appear exactly once in a term.

Linear type systems are the internal language of closed symmetric monoidal categories, much in the same way that simply typed lambda calculus is the language of Cartesian closed categories. More precisely, one may construct functors between the category of linear type systems and the category of closed symmetric monoidal categories.

Affine Type Systems

Affine types are a version of linear types allowing to *discard* (i.e. *not use*) a resource, corresponding to affine logic. An affine resource *can* only be used once, while a linear one *must* be used once.

Relevant Type System

Relevant types correspond to relevant logic which allows exchange and contraction, but not weakening, which translates to every variable being used at least once.

Ordered Type System

Ordered types correspond to noncommutative logic where exchange, contraction and weakening are discarded. This can be used to model stack-based memory allocation (contrast with linear types which can be used to model heap-based memory allocation). Without the exchange property, an object may only be used when at the top of the modelled stack, after which it is popped off resulting in every variable being used exactly once in the order it was introduced.

Gradual Typing

Gradually typed languages give us a better way: they embed the dynamic language in them, but we can also program in a statically typed style and have it interoperate with the dynamically typed code. This means new code can be written in a statically typed language while still being able to call the legacy dynamically typed code without having to sacrifice all of the benefits of static typing.

To a first approximation, a gradually typed language is a statically typed language with dynamic type errors, a distinguished dynamic type ?? and a distinguished way to coerce values from any type to and from the dynamic type (possibly causing type errors). Then a dynamically typed program can be compiled to the gradual language by translating the implicit dynamic type checking to explicit casts.

For a gradually typed language to deserve the name, it should be on the one hand *typed*, meaning the types have their intended categorical semantics as products, exponentials, etc and on the other hand it should satisfy *graduality*. Graduality of a language means that the transition from a very loose, dynamic style to a precise, statically typed style should be as smooth as possible. More concretely, it means that changing the types used in the program to be less dynamic should lead to a *refinement* of the program's behavior: if the term satisfies the new type, it should behave as before, but otherwise it should produce a dynamic type error.

We can formalize this idea by modeling our gradually typed language as a category *internal to preorders*: types and terms have related "dynamism" orderings (denoted by $\sqsubseteq$\sqsubseteq) and all type and term constructors are monotone with respect to these orderings. Then we can characterize the dynamic type as being the most dynamic type and the type error as a least dynamic term of each type. Making everything internal to preorders reproduces exactly the rules of type and term dynamism that programming language researchers have developed based on their operational intuitions.

Gradual Type Checking

A *gradual type checker* is a type checker that checks, at compile-time, for type errors in some parts of a program, but not others, as directed by which parts of the program have been annotated with types. For example, our prototype gradual type checker for Python does not give an error for the above program, reproduced again below.

```
def add1(x):

  return x + 1


class A:

  pass


a = A()

add1(a)
```

However, if the programmer adds a type annotation for the parameter x, as follows, then the type checker signals an error because the type of variable a is A, which is inconsistent with the type of parameter x of the add1 function, which is int.

```
def add1(x : int):

  return x + 1


class A:

  pass


a = A()

add1(a)
```

(Our rules for assigning static types to local variables such as a are somewhat complicated because Python does not have local variable declarations but in most cases we give the variable the same type as the expression on the right-hand side of the assignment.)

The gradual type checker deals with unannotated variables by giving them the unknown type (also called the *dynamic* type in the literature), which we abbreviate as "?" and by allowing implicit conversions from any type to ? and also from ? to any other type. For simplicity, suppose the + operator expects its arguments to be integers. The following version of add1 is accepted by the gradual type checker because we allow an implicit conversion from ? (the type of x) to int (the type expected by +).

```
def add1(x):

    return x + 1
```

Allowing the implicit converson from ? to int is unsafe, and is what gives gradual typing the flavor of dynamic typing. Just as with dynamic typing, the argument bound to x will be checked at run-time to make sure it is an integer before the addition is performed.

As mentioned above, the gradual type checker also allows implicit conversions from any type to type ?. For example, the gradual type checker accepts the following call to add1because it allows the implicit conversion from int (the type of 3) to ? (the implied type annotation for parameter x).

```
add1(3)
```

The gradual type checker also allows implicit conversions between more complicated types. For example, in the following program we have a conversion between different tuple types, from ? * int to int * int.

```
def g(p : int * int):

 return p


def f(x, y : int):

p = (x,y)

g(p)
```

In general, the gradual type checker allows an implicit conversion between two types if they are *consistent* with each other. We use the shorthand S ~ T to express that type S is consistent with type T. Here are some of the rules that define when two types are consistent:

1. For any type T, we have both ? ~ T and T ~ ?.

2. For any basic type B, such as int, we have B ~ B.

3. A tuple type T1 * T2 is consistent with another tuple type S1 * S2

   if T1 ~ S1 and T2 ~ S2. This rule generalizes in a straightforward way to tuples of arbitrary size.

4. A function type `fun(T1,...,Tn,R)` (the `T1`...`Tn` are the parameter types and `R` is the return type) is consistent with another function type `fun(S1,...,Sn,U)` if `T1` ~ `S1`...`Tn` ~ `Sn` and `R` ~ `U`.

We write S !~ T when S is not consistent with T.

So, for example,

- `int ~ int`

- `int !~ bool`

- `? ~ int`

- `bool ~ ?`

- `int * int ~ ?`

- `fun(?,?) ~ fun(int,int)`

- `? ~ fun(int,int)`

- `int * int !~ ? * bool`

Nominal Type System

In a nominal, or nominative, type system, two types are deemded to be the same if they have the same nameand a type T1 is deemed to be a (immediate) subtype of a type T2 if T1 is explicitly declared to be a subtype of T2.

In the following example, Employee is a subtype of Person because it is declared as such using keyword "extends" within its class declaration. Conversely, Product is not a subtype of Person because it lacks such an "extends" declaration.

```
class Person {

  public name: string;

}


class Employee extends Person {

  public salary: number;

}


class Manager extends Employee { }
```

```
class Product {

  public name: string;

  public price: number;

}
```

The subtype relation is transitive and thus Manager is not just a subtype of Employee but also of Person. Productis not a subtype of Person, although it provides the same members.

Most mainstream object-oriented languages use nominal subtyping, for example C++, C#, Java, Objective-C.

Classes are Nominally Typed

When you have two classes with the same structure, they still are not considered equivalent because Flow uses nominal typing for classes.

```
1 | // @flow

2 | class Foo { method(input: string) { /* ... */ } }

3 | class Bar { method(input: string) { /* ... */ } }

4 | let test: Foo = new Bar(); // Error!
```

If you wanted to use a class structurally you could do that by mixing them with objects as interfaces:

```
1   type Interface = {

2    method(value: string): void;

3   };

4

5   class Foo { method(input: string) { /* ... */ } }

6   class Bar { method(input: string) { /* ... */ } }

7

8   let test: Interface = new Foo(); // Okay.

9   let test: Interface = new Bar(); // Okay.
```

Structural Type System

Another possible standard for type checking is structural typing, which considers two types to be interchangeable if they have the same structure and support the same operations. Under structural typing, the types A and B defined above would be considered the same.

Structural typing may also be applied in a relatively loose manner. Perhaps the loosest variation on structural typing allows an argument to be passed to a function as long as every operation *that the function actually uses* is defined for the argument. This is duck typing. (The name comes from the *Duck Test*: "If it looks like a duck, swims like a duck, and quacks like a duck, then it's a duck.")

C++ checks template-parameter types using duck typing. The following function template ggt can be called with arguments of type A or B.

```
[C++]

template <typename T>

void ggt(T x)

{

    cout << x.h << " " << x.m << endl;

}
```

The addEm functions discussed earlier are examples of duck typing. Here they are again.

```
[C++]

template <typename T, typename U>

T addEm(T a, U b)

{

    return a + b;

}
[Python]

def addEm(a, b):

    return a + b
```

We have noted that C++ template-parameter types are checked using duck typing. Python, Lua, and some other dynamic languages check all function parameter types using duck typing. Both versions of addEm above can be called with arguments of any type, as long as all the operations used are defined for those types. In particular, both versions of addEm may be called with two integer arguments or with two string arguments.

Example

Objects in OCaml are structurally typed by the names and types of their methods.

Objects can be created directly (*immediate objects*) without going through a nominative class. Classes only serve as functions for creating objects.

```
# let x =
  object
    val mutable x = 5
    method get_x = x
    method set_x y = x <- y
  end;;
val x : < get_x : int; set_x : int -> unit > = <obj>
```

Here the OCaml interactive runtime prints out the inferred type of the object for convenience. Its type (< get_x : int; set_x : int -> unit >) is defined only by its methods. In other words, the type of x is defined by the method types "get_x : int" and "set_x : int -> unit" rather than by any name.

To define another object, which has the same methods and types of methods:

```
# let y =
  object
    method get_x = 2
    method set_x y = Printf.printf "%d\n" y
  end;;
val y : < get_x : int; set_x : int -> unit > = <obj>
```

OCaml considers them the same type. For example, the equality operator is typed to only take two values of the same type:

```
# x = y;;
- : bool = false
```

So they must be the same type, or else this wouldn't even type-check. This shows that equivalence of types is structural.

One can define a function that invokes a method:

```
# let set_to_10 a = a#set_x 10;;
val set_to_10 : < set_x : int -> 'a; .. > -> 'a = <fun>
```

The inferred type for the first argument (< set_x : int -> 'a; .. >) is interesting. The .. means that the first argument can be any object which has a "set_x" method, which takes an int as argument.

So it can be used on object x:

```
# set_to_10 x;;

- : unit = ()
```

Another object can be made that happens to have that method and method type; the other methods are irrelevant:

```
# let z =

  object

   method blahblah = 2.5

   method set_x y = Printf.printf "%d\n" y

  end;;

  val z : < blahblah : float; set_x : int -> unit > = <obj>
```

The "set_to_10" function also works on it:

```
 # set_to_10 z;;

 10

 - : unit = ()
```

This shows that compatibility for things like method invocation is determined by structure.

Let us define a type synonym for objects with only a "get_x" method and no other methods:

```
# type simpler_obj = < get_x : int >;;

type simpler_obj = < get_x : int >
```

The object x is not of this type; but structurally, x is of a subtype of this type, since x contains a superset of its methods. So x can be coerced to this type:

```
# (x :> simpler_obj);;

- : simpler_obj = <obj>

# (x :> simpler_obj)#get_x;;

- : int = 10
```

But not object z, because it is not a structural subtype:

```
# (z :> simpler_obj);;

This expression cannot be coerced to type simpler_obj = < get_x : int >;
```

```
it has type < blahblah : float; set_x : int -> unit > but is here used with
type

    < get_x : int; .. >

The first object type has no method get_x
```

This shows that compatibility for widening coercions are structural.

Strong and Weak Typing

Strong Typing

Programming languages in which variables have specific data types are strong typed. This implies that in strong typed languages, variables are necessarily bound to a particular data type. Python is strong typed, and so is Java. The distinction between strong typing and weak typing is more subtle and thus more difficult to grasp than is the distinction between static typing and dynamic typing. Consider the following example:

```
/* Python code */

>>> foo = "x"

>>> foo = foo + 2

Traceback (most recent call last):

  File "<pyshell#3>", line 1, in ?

    foo = foo + 2

TypeError: cannot concatenate 'str' and 'int' objects

>>>
```

In the above Python example (run from the Python shell), foo is of str type. In the second line, we're attempting to add 2 (an int) to a variable of str type. As we can see, a TypeError is returned, indicating that a str object cannot be concatenated with an int object. This is what characterizes strong typed languages: variables are bound to a particular data type.

Weak Typing

As opposed to strong typed languages, weak typed languages are those in which variables are not of a specific data type. It should be noted that this does not imply that variables do not have types; it does mean that variables are not "bound" to a specific data type. PHP and C are examples of weak typed languages. Consider the following:

```
/* PHP code */
```

```php
<?php

$foo = "x";

$foo = $foo + 2; // not an error

echo $foo;

?>
```

In this example, foo is initially a string type. In the second line, we add this string variable to 2, an integer. This is permitted in PHP, and is characteristic of all weak typed languages.

Now that we know about the two concepts, we can augment both of them to characterize any given language. Thus, Python is dynamic typed and strong typed; Java is static typed and strong typed; PHP is dynamic typed and weak typed; C is static typed and weak typed (owing to its casting ability).

Strongly-typed Features

Using strong-typing, the feature type is assigned or determined first, then the necessary properties listed and values provided.

In a XML implementation, this can result in relatively simple feature instances where the feature-type is given by an XML element name, and the properties are subelements with appropriate names.

```xml
<Road>

  <description> ... </description>

  <surfaceTreatment> Bitumen </surfaceTreatment>

  ...

</Road>
```

This is the usual GML encoding pattern.

The strong-typing approach is particularly suitable for domains where the items of interest are artefacts that are created or asserted (e.g. constructions, observation features), so their type is known *a priori*. Otherwise, the strong-typed features may thought of as "snapshots" of features representing the "current interpretation and model".

Weakly-typed Features

When applying a full weak-typing pattern, a generic feature has generic properties, and maybe a property that specifies (or refines) the "feature-type" itself. The value of this feature-type parameter may be selected from a controlled source (list or authority table), but does not directly affect other aspects of the feature description.

For maximum flexibility the feature has unlimited number of properties which are soft-typed themselves.

For a particular feature type, the weak-typed model should be isomorphic with the equivalent strong-typed model (i.e. with the same graph or tree structure) but the semantics are carried by a slightly different syntax. In an XML implementation this leads to less tidy instances, where semantic information occurs as element and attribute values rather than in tag names, for example:

```
<Feature type="Road">

  <property name="description" type="string"> ... </property>

  <property name="surfaceTreatment" type="token">Bitumen</property>

  ...

</Feature>
```

Like the strong-typed equivalent above, the data model for "Road" is exposed in the data instance, through the labelling and nesting of elements. The weak-typing pattern is much more flexible at "run-time" (i.e. in the instance), but provides no constraints on the structure according to feature-type.

The weak-typing approach is particularly suitable for domains where the classification of items of interest emerges from their properties, or where varying or evolving classification methodologies apply. The weak-type provided by the data supplier may even be treated as a "hint", and the user may take responsibility for classification on the basis of the properties and their values.

In this encoding, the way that such an feature might be built on-demand by a set of "joins" to a narrow database table of properties is quite obvious. Because of this, we can refer to the weak-typed model as more "normalised". In common with highly normalised database table schemas, the additional flexibility comes with an attendant processing burden.

Typing information == Schema Information

In the soft-typed pattern the encoding in the data instance is closer to a "schema-level" view. The typing information in the soft-typed version is essentially a "mini-schema language", using attributes and properties called (or functionally equivalent to) "name" and "type" etc. For example, the weakly-typed Road instance shown is almost the same as the W3C XML schema that defines the strong-typed version:

```
<element name="Road"><complexType><sequence>

  <element name="description" type="string"/>

  <element name="surfaceTreatment" type="token"/>

  ...

</sequence></complexType></element>
```

Just-in-time Schema

Another way of thinking about it is that, putting schema-level information in the instance is a kind of "just-in-time" schema. But if this is all we are doing, then why not generate a just-in-time XML Schema ? - i.e.

- The instance would be strong-typed, but

- The schemaLocation would refer to an XML Schema generated dynamically, for only this instance.

The disadvantage of this full-on just-in-time XML schema approach are:

- The "feature-type" catalogue becomes largely dynamic, rather than agreed in advance by a domain community, so

- Processing software must be fully XML schema-aware, and cannot be pre-configured for specific feature types.

A sensible "soft-typing" approach permits limited "schema" information *at selected positions* in an instance. This allows us to retain a set of generic feature-types, for which consuming software can be pre-configured if desired, with flexibility constrained to the necessary, more reasonable level.

Type Safety

A programming language or programming-language construct is type-safe if it forbids operations that are incorrect for the types on which they operate.

Some programming languages/constructs may discourage incorrect operations or make them difficult, without completely forbidding them. We may thus compare the level of type safety offered by two programming languages/constructs.

For example, the C++ printf function, inherited from the C Standard Library, is not type-safe. This function takes an arbitrary number of parameters. The first should be a format string containing references to the other parameters.

```
[C++]

printf("I am %d years old.", age);
```

The above inserts the value of variable age in place of the %d in the format string, on the assumption that age has type int. However, according to the Standard, the type of age is not checked. It could be a floating-point value or a pointer; the code would then compile, and a type error would slip by unnoticed.

In contrast, C++ stream I/O is type-safe.

```
[C++]

cout << "I am " << age << " years old.";
```

When the above code is compiled, the correct output function is chosen based on the type of the variable age.

Strong [*ick!*] & Weak [*ick!*]

Two unfortunate terms are often unfortunately used in discussions of type safety; the results are—you guessed it—unfortunate. The terms are strong typing (or strongly typed) and weak typing (or weakly typed). These generally have something to do with the overall level of type safety offered by a programming language.

The problem with this terminology is that it has no standard definition; it is used in different ways by different people, many of whom assume that their definition is the only standard one. I have seen (at least) three different definitions of "strongly typed" in common use. The C programming language is strongly typed by one of them and weakly typed by the other two.

Therefore:

> Avoid using the terms "strong" and "weak" typing, or "strongly" and "weakly" typed.

Nonetheless, the issue of how strictly type rules are enforced is an important one. When discussing it, we might speak informally of how one type system is "stronger" than another. If we wish to be formal, then we can talk about *soundness*.

Soundness

A static type system is sound if it guarantees that operations that are incorrect for a type will not be performed; otherwise it is unsound.

Haskell has a sound type system. The type system of C (and thus C++) is unsound. This might appear to be a criticism. However, the type system of C was deliberately designed to be unsound. Being able to interpret a value in memory in arbitrary ways makes C useful for low-level systems programming.

There does not seem to be any equivalent of soundness in the world of dynamic typing. However, we can still talk about whether a dynamic type system strictly enforces type safety.

Type Theory

Type theory is a mathematical technique widely used in computer science. In the formal methods community, type theory is at the basis of expressive specification languages and powerful proof assistant tools based on higher-order logic. From a practical point of view, type theory has been used to improve the quality of software systems by enabling the detection of errors before they become run-time problems.

A minimal type system, known as the Simple Type Theory, was proposed by Church in . In that theory, mathematical objects are of two kinds: terms and types. The terms of the Simple Type Theory are the terms of the λ-calculus, itself being a formalization of partial recursive functions proposed by Church . Types can be basic types or functional types A → B where A and B are types.

In λ-calculus, terms can be variables, functions, or applications. Only terms that follow a type discipline are considered to be valid. The type discipline is enforced by a set of typing rules. A typing rule says, for example, that a function f can be applied to a term x if and only if f has the type A → B and x has the type A. In that case, the application f(x) has the type B. Thanks to the typing rules, Russell's paradox cannot be expressed in the simple type theory.

Type checking is decidable in the simply typed λ-calculus. That is, it is decidable whether or not a term has a type according to the typing rules.

The simple type theory can be extended straightforwardly with simple data types such as Cartesian products, records, and disjoint unions. For this reason, simple types have been largely used by designers of programming languages. Indeed, most of the modern programming languages support, to some extent, a simply-typed system. In these languages, programs violating the type discipline are considered harmful, and therefore, they are rejected by the compiler. Thus, type checking is a powerful tool to eliminate run-time problems. For instance, in Pascal, boolean functions cannot be applied to integers. This restriction happens to be a simply typed rule enforced by the compiler. On the other hand, C supports a more liberal typing discipline; the compiler warns of some violations, but it seldom rejects a program. Almost every C-programmer knows the danger of this flexibility in the language.

When writing formal specifications, the choice of a typed language, in opposition to a language based on set theory, is not always evident. In contrast to programs, specifications are not supposed to be executable. Thus, a too restrictive type theory, as for example the simply typed λ-calculus, quickly becomes cumbersome to write enough abstract specifications. Several variants of type theories have been proposed in the literature, most of them are still convenient to write formal specifications and powerful enough to reject specifications that are undesirable.

Polymorphism and Data Types

A major improvement to the simple type theory, is the System F proposed by Girard. System F extends λ-calculus with quantification over types; that is, it introduces the notion of type parameters which is at the basis of the concept of polymorphism. In this system, generic data types as list, trees, etc. can be encoded. Type checking is still decidable in a type system that supports polymorphism and abstract data type declarations.

In programming languages, polymorphism allows for the reuse of code defined over structures parameterized by a type. For instance, a sort function is essentially the same whether it works over a list of integers or a list of strings. Polymorphic-typed languages exploit this uniformity without losing the ability to catch errors by enforcing a type discipline.

Although most of the specification languages based on higher-order logic support polymorphism, just a few modern programming languages implement it correctly.

The functional programming languages of the ML family are strongly typed languages that support algebraic data types and polymorphism. They use a type inference mechanism based on Milner's algorithm. Therefore, although these languages are strongly typed, the types of the expressions occurring in programs are automatically inferred by the compiler. Hence, ML programs are almost free of type declarations.

Object-oriented imperative languages such as Eiffel , C++, and Java support parametric classes, which is a form of polymorphism. However, object-oriented features, side effects, and polymorphism result in very complex type systems. Eiffel uses a rather complicated and ad-hoc type system, C++ follows the same liberal discipline of C with respect to type checking, and Java only supports single inheritance.

Dependent Types and Constructive Type Theories

Dependent types is the ability to define types that depend on expressions. For instance, in Pascal the type declaration array[1..10] of integers is a dependent-type declaration since this type depends on expressions 1 and 10. A general theory of dependent types, called LP, was proposed by Harper et al..

Dependent types, polymorphism, and inductive data types are supported by a very expressive extension to the λ-calculus called the Calculus of Inductive Constructions (CIC). This calculus is the logical framework of the proof assistant system Coq. Type checking is decidable in CIC and the calculus satisfies the strong normalization property, i.e., functions defined in the CIC formalism always terminate. The Calculus of Inductive Constructions also supports the propositions-as-types principle of the higher-order intuitionistic logic. According to this principle, a proof of a logical proposition A is the same as a term of type A. This isomorphism between proofs and terms is also known as the Curry-Howard isomorphism. In practice, the Curry-Howard isomorphism is used to extract a program from the constructive proof of the correctness of an algorithm. Programs extracted this way satisfy the termination property.

Although very simple dependent types such as arrays are used in most programming languages, general dependent types and constructive types are still hard to handle in programming languages. One notably exception is DML, a the conservative extension of ML with a restricted, but practical, form of dependent types.

Subtyping and Other Mysteries

In type theory every object has at most one type. A drawback of this postulate is that an object as the natural number 1 has to be different from the real number 1. A way to handle this problem is to introduce predicate subtyping, i.e., the ability to define new types by a predicate on previously defined types. For instance, the type nat can be defined as a subtype of real such that it contains only the numbers generated from 0 and +1. Via predicate subtyping the natural number 1 is also a real number.

The type theory of the general verification system PVS supports predicate subtyping. Unfortunately, general predicate subtyping rends type checking undecidable. In PVS, the type-checker returns a set of type correctness conditions (TCCs) that should be discharged by the user; these TCCs guarantee the type correction of the formal development. In practice, TCCs are not a problem since PVS provides a powerful theorem prover that implements several decision procedures and proof automation tools.

Due to the undecidability problem, general predicate subtyping is not used in programming languages. However, object-oriented programming languages opened the door to an interesting kind of structural subtyping: inheritance. Via inheritance, two structurally different types may share some elements. Related concepts to inheritance are those of overloading, that is, the ability to use the same name for different functions, and dynamic typing, that is, the ability for objects to change their types during the execution of a program.

References

- Walker, David (2002). «Substructural Type Systems». In Pierce, Benjamin C. Advanced Topics in Types and Programming Languages. MIT Press. pp. 3&ndash, 43. ISBN 0-262-16228-8

- What-is-gradual-typing: wphomes.soic.indiana.edu, Retrieved 09 July 2018

- Adam Petcher (1 April 2008). «Deciding Joinability Modulo Ground Equations in Operational Type Theory» (PDF). Retrieved 14 October 2010.

- Nominal-and-structural-typing: eclipse.org, Retrieved 11 April 2018

- Cook, W.R.; Hill, W.L.; Canning, P.S. (January 1990). «Inheritance is not subtyping». Proceedings of the Seventeenth Annual ACM Symposium on Principles of Programming Languages. San Francisco, California: 125–135. doi:10.1145/96709.96721

- Nominal-structural: flow.org, Retrieved 14 March 2018

- Aaron Stump (6 April 2009). «Verified Programming in Guru» (PDF). Archived from the original (PDF) on 29 December 2009. Retrieved 28 September 2010

- Strong-vs-weak-typing-for-features: confluence.csiro.au, Retrieved 28 May 2018

Common Programming Languages

A general purpose programming language is a programming language that is designed for writing software in a wide array of application domains. This chapter closely analyzes some general purpose programming languages in detail, such as C, C++, Java and Python.

C Programming Language

C is a general-purpose, high-level language that was originally developed by Dennis M. Ritchie to develop the UNIX operating system at Bell Labs. C was originally first implemented on the DEC PDP-11 computer in 1972.

In 1978, Brian Kernighan and Dennis Ritchie produced the first publicly available description of C, now known as the K&R standard.

The UNIX operating system, the C compiler, and essentially all UNIX application programs have been written in C. C has now become a widely used professional language for various reasons:

- Easy to learn
- Structured language
- It produces efficient programs
- It can handle low-level activities
- It can be compiled on a variety of computer platforms.

Facts About C

- C was invented to write an operating system called UNIX.
- C is a successor of B language which was introduced around the early 1970s.
- The language was formalized in 1988 by the American National Standard Institute (ANSI).
- The UNIX OS was totally written in C.
- Today C is the most widely used and popular System Programming Language.
- Most of the state-of-the-art software have been implemented using C.
- Today's most popular Linux OS and RDBMS MySQL have been written in C.

Reasons to use C

C was initially used for system development work, particularly the programs that make-up the operating system. C was adopted as a system development language because it produces code that runs nearly as fast as the code written in assembly language. Some examples of the use of C might be:

- Operating Systems
- Language Compilers
- Assemblers
- Text Editors
- Print Spoolers
- Network Drivers
- Modern Programs
- Databases
- Language Interpreters
- Utilities.

C Programs

A C program can vary from 3 lines to millions of lines and it should be written into one or more text files with extension ".c"; for example, hello.c. You can use "vi", "vim" or any other text editor to write your C program into a file.

Local Environment Setup

If you want to set up your environment for C programming language, you need the following two software tools available on your computer, (a) Text Editor and (b) The C Compiler.

Text Editor

This will be used to type your program. Examples of a few editors include Windows Notepad, OS Edit command, Brief, Epsilon, EMACS, and vim or vi.

The name and version of text editors can vary on different operating systems. For example, Notepad will be used on Windows, and vim or vi can be used on Windows as well as on Linux or UNIX.

The files you create with your editor are called the source files and they contain the program source codes. The source files for C programs are typically named with the extension ".c".

Before starting your programming, make sure you have one text editor in place and you have enough experience to write a computer program, save it in a file, compile it and finally execute it.

The C Compiler

The source code written in source file is the human readable source for your program. It needs to be "compiled" into machine language so that your CPU can actually execute the program as per the instructions given.

The compiler compiles the source codes into final executable programs. The most frequently used and free available compiler is the GNU C/C++ compiler, otherwise you can have compilers either from HP or Solaris if you have the respective operating systems.

Installation on UNIX/Linux

If you are using Linux or UNIX, then check whether GCC is installed on your system by entering the following command from the command line:

```
$ gcc -v
```

If you have GNU compiler installed on your machine, then it should print a message as follows:

```
Using built-in specs.

Target: i386-redhat-linux

Configured with: ../configure --prefix=/usr .......

Thread model: posix

gcc version 4.1.2 20080704 (Red Hat 4.1.2-46)
```

If GCC is not installed, then you will have to install it yourself using the detailed instruction.

Installation on Mac OS

If you use Mac OS X, the easiest way to obtain GCC is to download the Xcode development environment from Apple's web site and follow the simple installation instructions. Once you have Xcode setup, you will be able to use GNU compiler for C/C++.

Installation on Windows

To install GCC on Windows, you need to install MinGW. To install MinGW, go to the MinGW homepage, www.mingw.org, and follow the link to the MinGW download page. Download the latest version of the MinGW installation program, which should be named MinGW-<version>.exe.

While installing Min GW, at a minimum, you must install gcc-core, gcc-g++, binutils, and the MinGW runtime, but you may wish to install more.

Add the bin subdirectory of your MinGW installation to your PATHenvironment variable, so that you can specify these tools on the command line by their simple names.

After the installation is complete, you will be able to run gcc, g++, ar, ranlib, dlltool, and several other GNU tools from the Windows command line.

Program Structure

Hello World Example

A C program basically consists of the following parts:

- Preprocessor Commands

- Functions

- Variables

- Statements & Expressions

- Comments.

Let us look at a simple code that would print the words "Hello World":

```c
#include <stdio.h>


int main() {

  /* my first program in C */

  printf("Hello, World! \n");


  return 0;

}
```

Let us take a look at the various parts of the above program:

- The first line of the program *#include <stdio.h>* is a preprocessor command, which tells a C compiler to include stdio.h file before going to actual compilation.

- The next line *int main()* is the main function where the program execution begins.

- The next line /*...*/ will be ignored by the compiler and it has been put to add additional comments in the program. So such lines are called comments in the program.

- The next line *printf(...)* is another function available in C which causes the message "Hello, World!" to be displayed on the screen.

- The next line return 0; terminates the main() function and returns the value 0.

Compile and Execute C Program

Let us see how to save the source code in a file, and how to compile and run it. Following are the simple steps:

- Open a text editor and add the above-mentioned code.

- Save the file as *hello.c*

- Open a command prompt and go to the directory where you have saved the file.

- Type *gcc hello.c* and press enter to compile your code.

- If there are no errors in your code, the command prompt will take you to the next line and would generate *a.out* executable file.

- Now, type *a.out* to execute your program.

- You will see the output *"Hello World"* printed on the screen.

```
$ gcc hello.c

$ ./a.out

Hello, World!
```

Make sure the gcc compiler is in your path and that you are running it in the directory containing the source file hello.c.

Basic Syntax

Tokens in C

A C program consists of various tokens and a token is either a keyword, an identifier, a constant, a string literal, or a symbol. For example, the following C statement consists of five tokens:

```
printf("Hello, World! \n");
```

The individual tokens are:

```
printf

(

"Hello, World! \n"

)

;
```

Semicolons

In a C program, the semicolon is a statement terminator. That is, each individual statement must be ended with a semicolon. It indicates the end of one logical entity.

Given below are two different statements:

```
printf("Hello, World! \n");

return 0;
```

Comments

Comments are like helping text in your C program and they are ignored by the compiler. They start with /* and terminate with the characters */ as shown below:

```
/* my first program in C */
```

You cannot have comments within comments and they do not occur within a string or character literals.

Identifiers

A C identifier is a name used to identify a variable, function, or any other user-defined item. An identifier starts with a letter A to Z, a to z, or an underscore '_' followed by zero or more letters, underscores, and digits (0 to 9).

C does not allow punctuation characters such as @, $, and % within identifiers. C is a case-sensitive programming language. Thus, *Manpower* and *manpower* are two different identifiers in C. Here are some examples of acceptable identifiers:

```
mohd    zara   abc   move_name a_123

myname50  _temp  j   a23b9    retVal
```

Keywords

The following list shows the reserved words in C. These reserved words may not be used as constants or variables or any other identifier names.

auto	else	long	switch
break	enum	register	typedef
case	extern	return	union
char	float	short	unsigned
const	for	signed	void
continue	goto	sizeof	volatile
default	if	static	while
do	int	struct	_Packed
double			

Whitespace in C

A line containing only whitespace, possibly with a comment, is known as a blank line, and a C compiler totally ignores it.

Whitespace is the term used in C to describe blanks, tabs, newline characters and comments. Whitespace separates one part of a statement from another and enables the compiler to identify where one element in a statement, such as int, ends and the next element begins. Therefore, in the following statement –

```
int age;
```

there must be at least one whitespace character (usually a space) between int and age for the compiler to be able to distinguish them. On the other hand, in the following statement –

```
fruit = apples + oranges;   // get the total fruit
```

no whitespace characters are necessary between fruit and =, or between = and apples, although you are free to include some if you wish to increase readability.

Benefits of C Language

1. As a middle level language, C combines the features of both high level and low level languages. It can be used for low-level programming, such as scripting for drivers and kernels and it also supports functions of high level programming languages, such as scripting for software applications etc.

2. C is a structured programming language which allows a complex program to be broken into simpler programs called functions. It also allows free movement of data across these functions.

3. Various features of C including direct access to machine level hardware APIs, presence of C compilers, deterministic resource use and dynamic memory allocation make C language an optimum choice for scripting applications and drivers of embedded systems.

4. C language is case-sensitive which means lowercase and uppercase letters are treated differently.

5. C is highly portable and is used for scripting system applications which form a major part of Windows, UNIX and Linux operating system.

6. C is a general purpose programming language and can efficiently work on enterprise applications, games, graphics, and applications requiring calculations etc.

7. C language has a rich library which provides a number of built-in functions. It also offers dynamic memory allocation.

8. C implements algorithms and data structures swiftly, facilitating faster computations in programs. This has enabled the use of C in applications requiring higher degrees of calculations like MATLAB and Mathematica.

Disadvantages of C Language

1. C does not have concept of OOPs, that's why C++ is developed.

2. There is no runtime checking in C language.

3. There is no strict type checking. For example, we can pass an integer value.

4. for the floating data type.

5. C doesn't have the concept of namespace.

6. C doesn't have the concept of constructor or destructor.

C++

C++ is an enhanced C language typically used for object oriented programming. It traces its origins back well over thirty years. Although it's far from the oldest computer language, it's one of the older ones that is in common usage today – so you might say it gets an A for its ability to adapt to changing technological times.

C++ was developed by Bjarne Stroustrup, who did the first development work as part of his PhD project. During the early years, he called the language "C with Classes". He had begun developing a new language because he felt that no existing language was ideal for large scale projects. Later, when he was working at AT&T Bell Labs, he again felt limited. He dusted off his "C with Classes" and added features of other languages. Simula had a strong influence; AlLGOL 68 played a role. Ultimately, a lot more than classes got added: virtual functions, templates, and operator overloading. *C++has influenced later languages like PHP, Java, and (not surprisingly) C# (C-Sharp).*

C++ has grown far beyond a one man operation. The name actually came from another developer, Rick Mascitti. It was partly a play on the name of the "++" operator and partly a reference to the enhancement.

The language was first standardized in 1998. Standards were again issued in 2003, 2007, and 2011. C++ is maintained by the ISO, a large standards committee. The current version is C++11. the biggest improvement is in abstraction mechanisms. Among the other goals of the most recent revision: to make C++ a better language for embedded systems and to better support novices.

Development has been guided by certain ideals. C++ strives to be portable; there is an attempt to avoid reliance on features that are platform-dependent.

Goals of the most recent revision include: to make C++ a better language for embedded systems and to better support novices. The standard, of course, isn't all there is; there are libraries that exist outside it.

Syntax and Structure of C++ Program

Here we will discuss one simple and basic C++ program to print "Hello this is C++" and its structure in parts with details and uses.

First C++ Program

```
#include <iostream.h>

using namespace std;

int main()

{

cout << "Hello this is C++";

}
```

Header files are included at the beginning just like in C program. Here iostream is a header file which provides us with input & output streams. Header files contained predeclared function libraries, which can be used by users for their ease.

Using namespace std, tells the compiler to use standard namespace. Namespace collects identifiers used for class, object and variables. NameSpace can be used by two ways in a program, either by the use of using statement at the beginning, like we did in above mentioned program or by using name of namespace as prefix before the identifier with scope resolution (::) operator.

Example : `std::cout << "A";`

main(), is the function which holds the executing part of program its return type is int.

cout <<, is used to print anything on screen, same as printf in C language. cin and cout are same as scanf and printf, only difference is that you do not need to mention format specifiers like, %d for int etc, in cout & cin.

Comments

For single line comments, use // before mentioning comment, like

```
cout<<"single line";  // This is single line comment
```

For multiple line comment, enclose the comment between /* and */

```
/*this is

 a multiple line

 comment */
```

Using Classes

Classes name must start with capital letter, and they contain data variables and member functions.

```
class Abc

{

 int i;        //data variable

 void display()       //Member Function

 {

   cout<<"Inside Member Function";

 }

}; // Class ends here


int main()

{

 Abc obj; // Creatig Abc class's object

 obj.display(); //Calling member function using class object

}
```

This is how class is defined, its object is created and the member functions are used.

Variables can be declared anywhere in the entire program, but must be declared, before they are used. Hence, we don't need to declare variable at the start of the program.

Variables

Variable are used in C++, where we need storage for any value, which will change in program. Variable can be declared in multiple ways each with different memory requirements and functioning. Variable is the name of memory location allocated by the compiler depending upon the datatype of the variable.

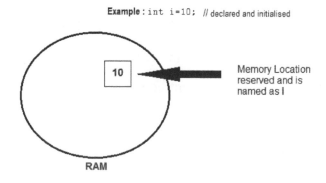

Example : int i=10; // declared and initialised

10

Memory Location reserved and is named as i

RAM

Basic Types of Variables

Each variable while declaration must be given a datatype, on which the memory assigned to the variable depends. Following are the basic types of variables,

bool	For variable to store boolean values(True or False)
char	For variables to store character types.
int	for variable with integral values
float and double are also types for variables with large and floating point values	

Declaration and Initialization

Variable must be declared before they are used. Usually it is preferred to declare them at the starting of the program, but in C++ they can be declared in the middle of program too, but must be done before using them.

Example :

```
int i;    // declared but not initialised

char c;

int i, j, k; // Multiple declaration
```

Initialization means assigning value to an already declared variable,

```
int i;   // declaration

i = 10; // initialization
```

Initialization and declaration can be done in one single step also,

```
int i=10;     //initialization and declaration in same step

int i=10, j=11;
```

If a variable is declared and not initialized by default it will hold a garbage value. Also, if a variable is once declared and if try to declare it again, we will get a compile time error.

```
int i,j;

i=10;

j=20;

int j=i+j;  //compile time error, cannot redeclare a variable in same scope
```

Scope of Variables

All the variables have their area of functioning, and out of that boundary they don't hold their value, this boundary is called scope of the variable. For most of the cases its between the curly braces,in which variable is declared that a variable exists, not outside it. We can broadly divide variables into two main types:

- Global Variables
- Local variables

Global Variables

Global variables are those, which ar once declared and can be used throughout the lifetime of the program by any class or any function. They must be declared outside the main() function. If only declared, they can be assigned different values at different time in program lifetime. But even if they are declared and initialized at the same time outside the main() function, then also they can be assigned any value at any point in the program.

Example : Only declared, not initialized

```
include <iostream>

using namespace std;

int x;          // Global variable declared

int main()

{

 x=10;          // Initialized once

 cout <<"first value of x = "<< x;

 x=20;          // Initialized again

 cout <<"Initialized again with value = "<< x;

}
```

Local Variables

Local variables are the variables which exist only between the curly braces, in which its declared. Outside that they are unavailable and leads to compile time error.

Example :

```
include <iostream>

using namespace std;

int main()

{

 int i=10;

 if(i<20)     // if condition scope starts
```

```
{
  int n=100;   // Local variable declared and initialized
}          // if condition scope ends
 cout << n;   // Compile time error, n not available here
}
```

Some Special Types of Variable

There are also some special keywords, to impart unique characteristics to the variables in the program.

1. Final - Once initialized, its value cant be changed.
2. Static - These variables holds their value between function calls.

Example :

```
#include <iostream.h>
using namespace std;
int main()
{
 final int i=10;
 static int y=20;
}
```

Operators in C++

Operators are special type of functions, that takes one or more arguments and produces a new value. For example : addition (+), substraction (-), multiplication (*) etc, are all operators. Operators are used to perform various operations on variables and constants.

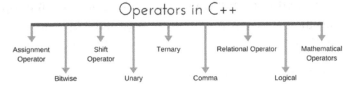

Operators in C++

Assignment Operator | Shift Operator | Ternary | Relational Operator | Mathematical Operators

Bitwise | Unary | Comma | Logical

Types of Operators

1. Assignment Operator
2. Mathematical Operators

3. Relational Operators

4. Logical Operators

5. Bitwise Operators

6. Shift Operators

7. Unary Operators

8. Ternary Operator

9. Comma Operator.

Assignment Operator (=)

Operates '=' is used for assignment, it takes the right-hand side (called rvalue) and copy it into the left-hand side (called lvalue). Assignment operator is the only operator which can be overloaded but cannot be inherited.

Mathematical Operators

There are operators used to perform basic mathematical operations. Addition (+) , subtraction (-) , diversion (/) multiplication (*) and modulus (%) are the basic mathematical operators. Modulus operator cannot be used with floating-point numbers.

C++ and C also use a shorthand notation to perform an operation and assignment at same type. *Example,*

```
int x=10;

x += 4 // will add 4 to 10, and hence assign 14 to X.

x -= 5 // will subtract 5 from 10 and assign 5 to x.
```

Relational Operators

These operators establish a relationship between operands. The relational operators are : less than (<) , grater thatn (>) , less than or equal to (<=), greater than equal to (>=), equivalent (==) and not equivalent (!=).

You must notice that assignment operator is (=) and there is a relational operator, for equivalent (==). These two are different from each other, the assignment operator assigns the value to any variable, whereas equivalent operator is used to compare values, like in if-else conditions, *Example:*

```
int x = 10; //assignment operator

x=5;     // again assignment operator

if(x == 5)  // here we have used equivalent relational operator, for com-
parison

{
```

```
    cout <<"Successfully compared";

}
```

Logical Operators

The logical operators are AND (&&) and OR (||). They are used to combine two different expressions together.

If two statement are connected using AND operator, the validity of both statements will be considered, but if they are connected using OR operator, then either one of them must be valid. These operators are mostly used in loops (especially while loop) and in Decision making.

Bitwise Operators

There are used to change individual bits into a number. They work with only integral data types like char, int and long and not with floating point values.

- Bitwise AND operators &.
- Bitwise OR operator |.
- And bitwise XOR operator ^.
- And, bitwise NOT operator ~.

They can be used as shorthand notation too, & = , |= , ^= , ~= etc.

Shift Operators

Shift Operators are used to shift Bits of any variable. It is of three types,

1. Left Shift Operator <<.
2. Right Shift Operator >>.
3. Unsigned Right Shift Operator >>>.

Unary Operators

These are the operators which work on only one operand. There are many unary operators, but increment ++ and decrement -- operators are most used.

Other Unary Operators : address of &, dereference *, new and delete, bitwise not ~, logical not !, unary minus - and unary plus +.

Ternary Operator

The ternary if-else ? : is an operator which has three operands.

```
int a = 10;

a > 5 ? cout << "true" : cout << "false"
```

Comma Operator

This is used to separate variable names and to separate expressions. In case of expressions, the value of last expression is produced and used.

Example :

```
int a,b,c; // variables declaration using comma operator

a=b++, c++; // a = c++ will be done.
```

Size of Operator in C++

Size of is also an operator not a function, it is used to get information about the amount of memory allocated for data types & Objects. It can be used to get size of user defined data types too.

size of operator can be used with and without parentheses. If you apply it to a variable you can use it without parentheses.

```
cout << sizeOf(double);   //Will print size of double

int x = 2;

int i = sizeOf x;
```

Typedef Operator

Typedef is a keyword used in C language to assign alternative names to existing types. Its mostly used with user defined data types, when names of data types get slightly complicated. Following is the general syntax for using typedef,

typedef *existing_name alias_name*

Lets take an example and see how typedef actually works.

```
typedef unsigned long ulong;
```

The above statement define a term ulong for an unsigned long type. Now this ulong identifier can be used to define unsigned long type variables.

```
ulong i, j;
```

Typedef and Pointers

Typedef can be used to give an alias name to pointers also. Here we have a case in which use of typedef is beneficial during pointer declaration.

In Pointers * binds to the right and not the left.

```
int* x, y ;
```

By this declaration statement, we are actually declaring **x** as a pointer of type int, whereas **y** will be declared as a plain integer.

```
typedef int* IntPtr ;

IntPtr x, y, z;
```

But if we use typedef like in above example, we can declare any number of pointers in a single statement.

Real-world Applications of C++

Games

C++ overrides the complexities of 3D games, optimizes resource management and facilitates multiplayer with networking. The language is extremely fast, allows procedural programming for CPU intensive functions and provides greater control over hardware, because of which it has been widely used in development of gaming engines. For instance, the science fiction game Doom 3 is cited as an example of a game that used C++ well and the Unreal Engine, a suite of game development tools, is written in C++.

Graphic User Interface (GUI) Based Applications

Many highly used applications, such as Image Ready, Adobe Premier, Photoshop and Illustrator, are scripted in C++.

Web Browsers

With the introduction of specialized languages such as PHP and Java, the adoption of C++ is limited for scripting of websites and web applications. However, where speed and reliability are required, C++ is still preferred. For instance, a part of Google's back-end is coded in C++, and the rendering engine of a few open source projects, such as web browser Mozilla Firefox and email client Mozilla Thunderbird, are also scripted in the programming language.

Advance Computations and Graphics

C++ provides the means for building applications requiring real-time physical simulations, high-performance image processing, and mobile sensor applications. Maya 3D software, used for integrated 3D modeling, visual effects and animation, is coded in C++.

Database Software

C++ and C have been used for scripting MySQL, one of the most popular database management software. The software forms the backbone of a variety of database-based enterprises, such as Google, Wikipedia, Yahoo and YouTube etc.

Operating Systems

C++ forms an integral part of many of the prevalent operating systems including Apple's OS X and various versions of Microsoft Windows, and the erstwhile Symbian mobile OS.

Enterprise Software

C++ finds a purpose in banking and trading enterprise applications, such as those deployed by Bloomberg and Reuters. It is also used in development of advanced software, such as flight simulators and radar processing.

Medical and Engineering Applications

Many advanced medical equipments, such as MRI machines, use C++ language for scripting their software. It is also part of engineering applications, such as high-end CAD/CAM systems.

Compilers

A host of compilers including Apple C++, Bloodshed Dev-C++, Clang C++ and MINGW make use of C++ language. C and its successor C++ are leveraged for diverse software and platform development requirements, from operating systems to graphic designing applications. Further, these languages have assisted in the development of new languages for special purposes like C#, Java, PHP, Verilog etc.

Java

Java programming language was originally developed by Sun Microsystems which was initiated by James Gosling and released in 1995 as core component of Sun Microsystems' Java platform (Java 1.0 [J2SE]).

The latest release of the Java Standard Edition is Java SE 8. With the advancement of Java and its widespread popularity, multiple configurations were built to suit various types of platforms. For example: J2EE for Enterprise Applications, J2ME for Mobile Applications.

The new J2 versions were renamed as Java SE, Java EE, and Java ME respectively. Java is guaranteed to be Write Once, Run Anywhere.

Java is:

- Object oriented – In Java, everything is an Object. Java can be easily extended since it is based on the Object model.

- Platform independent – Unlike many other programming languages including C and C++, when Java is compiled, it is not compiled into platform specific machine, rather into platform independent byte code. This byte code is distributed over the web and interpreted by the Virtual Machine (JVM) on whichever platform it is being run on.

- Simple – Java is designed to be easy to learn. If you understand the basic concept of OOP Java, it would be easy to master.

- Secure – With Java's secure feature it enables to develop virus-free, tamper-free systems. Authentication techniques are based on public-key encryption.

- Architecture-neutral – Java compiler generates an architecture-neutral object file format, which makes the compiled code executable on many processors, with the presence of Java runtime system.

- Portable – Being architecture-neutral and having no implementation dependent aspects of the specification makes Java portable. Compiler in Java is written in ANSI C with a clean portability boundary, which is a POSIX subset.

- Robust – Java makes an effort to eliminate error prone situations by emphasizing mainly on compile time error checking and runtime checking.

- Multithreaded – With Java's multithreaded feature it is possible to write programs that can perform many tasks simultaneously. This design feature allows the developers to construct interactive applications that can run smoothly.

- Interpreted – Java byte code is translated on the fly to native machine instructions and is not stored anywhere. The development process is more rapid and analytical since the linking is an incremental and light-weight process.

- High performance – With the use of Just-In-Time compilers, Java enables high performance.

- Distributed – Java is designed for the distributed environment of the internet.

- Dynamic – Java is considered to be more dynamic than C or C++ since it is designed to adapt to an evolving environment. Java programs can carry extensive amount of run-time information that can be used to verify and resolve accesses to objects on run-time.

Tools you will Need

For performing the examples discussed in this tutorial, you will need a Pentium 200-MHz computer with a minimum of 64 MB of RAM (128 MB of RAM recommended).

You will also need the following softwares:

- Linux 7.1 or Windows xp/7/8 operating system.

- Java JDK 8.

- Microsoft Notepad or any other text editor.

Local Environment Setup

If you are still willing to set up your environment for Java programming language, then this section guides you on how to download and set up Java on your machine. Following are the steps to set up the environment.

Follow the instructions to download Java and run the .exe to install Java on your machine. Once you installed Java on your machine, you will need to set environment variables to point to correct installation directories.

Setting up the Path for Windows

Assuming you have installed Java in *c:\Program Files\java\jdk* directory:

- Right-click on 'My Computer' and select 'Properties'.

- Click the 'Environment variables' button under the 'Advanced' tab.

- Now, alter the 'Path' variable so that it also contains the path to the Java executable. Example, if the path is currently set to 'C:\WINDOWS\SYSTEM32', then change your path to read 'C:\WINDOWS\SYSTEM32;c:\Program Files\java\jdk\bin'.

Setting up the Path for Linux, UNIX, Solaris, FreeBSD

Environment variable PATH should be set to point to where the Java binaries have been installed. Refer to your shell documentation, if you have trouble doing this.

Example, if you use *bash* as your shell, then you would add the following line to the end of your '.bashrc: export PATH = /path/to/java:$PATH'

Popular Java Editors

To write your Java programs, you will need a text editor. There are even more sophisticated IDEs available in the market. But for now, you can consider one of the following:

- Notepad – On Windows machine, you can use any simple text editor like Notepad (Recommended for this tutorial), TextPad.

- Netbeans – A Java IDE that is open-source and free.

- Eclipse – A Java IDE developed by the eclipse open-source community.

When we consider a Java program, it can be defined as a collection of objects that communicate via invoking each other's methods. Let us now briefly look into what do class, object, methods, and instance variables mean.

- Object – Objects have states and behaviors. Example: A dog has states - color, name, breed as well as behavior such as wagging their tail, barking, eating. An object is an instance of a class.

- Class – A class can be defined as a template/blueprint that describes the behavior/state that the object of its type supports.

- Methods – A method is basically a behavior. A class can contain many methods. It is in methods where the logics are written, data is manipulated and all the actions are executed.

- Instance Variables – Each object has its unique set of instance variables. An object's state is created by the values assigned to these instance variables.

First Java Program

Let us look at a simple code that will print the words *Hello World*.

Example

```
public class MyFirstJavaProgram {

   /* This is my first java program.
   * This will print 'Hello World' as the output
   */

   public static void main(String []args) {
    System.out.println("Hello World"); // prints Hello World
   }

}
```

Let's look at how to save the file, compile, and run the program. Please follow the subsequent steps:

- Open notepad and add the code as above.
- Save the file as: MyFirstJavaProgram.java.
- Open a command prompt window and go to the directory where you saved the class. Assume it's C:\.
- Type 'javac MyFirstJavaProgram.java' and press enter to compile your code. If there are no errors in your code, the command prompt will take you to the next line (Assumption : The path variable is set).
- Now, type ' java MyFirstJavaProgram ' to run your program.
- You will be able to see ' Hello World ' printed on the window.

Output

```
C:\> javac MyFirstJavaProgram.java
C:\> java MyFirstJavaProgram
Hello World
```

Basic Syntax

About Java programs, it is very important to keep in mind the following points.

- Case Sensitivity – Java is case sensitive, which means identifier Hello and hello would have different meaning in Java.
- Class Names – For all class names the first letter should be in Upper Case. If several words are used to form a name of the class, each inner word's first letter should be in Upper Case.

Example: *class MyFirstJavaClass*.

- Method Names – All method names should start with a Lower Case letter. If several words are used to form the name of the method, then each inner word's first letter should be in Upper Case.

  Example: *public void myMethodName()*.

- Program File Name – Name of the program file should exactly match the class name.

  When saving the file, you should save it using the class name (Remember Java is case sensitive) and append '.java' to the end of the name (if the file name and the class name do not match, your program will not compile).

  Example: Assume 'MyFirstJavaProgram' is the class name. Then the file should be saved as 'MyFirstJavaProgram.java'.

- Public static void main(String args[]) – Java program processing starts from the main() method which is a mandatory part of every Java program.

Java Identifiers

All Java components require names. Names used for classes, variables, and methods are called identifiers.

In Java, there are several points to remember about identifiers. They are as follows:

- All identifiers should begin with a letter (A to Z or a to z), currency character ($) or an underscore (_).

- After the first character, identifiers can have any combination of characters.

- A key word cannot be used as an identifier.

- Most importantly, identifiers are case sensitive.

- Examples of legal identifiers: age, $salary, _value, __1_value.

- Examples of illegal identifiers: 123abc, -salary.

Java Modifiers

Like other languages, it is possible to modify classes, methods, etc., by using modifiers. There are two categories of modifiers:

- Access Modifiers – default, public , protected, private

- Non-access Modifiers – final, abstract, strictfp.

Java Variables

Following are the types of variables in Java:

- Local Variables

- Class Variables (Static Variables)
- Instance Variables (Non-static Variables).

Java Arrays

Arrays are objects that store multiple variables of the same type. However, an array itself is an object on the heap. We will look into how to declare, construct, and initialize in the upcoming chapters.

Java Enums

Enums were introduced in Java 5.0. Enums restrict a variable to have one of only a few predefined values. The values in this enumerated list are called enums.

With the use of enums it is possible to reduce the number of bugs in your code.

For example, if we consider an application for a fresh juice shop, it would be possible to restrict the glass size to small, medium, and large. This would make sure that it would not allow anyone to order any size other than small, medium, or large.

Example

```
class FreshJuice {

  enum FreshJuiceSize{ SMALL, MEDIUM, LARGE }

  FreshJuiceSize size;

}


public class FreshJuiceTest {


  public static void main(String args[]) {

    FreshJuice juice = new FreshJuice();

    juice.size = FreshJuice.FreshJuiceSize.MEDIUM ;

    System.out.println("Size: " + juice.size);

  }

}
```

The above example will produce the following result:

Output:

```
Size: MEDIUM
```

Note – Enums can be declared as their own or inside a class. Methods, variables, constructors can be defined inside enums as well.

Java Keywords

The following list shows the reserved words in Java. These reserved words may not be used as constant or variable or any other identifier names.

abstract	assert	boolean	break
byte	case	catch	char
class	const	continue	default
do	double	else	enum
extends	final	finally	float
for	goto	if	implements
import	instanceof	int	interface
long	native	new	package
private	protected	public	return
short	static	strictfp	super
switch	synchronized	this	throw
throws	transient	try	void
volatile	while		

Comments in Java

Java supports single-line and multi-line comments very similar to C and C++. All characters available inside any comment are ignored by Java compiler.

Example

```
public class MyFirstJavaProgram {


   /* This is my first java program.

   * This will print 'Hello World' as the output

   * This is an example of multi-line comments.

   */


   public static void main(String []args) {

   // This is an example of single line comment
```

```
        /* This is also an example of single line comment. */

        System.out.println("Hello World");

    }

}
```

Output:

```
Hello World
```

Using Blank Lines

A line containing only white space, possibly with a comment, is known as a blank line, and Java totally ignores it.

Inheritance

In Java, classes can be derived from classes. Basically, if you need to create a new class and here is already a class that has some of the code you require, then it is possible to derive your new class from the already existing code.

This concept allows you to reuse the fields and methods of the existing class without having to rewrite the code in a new class. In this scenario, the existing class is called the superclass and the derived class is called the subclass.

Interfaces

In Java language, an interface can be defined as a contract between objects on how to communicate with each other. Interfaces play a vital role when it comes to the concept of inheritance.

An interface defines the methods, a deriving class (subclass) should use. But the implementation of the methods is totally up to the subclass.

Applications of Java

Every enterprise uses Java in one way or other. As per Oracle, more than 3 billion devices run applications designed on the development platform. Java is used to design the following applications:

- Desktop GUI applications.
- Embedded systems.
- Web applications, including eCommerce applications, front and back office electronic trading systems, settlement and confirmation systems, data processing projects, and more.
- Web servers and application servers.
- Mobile applications including Android applications.
- Enterprise applications.

- Scientific applications

- Middleware products.

Advantages of Java

- Java offers higher cross- functionality and portability as programs written in one platform can run across desktops, mobiles, embedded systems.

- Java is free, simple, object-oriented, distributed, supports multithreading and offers multimedia and network support.

- Java is a mature language, therefore more stable and predictable. The Java Class Library enables cross-platform development.

- Being highly popular at enterprise, embedded and network level, Java has a large active user community and support available.

- Unlike C and C++, Java programs are compiled independent of platform in *byte-code*language which allows the same program to run on any machine that has a JVM installed.

- Java has powerful development tools like Eclipse SDK and NetBeans which have debugging capability and offer integrated development environment.

- Increasing language diversity, evidenced by compatibility of Java with Scala, Groovy, JRuby, and Clojure.

- Relatively seamless forward compatibility from one version to the next

Disadvantages of Java

- Performance: SIgnificantly slower and more memory-consuming than natively compiled languages such as C or C++.

- Look and feel: The default look and feel of GUI applications written in Java using the Swing toolkit is very different from native applications.

- Single-paradigm language: The addition of static imports in Java 5.0 the procedural paradigm is better accommodated than in earlier versions of Java.

Python

Python is a general-purpose language. It has wide range of applications from Web development (like: Django and Bottle), scientific and mathematical computing (Orange, SymPy, NumPy) to desktop graphical user Interfaces (Pygame, Panda3D).

The syntax of the language is clean and length of the code is relatively short. It's fun to work in Python because it allows you to think about the problem rather than focusing on the syntax.

Features of Python Programming

1. **A simple language which is easier to learn:**

    Python has a very simple and elegant syntax. It's much easier to read and write Python programs compared to other languages like: C++, Java, C#. Python makes programming fun and allows you to focus on the solution rather than syntax.

    If you are a newbie, it's a great choice to start your journey with Python.

2. **Free and open-source:**

    You can freely use and distribute Python, even for commercial use. Not only can you use and distribute softwares written in it, you can even make changes to the Python's source code.

    Python has a large community constantly improving it in each iteration.

3. **Portability:**

    You can move Python programs from one platform to another, and run it without any changes. It runs seamlessly on almost all platforms including Windows, Mac OS X and Linux.

4. **Extensible and Embeddable:**

    Suppose an application requires high performance. You can easily combine pieces of C/C++ or other languages with Python code.

    This will give your application high performance as well as scripting capabilities which other languages may not provide out of the box.

5. **A high-level, interpreted language:**

    Unlike C/C++, you don't have to worry about daunting tasks like memory management, garbage collection and so on.

    Likewise, when you run Python code, it automatically converts your code to the language your computer understands. You don't need to worry about any lower-level operations.

6. **Large standard libraries to solve common tasks:**

    Python has a number of standard libraries which makes life of a programmer much easier since you don't have to write all the code yourself. For example: Need to connect MySQL database on a Web server? You can use MySQLdb library using `import MySQLdb`.

    Standard libraries in Python are well tested and used by hundreds of people. So you can be sure that it won't break your application.

7. **Object-oriented:**

    Everything in Python is an object. Object oriented programming (OOP) helps you solve a complex problem intuitively.

    With OOP, you are able to divide these complex problems into smaller sets by creating objects.

Applications of Python

Web Applications

You can create scalable Web Apps using frameworks and CMS (Content Management System) that are built on Python. Some of the popular platforms for creating Web Apps are: Django, Flask, Pyramid, Plone, Django CMS.

Sites like Mozilla, Reddit, Instagram and PBS are written in Python.

Scientific and Numeric Computing

There are numerous libraries available in Python for scientific and numeric computing. There are libraries like: SciPy and NumPy that are used in general purpose computing. And, there are specific libraries like: EarthPy for earth science, AstroPy for Astronomy and so on.

Also, the language is heavily used in machine learning, data mining and deep learning.

Creating Software Prototypes

Python is slow compared to compiled languages like C++ and Java. It might not be a good choice if resources are limited and efficiency is a must.

However, Python is a great language for creating prototypes. For example: You can use Pygame (library for creating games) to create your game's prototype first. If you like the prototype, you can use language like C++ to create the actual game.

Good Language to Teach Programming

Python is used by many companies to teach programming to kids and newbies.

It is a good language with a lot of features and capabilities. Yet, it's one of the easiest language to learn because of its simple easy-to-use syntax.

Reasons to Choose Python as First Language

Simple Elegant Syntax

Programming in Python is fun. It's easier to understand and write Python code. **Why?** The syntax feels natural. Take this source code for an example:

```
1. a = 2
2. b = 3
3. sum = a + b
print(sum)
```

Even if you have never programmed before, you can easily guess that this program adds two numbers and prints it.

Not Overly Strict

You don't need to define the type of a variable in Python. Also, it's not necessary to add semicolon at the end of the statement.

Python enforces you to follow good practices (like proper indentation). These small things can make learning much easier for beginners.

Expressiveness of the Language

Python allows you to write programs having greater functionality with fewer lines of code. Here's a link to the source code of Tic-tac-toe game with a graphical interface and a smart computer opponent in less than 500 lines of code. This is just an example.

References

- Benefits-c-language-programming-languages: geeksforgeeks.org, Retrieved 22 May 2018
- What-are-advantages-and-disadvantages: thecrazyprogrammer.com, Retrieved 29 June 2018
- Variables-scope-details: studytonight.com, Retrieved 19 April 2018
- Applications-of-c-c-plus-plus-in-the-real-world: invensis.net, Retrieved 20 April 2018
- Benefits-of-java-over-other-programming-languages: invensis.net, Retrieved 10 May 2018
- Python-programming: programiz.com, Retrieved 16 March 2018

Permissions

All chapters in this book are published with permission under the Creative Commons Attribution Share Alike License or equivalent. Every chapter published in this book has been scrutinized by our experts. Their significance has been extensively debated. The topics covered herein carry significant information for a comprehensive understanding. They may even be implemented as practical applications or may be referred to as a beginning point for further studies.

We would like to thank the editorial team for lending their expertise to make the book truly unique. They have played a crucial role in the development of this book. Without their invaluable contributions this book wouldn't have been possible. They have made vital efforts to compile up to date information on the varied aspects of this subject to make this book a valuable addition to the collection of many professionals and students.

This book was conceptualized with the vision of imparting up-to-date and integrated information in this field. To ensure the same, a matchless editorial board was set up. Every individual on the board went through rigorous rounds of assessment to prove their worth. After which they invested a large part of their time researching and compiling the most relevant data for our readers.

The editorial board has been involved in producing this book since its inception. They have spent rigorous hours researching and exploring the diverse topics which have resulted in the successful publishing of this book. They have passed on their knowledge of decades through this book. To expedite this challenging task, the publisher supported the team at every step. A small team of assistant editors was also appointed to further simplify the editing procedure and attain best results for the readers.

Apart from the editorial board, the designing team has also invested a significant amount of their time in understanding the subject and creating the most relevant covers. They scrutinized every image to scout for the most suitable representation of the subject and create an appropriate cover for the book.

The publishing team has been an ardent support to the editorial, designing and production team. Their endless efforts to recruit the best for this project, has resulted in the accomplishment of this book. They are a veteran in the field of academics and their pool of knowledge is as vast as their experience in printing. Their expertise and guidance has proved useful at every step. Their uncompromising quality standards have made this book an exceptional effort. Their encouragement from time to time has been an inspiration for everyone.

The publisher and the editorial board hope that this book will prove to be a valuable piece of knowledge for students, practitioners and scholars across the globe.

Index